THE CREATIVE ARTIST'S LEGAL GUIDE

D1284289

DATE DUE

The Roxy Theater in Pacific Beach, California, 1980
(Photo by John Fry, used with permission)

THE CREATIVE ARTIST'S LEGAL GUIDE

COPYRIGHT, TRADEMARK, AND CONTRACTS
IN FILM AND DIGITAL MEDIA PRODUCTION

BILL SEITER & ELLEN SEITER

Yale UNIVERSITY PRESS/NEW HAVEN & LONDON

Yale University Press books may be purchased in quantity for educational, business, or promotional use. For information, please e-mail sales.press@ yale.edu (U.S. office) or sales@yaleup.co.uk (U.K. office).

Designed by Mary Valencia.
Set in Sabon and Eureka Sans types by Integrated Publishing Solutions.
Printed in the United States of America.

Library of Congress Cataloging-in-Publication Data
Seiter, William J., 1953–
The creative artist's legal guide : copyright, trademark, and contracts in film and digital media production / Bill Seiter, Ellen Seiter.
   p. cm.
  Includes bibliographical references and index.
  ISBN 978-0-300-16119-9 (alk. paper)
   1. Intellectual property—United States. 2. Copyright and electronic data processing—United States. 3. Digital media—Law and legislation—United States. 4. Copyright—United States. 5. Trademarks—Law and legislation—United States. 6. Copyright—Fictitious characters—United States. 7. Contracts—United States. 8. Fair use (Copyright)—United States. I. Seiter, Ellen, 1957– II. Title.
  KF2979.S45 2012
  346.7304'82—dc23   2011052838

A catalogue record for this book is available from the British Library.

This paper meets the requirements of ANSI/NISO Z39.48–1992 (Permanence of Paper).

10 9 8 7 6 5 4 3 2 1

To our sister Rose

CONTENTS

PREFACE

Students and professionals in film and media arts today encounter a continuous feed of breaking news about intellectual property. Cutting-edge legal developments, deals, and disputes revolving around copyright, trademarks, and rights of privacy and publicity are reported daily in the most sensational terms. Aspiring filmmakers witness a spectacle of legal happenings involving litigators and lobbyists, First Amendment Davids and big-business Goliaths, record-breaking deals and contracts gone sour. This endless pageant could remain a tale of sound and fury signifying nothing to you—the creative artist—until you get a solid grip on the core legal concepts.

The Creative Artist's Legal Guide is here to help students and teachers, creative entrepreneurs, and professionals cut through the clutter and meet head-on the intellectual property challenges posed by today's complex media environment. It will empower you to understand what questions to ask and what situations to avoid. Our book demystifies the law that surrounds film, animation, video games, and new media so that when your turn comes to dealing with the lawyers, agents, executives, and other players who trade in IP and business law all day long, seven days a week, you will deal with confidence.

What must you do to copyright your screenplay? How do you clear rights for your latest film project? Is there a way to steer clear of legal trouble while producing a mockumentary about a bodybuilder turned movie star turned governor turned gossip-page headliner? How do you figure out whether a vintage novel is in the public domain? How do you determine whether a cool-sounding trademark you dreamed up for your production company is available? Do those cute woodland creatures you storyboarded for your new cartoon come too close for comfort to Bambi's pals? What types of contracts must you sew up to stitch together your transmedia storytelling project across multiple platforms? How will you defend yourself if a famous brand objects to your unorthodox depiction of their trademarked product in your artwork? How do you nail down copyright and trademark rights overseas to be able to reach foreign audiences and markets?

This comprehensive user-friendly guide explains intellectual property—its roots, internal logic, and regional variations—applied to fiction, screenwriting, various forms of filmmaking from celluloid to digital, animation, video gaming, and other creative media.

Chapter 1 walks you through the ins and outs of copyrights: how to get them, how to protect them, how to deal in them, how to fight with them, and how to take them abroad.

Chapter 2 does the same for trademarks, so different from copyrights, yet vital to creative content branding in your media-rich world, and to the commercial mechanics of everything from film financing to celebrity endorsements to video gaming to merchandise licensing to social networking sites and mobile content distribution.

Chapter 3 probes the pitfalls that lurk within the rules of the game laid down by schools, guilds, and studios, rules that can take away or limit your rights in the work you create, so that you can approach the institutions that may make or break you with eyes wide open.

Chapter 4 pilots you through the swamp waters of entertainment and other media-driven contracts, as you negotiate the transmedia epic of a lifetime with a cast of hungry industry crocodiles.

Chapter 5 explains rights of publicity and privacy, and the importance of taking them into account at the front end of your media productions.

Chapter 6 rounds out the tour with a look at the laws and legal structures governing the Internet and new media, and the ways copyright, trademark, and other concepts mapped out in the first five chapters affect the genesis, distribution, and protection of creative works in a virtual world.

By arming the content creator with practical legal information and career guidance, this book will help you protect your work from those seeking, sometimes unfairly, to profit from it. Potential profiteers run the gamut from teachers, employers, internship supervisors, and talent agents to amateur copycats and professional counterfeiters, to the many outfits that require you to surrender your IP rights if you want to play in their sandbox—from social networking, virtual reality, and other user-generated content sites to universities, studios, and other media producers, large and small.

By immersing you in emergent issues in law and media studies, *The Creative Artist's Legal Guide* will also supply you with the tools you need to operate as a savvy digital citizen, a politically informed artist, and a global sophisticate in the new media universe.

We come to this book as a pair of siblings with three decades of experience along parallel professional paths: Bill as a lawyer specializing in copyright, trademark, business, and international law; Ellen as a professor, researcher, and widely published critic in film, television, and new media studies. Our education in film began in the 1960s at the second-run Roxy Theater in Pacific Beach, California, where on Friday nights our mother would take us, along with brothers Frank and Charles and sister Rose, to marvel at the art and artistry of Sergio Leone and Clint Eastwood, Ennio Morricone and Nino Rota, Elizabeth Taylor and Jean Simmons, Kirk Douglas and Robert Mitchum, Burt Lancaster, Sidney Poitier, Sophia Loren, Federico Fellini, and Akira Kurosawa.

Pacific Beach is also where we learned how to swim. With this book we aim to teach you how to swim the often shark-infested waters of intellectual property, entertainment, and media law with complete artistic impunity.

CHAPTER 1

Copyright

... the only visible form that evil assumes is an attempt on private property.

—Umberto Eco, "The Myth of Superman," 1962

One of these days you're going to get a "cease and desist" letter.

It will be from a law firm you never heard of, written on behalf of a client you may or may not have heard of. It is called a cease and desist letter because it demands you cease doing something their client doesn't like, and desist from ever, ever doing it again. It will have some nasty things to say about a creative project you are on the brink of releasing, or a project you just released, or a project you released ages ago. It will follow a script more or less like this:

- Lawyer mentions the client he or she represents, and says how great they are.
- Lawyer says the client owns one or more copyrighted works, likewise great.
- Lawyer mentions copyright registrations the client owns, if any.
- Lawyer says your work infringes or will infringe the client's work.
- Lawyer says how shameful this is, and how it hurts the client.
- Lawyer demands you stop producing, distributing, or selling your work.
- Lawyer demands you promise in writing never to do it again.
- Lawyer demands you provide an accounting of your ill-gotten profits.
- Lawyer threatens lawsuit and other dire consequences if you don't comply.
- Lawyer demands a reply within a matter of days.
- Lawyer reserves all of the client's rights and remedies.

Your first impulse may be to drop the letter behind the sofa and ignore it. Don't.

You can't afford to ignore it.

And it's nothing you can't cope with.

You may be suffering a little fear of the unknown, but it's a fear you can conquer.

All you need to do is read this chapter.

The Copyright Act of the United States is a federal statute enacted by Congress. It tells how to get copyrights, how to protect copyrights, how to deal in copyrights, how to fight with copyrights, and how to handle copyrights abroad.

Congress has you at a disadvantage. They've had over two centuries to write the Copyright Act. You don't have two centuries. But don't despair. You can learn what you need to know about copyrights in about two hours.

Because copyright law isn't complicated.

The world we live in is complicated.

GETTING COPYRIGHTS

The Copyright Act creates rights in *original works of authorship* fixed in any *tangible medium of expression*. The current Copyright Act of 1976 is the sixth version of a law that has been amended often, and overhauled once every generation or so. Congress keeps having to play catch-up with new media. But Congress need never play alone, because new media inevitably spawn new lobbyists. Over the years, Congress and the copyright lobby have drilled numerous pigeonholes into the law to accommodate various new media and new types of artistic work. Meanwhile, under the Copyright Act, old media, like old soldiers, never die. They just fade away, leaving sometimes quaint terminology in their wake, in remembrance of things past.

You can think of copyright law as an arms race between content creators and content users, and the rise of the Internet as tantamount to the advent of the atomic bomb. The Web and digital media have radically transformed the way we produce and consume content, and indeed transformed the very nature of what you and your audience consider art. Where this arms race gets tricky for you, as a media artist of the twenty-first century, is that you are sure to fight on both sides of the copyright battlefront, sometimes as creator of your own content, sometimes as user of other people's content. In Chapter 6 we will take an in-depth look at some specific ways in which copyright and other areas of law have impacted and been impacted by the Internet and new media. But we need to learn to walk before we can run. So let's take a walk right now around the copyright block.

What does it take to make an "original work of authorship"?

A PIECE OF WORK

For there to be a copyright, there has to be a "work" expressed in tangible form, because what copyright protects is the artistic or literary expression contained in the work, not the ideas the work expresses.

Yet not all species of artistic activity are protected species under the Copyright Act. It contains a fixed list of protected works. Congress started the list in 1790 with books, maps, and charts. It tacked on musical compositions in 1834, dramatic compositions in 1856, photographs in 1865, music for public performance in 1897, motion pictures in 1912, sound recordings in 1971, computer programs in 1980, and architectural works in 1990.

"Original works of authorship" currently include the following protected species:

Literary works are nondramatic textual works, expressed in words, numbers, or other verbal or numerical symbols, which may include accompanying illustrations. Literary works include such things as novels, nonfiction books, poetry, speeches, dissertations, and computer programs.

Pictorial, graphic, and sculptural works include two- and three-dimensional works of fine art, graphic art, and applied art, photographs, prints and art reproductions, maps, globes, charts, diagrams, models, and technical drawings.

Musical works can be original songs or other musical compositions, original arrangements or other new versions of earlier compositions to which new copyrightable content has been added. Musical works include any lyrics or other words accompanying the music.

Dramatic works include plays, film treatments, screenplays, scripts for radio, and teleplays for television. This also includes any music accompanying the dramatic text.

Pantomimes and choreographic works can be copyrighted too, but to be a work under the Copyright Act, the pantomime or choreography has to be written down or recorded.

Sound recordings are works that result from fixing a series of sounds, musical, spoken, or otherwise, in a material medium such as a disk, tape, or record. Sound recordings do not include the sounds accompanying a motion picture or other audiovisual work, because these sounds fall into the next pigeonhole—the pigeonhole Hollywood built.

Audiovisual works are works that consist of a series of related images which are intended to be shown by the use of a machine or device, such as a projector, a viewer, or electronic equipment, together with accompanying sounds, if any.

An audiovisual work can be embodied on film, tape, digital media, or any other medium that enables the work to be shown. *Motion pictures* are a subset of audiovisual works, and consist of a series of related images which impart an impression of motion when shown in succession. As with other audiovisual works, any accompanying sounds are considered part of the motion picture.

Architectural works consist of the design of a building as embodied in any tangible medium of expression, including the building itself, a model of it, or architectural plans or drawings for it. The work includes the overall form as well as the arrangement and composition of spaces and elements in the design, but does not include individual standard architectural features.

ORIGINAL SPIN

For there to be a copyright, the work needs to be—at least in part—"original."

Originality is a constitutional requirement because the source of Congress's power to enact copyright laws in the first place is Article I, Section 8, clause 8, of the U.S. Constitution, which empowers Congress: "To promote the Progress of Science and useful Arts, by securing for limited Times to Authors and Inventors the exclusive Right to their respective Writings and Discoveries." This clause enabled Congress to enact a patent law allowing inventors to obtain patents in new inventions for a limited period of time. It also enabled Congress to enact the Copyright Act, granting authors and artists copyrights in new literary and artistic works for a limited period of time.

"Originality" here does not mean novelty. Nor is it a matter of artistic taste. It just means the work has to be independently created by the author, as opposed to being copied from other works, and it has to possess at least some minimal degree of creativity.

THE IMPORTANCE OF BEING AUTHOR

For there to be a copyright, the work needs to have an "author."

A bird can sing. But it can't copyright a thing. It's not an author.

You can be an author. You can record the bird singing and create an original work of authorship in the form of a sound recording. Whether you end up owning the copyright, or anything more than the shirt on your back, is another matter.

Copyright in an original work of authorship springs to life the moment the work is created in fixed form. The morning you taped that red, red robin, after being so rudely awakened, you weren't losing sleep, you were gaining a copyright. Normally, the creator of the work is its author and the copyright belongs to the creator as author. However, there is a giant exception to this which, like money, makes the entertainment world go round. It is called the *work-for-hire* exception.

The Copyright Act defines a "work made for hire" as either:

(1) a work prepared by an employee within the scope of his or her employment, or

(2) a work specially ordered or commissioned for use as a part of a motion picture or other audiovisual work, as a translation, as a supplementary work, as a compilation, as an instructional text, as a test, as answer material for a test, or as an atlas, if the parties expressly agree in a written instrument signed by them that the work shall be considered a work made for hire.

The upshot of this definition, if your work on a project is a "work made for hire," is that you do not own any copyright in what you create on the project. The folks footing the bill do. If you guess major studios had something to do with Congress putting motion pictures and other audiovisual works first and foremost in clause 2 above, you guessed right. Sound recordings didn't make it into clause 2, but don't think the recording industry didn't try.

As a result of the work-for-hire exception, creative artists in motion picture and other audiovisual productions—be they writers, directors, composers, animators, actors, voices, musicians, camera people, sound people, FX geeks, graphic artists, set designers, or costume designers—nearly always fall under one of two categories of talent, neither of which ever owns copyright in what they create, because their works are works made for hire:

• Employees do not own copyright, because the works of an employee prepared within the scope of his or her employment automatically belong to the employer.

• Freelancers who sign work-for-hire agreements do not own copyright, because their contracted works automatically belong to the party who commissioned the work.

If your creative work falls outside the work-for-hire exception, you own the copyright. It is yours to use, license, sell, give away for free, or sit on, as you see fit. Someone who wants to own the rights in your work could buy the rights from you, but in that case the buyer would have to obtain from you a signed copyright assignment explicitly transferring the copyright.

For good reason, studios and independent producers coordinating a film or TV production like the work-for-hire concept. They don't want to have to chase the talent all over hell's half acre for copyright assignments each time the talent creates a copyrightable work in the course of pre-production, production, or post-production and it ends up part of the show. They don't want to be up a creek every time a creative artist walks off the job or tries to play hold-up artist. They don't want to be sandbagged after releasing a show by claims the talent had rights in the finished product. Work for hire obviates these headaches.

If you happen to be a starving artist slaving away on a production, you may resent having to sign a work-for-hire agreement stating you never own copyright in what you create. But if the point is non-negotiable—and it almost always is—the best you can do is read the work-for-hire provisions in your contract carefully and understand what they say. If you happen to be an aspiring or actual motion picture producer, you will come to appreciate the way work-for-hire agreements make the process of piecing together a clean chain of title for the motion pictures you produce much more manageable than the alternative, which would involve hand-stitching a motley quilt of copyright assignments obtained one by one from your motley crew. Used legitimately, the work-for-hire exception is a legitimate tool to help bring creative work to fruition, and we'll be surprised if you don't avail yourself of it, sooner or later.

A TANGIBLE MEDIUM

Finally, for there to be a copyright, the original work of authorship must be fixed in a "tangible medium of expression." The medium must enable the work to be perceived, reproduced, or otherwise communicated, either directly through the human senses or with the aid of a machine or device, for instance, a movie projector or an MP3 player. Works can be fixed in all sorts of material objects.

The Copyright Act divides the universe of media into *copies* and *phonorecords*.

Phonorecords are material objects in which sounds—other than sounds accompanying a motion picture or other audiovisual work—are fixed by any method now known or to be developed in the future, and from which the sounds can be perceived, reproduced, or otherwise communicated, either directly or with the aid of a machine or device. A phonorecord can be a phonograph record, or any other material object embodying sound recordings, such as a cassette tape, CD, MP3 file, and other digital media, including formats developed in the future.

Copies are any material objects other than phonorecords in which a work is fixed, for instance, printed books and magazines, newspapers, handwritten or typewritten manuscripts, film prints, negatives, DVDs, videotapes, computer hard drives, flash drives and diskettes, and including formats developed in the future. A motion picture print with sound is not a "phonorecord" even though it contains sounds. It is a "copy."

DERIVATIVE WORKS

Many copyrightable works build on preexisting materials. For instance, a motion picture is a type of audiovisual work. If it is filmed based on a screenplay and features recorded music, the film is a derivative work of the screenplay, and it is also a derivative work of the recorded music. The screenplay and the recorded music are each separately copyrightable. The film is also copyrightable as a *derivative work*.

In turn, if the screenplay is based on a novel, it is a derivative work of the novel, and if the recorded music is a recording of a song, the recording is a derivative work of the song, which is a musical work consisting of music and accompanying lyrics.

Since a derivative work is based upon one or more preexisting works, the copyright in a derivative work extends only to the material contributed by the author of the derivative work. In creating a motion picture, the filmmaker gets a copyright in the film, as a derivative work, but the filmmaker does not thereby get to hijack the separate copyrights in the screenplay and the recorded music, or in the novel or song underlying them. Those separate copyrights remain with their authors or owners, unless the filmmaker comes along and buys them out.

In a related vein are two special types of works recognized under the Copyright Act. A *compilation* is a work formed by the collection and assembling of preexisting materials or data that are selected or arranged in such a way that the resulting work as a whole is an original work of authorship. Compilations include things like collections of public domain sheet music, recorded music, photographs and clip art, and automated databases. Compilations include *collective works,* in which a number of contributions from different sources are assembled together, such as an anthology, a magazine, or a music album featuring music by multiple artists. Copyright in each separate contribution to a collective work, owned by the author of that contribution, is distinct and separate from the copyright in the collective work as a whole, which is held by the author of the collection.

THINGS NOT COPYRIGHTABLE

The list of protected species under the Copyright Act is not open-ended. Lots of things are ineligible for copyright protection. If your creation is not on the list of "original works of authorship" covered above, it is not protected by copyright.

Here is a short list of unprotected species:

Works Not Fixed in a Tangible Medium

You're a natural-born comedian. Your stand-up routine is hilarious. All your friends tell you so. You just haven't gotten around to writing any of it down, recording it, or filming it. You're a piece of work, your friends all say. But your monologue is *not* a work under copyright. It's unprotected, because it hasn't been fixed in a tangible medium of expression. Go write it down. Now. Shut the book. We'll wait. Go save the monologue. Just do it.

Titles, Slogans, and Other Short Stuff

Come to think of it, JUST DO IT® just happens to be a registered trademark of Nike, Inc. But it's not copyrightable. Short combinations of words such as titles, names, slogans, mottoes, catchwords, catchphrases, and short advertising expressions are not protected by copyright. To be copyrightable, a work must contain at least a certain minimum amount of authorship in the form of original literary, musical, pictorial, or graphic expression. Titles, names, slogans, and other short phrases, however clever, don't make the copyright grade. You can copyright a novel, but not the title of a novel. On the other hand, you may be able to trademark the title and the names of characters in the novel, under certain circumstances, and we'll get a chance to do so in Chapter 2.

Familiar Symbols and Familiar Designs

Wouldn't it be outrageous if you could copyright the © symbol?

Well, you can't. Other people need to be able to use it without asking your permission. But what if you painted a © on a canvas or created a weird computer graphic of a ©? The resulting art might be a work original enough to qualify for copyright protection. The same goes for common geometric shapes, and things like a cross, a fleur-de-lis, or the peace sign. In their generic form, they aren't copyrightable, but any familiar symbol can become the subject of an originally rendered artistic work that is.

Useful Articles

Designs for "useful articles" such as fashion apparel, automobile bodies, and household appliances are currently not protected by copyright, but the design of a useful article is copyrightable to the extent that its pictorial, graphic, or sculptural features can be identified separately from the utilitarian aspects of the article and are capable of existing independently of the utilitarian side.

The line between uncopyrightable works of industrial design and copyrightable works of applied art can get fuzzy at times. But it is clear that two-dimensional photos, paintings, cartoon drawings, and graphic art are identifiable separately from the useful article when printed on stuff like t-shirts, mugs, toys, and lunch boxes, and being able to copyright these goodies and enforce the trademarks associated with them is what protects the lion's share of licensed movie merchandise.

Faced with this "useful article" dilemma, the fashion biz has lobbied long and hard for a little respect in Congress. As this book went to print, the U.S. Senate was set to vote on a bill dubbed the Innovative Design Protection and Piracy Prevention Act, which would provide a short three-year term of copyright protection for new and original fashion apparel and accessory designs to prohibit substantially identical knockoffs.

U.S. Government Works

We didn't have to go hat in hand to Congress for permission to quote from the Copyright Act, or stop and think about whether our use of it constitutes the kind of "fair use" that exempts us from having to ask permission. That's because the Copyright Act is in the public domain. This law was made for you and us. Works of the U.S. government, prepared by a federal officer or employee as part of his or her official duties, are not copyrightable under U.S. law, although Uncle Sam can claim copyright in them overseas. On the other hand, works created by federal government contractors can be protected under copyright, and so can works of state and local governments and works created by their contractors. Keep this in mind if you venture into creating documentary, investigative, or other creative works that draw on such materials, because then you may well have to delve into fair use issues, discussed later in this chapter.

Ideas

Copyright protection for an original work of authorship does not extend to any idea contained in it. A book about law can be copyrighted, but the idea of putting in the book a hypothetical case study to illustrate key points cannot. Even if someone else originated the idea in an earlier book protected by copyright, the idea remains free for us and the rest of the world to use.

Which gives us an idea.

This book could use a hypothetical.

Which gives us another idea.

Our hypothetical may as well start with you.

HISPANIOLA—THE HYPOTHETICAL

One fine day, you're slaving away at your laptop when you feel a sudden urge to pry your fingers off the keyboard, take a break from your latest work in progress, turn your back on your so-called social network, quit your browser and escape the virtual world. What you need, you tell yourself as you head out the door, is some fresh air. But around the corner, just down the street, the sunlit glint of a plate-glass display window catches your eye.

Marlow has reshuffled his wares. Atop a faded red velvet tablecloth draped over a pair of orange crates stands a leaning tower of hardbound classics, straddled by an open first edition *Mark of Zorro* flaunting a dubious Johnston McCulley autograph on the flyleaf. Bumping up against the classics is a dusty stack of comic books topped by *Green Hornet Fights Crime*, Issue #34. Dangling over Zorro in midair is a replica samurai sword jerry-rigged with nylon fishing line, perhaps Made in Occupied Japan, but more likely pilfered from the props department the morning after *Kill Bill: Vol. 2*. Higher still in aerial combat soar the Creature from the Black Lagoon, glued to the gills from an Aurora model kit, and a vintage Barbie in bermudas and midriff bolero top, flirtatiously flinging Yu-Gi-Oh! cards at the amphibious loner. You draw a deep breath and enter the shop, setting off the inevitable brass bells hung over the door.

"Marlow's Collectibles" isn't organized like the Internet.

There are no sponsored links, no banner ads, no pop-ups, no streaming media, no apps, no social networking (unless you call talking to Marlow social networking), and no search engines (except Marlow). The shop is an ill-lit gauntlet of mismatched bookcases crammed floor to ceiling with musty gilded volumes, dog-eared paperbacks, manga, DVDs, videocassettes, CDs, LPs, 45s, 78s, eight-track tapes, dolls, toys, and other sundry flotsam and jetsam washed up without discrimination on basis of genre or taste from the boundless sea of entertainment and the arts. The place is an absolute mess, but you are drawn here every once in a while when you feel creatively blocked, because you know a little secret:

Marlow's is full of ideas and other cool free stuff.

Chances are, you tell yourself, a lot of these books are in the public domain, long out of print, totally forgotten, their copyrights expired, authors dead, publishers bankrupted. You may see yourself as a screenwriter, a filmmaker, an animator, a video game artist, or something else entirely, but you realize that Marlow's is a goldmine of ideas free for the taking, a graveyard of underappreciated themes, plots, twists, characters, and settings just waiting for you to breathe fresh life into them.

You take a walk down the aisle, sampling the goods. Wedged between a pair of *Pirates of the Caribbean* Series 1 action figures, Jack Sparrow and Captain Barbossa embalmed in their original packaging, you spy a faux parchment leatherette book with ornate black letters inscribed down the spine—the two I's tricked out to look like daggers, promising intrigue, danger, and blood.

You pull the book off the shelf, and inspect the front cover:

HISPANIOLA
A Sequel to Treasure Island
by
Bonnie Charlotte

You pull up a footstool and begin to read.

The prologue recaps how in Robert Louis Stevenson's *Treasure Island*, the boy narrator Jim Hawkins got a crash course in the nature of good and evil, conflicted as he was between his sage yet square mentors Squire Trelawney and Doctor Livesey, on one hand, and the edgy gangster charisma of Long John Silver on the other. Jim and the good guys barely survive the bad guys' harrowing attack on their island stockade, their good ship *Hispaniola* maroons the pirates and limps back to Bristol, and they divvy up the modest fraction of Captain Flint's fabled treasure they managed to unearth before all hell broke loose. Having learned his lesson, young Jim swears off treasure hunting with dodgy seafarers. As far as Jim's concerned, the bulk of Flint's silver can remain buried forever where Flint hid it. Nothing could ever bring him back to that accursed island.

That was then.

Fast forward thirty years, and *Hispaniola* the sequel finds Hawkins in midlife crisis as proprietor of the Admiral Benbow Inn in Kingston, Jamaica. Thirty years on the make have rather frayed Jim's ethical underpinnings. He's running rum, running guns, and in up to his neck fencing stolen booty. The Benbow is a one-stop den of iniquity catering to the lowest rung of Caribbean nautical society. It seems Squire Trelawney and Doctor Livesey's formative influence wasn't so formative after all. Long John Silver has won the tug of war for Jim's heart and mind. At forty-something, Hawkins is a dirtbag. A graphic image of this piece of work takes shape in your mind's eye.

Enter *Hispaniola*'s heroine, nineteen-year-old orphan Lucia Bonaire, with her kid sister Dominica and a half dozen more young ladies sporting late-eighteenth-

Jim Hawkins

century pirate gear. As they enter the inn, one of the rude boys loafing round the bar gets fresh with Dominica. Lucia changes his tune with a rum bottle across the forehead, then proceeds to the back room, where she meets with Hawkins, who pitches her a plan to sail for Treasure Island on his newly refurbished schooner *Hispaniola*.

It has taken him thirty years to track down Flint's real treasure map, and now he means to recoup Flint's silver. But he needs a trustworthy crew. If Lucia and her girls want the gig, it's theirs. Hawkins promises it'll be share and share alike. Lucia is reluctant to throw in with him, but good intentions compel her nonetheless. Some call her a pirate; Lucia calls herself a social entrepreneur. She and the girls took out a subprime mortgage to establish a fixer-upper old folk's home for indigent retired pirates, the Casa Antiqua, but now, perilously short of funds to stave off foreclosure, and with no alternative in sight, Lucia signs on with Hawkins. You can picture Lucia right now.

Lucia Bonaire

She and her crew leave the Benbow to go rethatch the Casa's roof, and Hawkins slinks off to the waterfront to inspect his ship. In the captain's quarters Hawkins conspires with his unsavory female first mate Ripley. They hatch a plan to stow away a shadow crew of a dozen of the Benbow's worst degenerates, then double-cross Lucia's team on Treasure Island, as soon as the girls find the silver and accomplish the heavy lifting. Ripley signals approval of her boss's scheme with a horrid, sycophantic cackle, confirming one's worst suspicions about the state of British dental care in the 1790s.

OMG, you tell yourself. You're not that into pirates, but this has potential.

A film treatment starts writing itself in your head. Good-apple-gone-bad Hawkins and sleazy henchwoman Ripley are compelling characters. So are the girl pirates with hearts of gold: daring Lucia and her ingénue sis Dominica—Martinique, the runaway Haitian slave—Montserrat, the French consul's rebellious daughter—Kitty, the indentured Irish maidservant—Guadeloupe, the renegade Puerto Rican sugar heiress—Jade, the Chinese short-order cook with culinary dreams—and Saba, the mysterious Taíno Indian princess. In the right hands, *Hispaniola* would make an awesome transmedia franchise. With a little help from your friends and some financial backing, you could produce, write, and direct a live action film, adapt the film into a cartoon, turn that into a video game, and generate the myriad media and merchandise spin-offs, from interactive sites to dolls to toys to Halloween costumes, that *Hispaniola*'s hip-to-be-square heroines and rotten-to-the-core baddies cry out for. You wonder who, if anyone, holds rights in this treasure chest of a book.

You storm down the aisle brandishing *Hispaniola*.

Found something, have we? asks Marlow, gazing up through rimless tinted specs that give him a passing resemblance to Mad Mod from *Teen Titans*. He lifts his noble aquiline nose out of an especially gory volume of *Bleach* splayed open on his creaky oak desk.

In a town where Brit accents real and fake have been a dime a dozen for a century, this veteran of stage and scene sounds like the genuine article, even though he drifts from Yorkshire to Cheshire to Worcestershire and points south with random poetic license. Rumor has it that after a sufficiently lengthy string of bad reviews helped him decide an actor's life was not for him, Marlow put his law degree to work as a studio hired gun back in the bad old days, and that he knows every trick in the book.

Can you borrow *Hispaniola* for a day or two? you ask.

Marlow shrugs. It's not as if you came in to buy anything.

You have a hunch it would make a great movie.

Brilliant, Marlow concedes.

If you can just make it happen without getting ripped off in the process.

Aye, there's the rub, grins Marlow.

But there's a lot to tackle, including the legal.

Indeed, there is.

For starters, you just need to figure out whether *Hispaniola* is in the public domain.

For starters, yes.

You're just not sure how to go about it.

Marlow sighs. He juts his pointy chin at the book tucked under your arm.

It's *The Creative Artist's Legal Guide.*

THE RIGHTS COPYRIGHT CREATES

The Copyright Act grants the owner of a copyrighted work several ex-clusive rights. *Reproduction rights* control who can reproduce copies of the work. *Distribution rights* entitle the owner to decide who can distribute copies to the public. *Performance rights,* in the case of a literary, musical, or dramatic work, or a motion picture or other audiovisual work, entitle the owner to decide who can perform the work publicly, and *digital perfor-mance rights,* in the case of a sound recording, do so for public digital audio transmission. *Display rights,* in the case of a literary, musical, dramatic, pictorial, graphic, or sculptural work, or the individual images of a mo-tion picture or other audiovisual work, govern display of the work publicly, such as in an art gallery or on a Web site. Most important for media artists in the scheme of things, after reproduction and distribution rights, are *de-rivative rights,* which entitle the owner of a copyrighted work to decide who can create derivative works based upon the original.

These exclusive rights equip the copyright owner to deal in copyrights, and arm the owner to fight with copyrights, but they don't last forever, and the owner needs to take a few protective steps to make sure they can be enforced if push comes to shove.

PROTECTING COPYRIGHTS

The copyright in an original work of authorship springs to life the moment the work is created and fixed in a tangible medium of expression. There are, however, several things the owner should do to protect his or her copyrights and their effectiveness.

KEEPING TRACK

Keeping a clear paper or digital record of the date or dates you create a work is key, because down the road you may run into somebody who claims he or she created a similar work before you created yours. The kind of paper or digital record you keep will depend on the medium or media in which you tangibly fix your work. You needn't obsess over it, though, and a little common sense in your approach to organizing your work and keeping records will go a long way.

If your work is a derivative work based on one or more underlying works, you will need to keep track of each underlying work you used. For each, you will need to document whether it is one you already own yourself, one you bought from the owner and for which you received a signed copyright assignment, one you licensed from the owner under a signed copyright license, one you got permission from the owner to use for free, one you didn't need permission for because it is in the public domain, or one you didn't need permission for because your use counts as fair use.

For your latest project, Bonnie Charlotte's novel *Hispaniola* is the core underlying work on which you hope to base your movie *Hispaniola*. You will have to document how you acquire the right to use it. But you will also deploy many additional underlying works in order to make your derivative work. Keeping track of all of them will enable you to piece together a *chain of title* giving your film a clean bill of copyright health, so that you and the industry players with whom you end up coming to terms can use it, sell it, distribute it, and license it without fear of third-party copyright claims.

PUBLICATION

Publication of a work used to be a prerequisite to obtaining a copyright, but not anymore. The publication requirement was abolished in the Copyright Act of 1976, which came into effect on January 1, 1978. This magic date will come back to haunt us later when we delve into calculating how long copyrights last.

Under current law, copyright springs to life automatically when a work is fixed in a copy or phonorecord for the first time, and does not hinge on publication. Publication, though, remains a significant legal step in the life of a copyrighted work because several other things *do* hinge on it.

First, some of the advantages of registering a copyright are available only if the registration occurs within specified time periods after publication.

Second, the year of publication determines how long copyright lasts for "works made for hire" (and for "anonymous" and "pseudonymous" works, registered works whose author's identity is not revealed in Copyright Office records).

Third, in order to register a copyright, the Copyright Office imposes deposit requirements, and these differ depending on whether the work is unpublished or published.

Fourth, whether you register the copyright or not, works published in the United States are subject to mandatory deposit with the Library of Congress, to help bulk up its collection of books, photographs, films, TV shows, and music, and this mandatory deposit requirement kicks in immediately upon publication.

The Copyright Act defines "publication" as the distribution of copies or phonorecords of a work to the public by sale or other transfer of ownership, or by rental, lease, or lending. Think of "publication" as equivalent to exercising the author's distribution right. "To the public" means distribution to people under no express or implied restrictions on disclosure of the contents. For example, if you write a film treatment for *Hispaniola* and selectively circulate it to friends or potential business partners, you haven't published the treatment.

Public performance or display of a work does not, by itself, amount to publication. Any form of dissemination of a work in which the material object does not change hands, such as on television, is generally not a publication, no matter how many people can view or listen to the performance. However, when copies or phonorecords are offered for sale or lease to a group of wholesalers, broadcasters, or motion picture theaters or exchanges, publication does occur, if the purpose is further distribution to the public, public performance, or public display.

The sale of a phonorecord is not only a publication of the sound recording on it, but also amounts to a publication of the underlying work. For instance, the public release of a music CD or MP3 is a publication of the recording, and also a publication of the song or songs contained in the recording.

COPYRIGHT NOTICE

Putting a copyright notice on copies or phonorecords of a work used to be a prerequisite to obtaining a copyright, but not anymore. This requirement was eliminated as of March 1, 1989, another magic date, when the United States joined the Berne Convention, a key international copyright treaty. Though no longer legally required for works published on and after March 1, 1989, it is still a good idea to put a copyright notice on new works. Also, since prior law did require notice, a copyright notice or lack of notice can become legally crucial when you need to size up the validity of copyright in older works.

Use of a copyright notice on any work you publish, or distribute privately in unpublished form, helps protect you, because it tells others the work is protected by copyright, identifies the copyright owner and, if it is published, shows the year of publication. If later on your work is infringed, a proper notice of copyright appearing on a copy to which the infringer had access precludes the infringer from rolling his or her eyes and pleading "innocent infringement."

A copyright notice should contain three things:

- a copyright symbol
- the year of first publication of the work, if published
- the name of the owner or owners of the copyright.

Example: © 2012 Bill Seiter, Ellen Seiter, and Yale University.

There. Don't say we didn't warn you.

The symbol ©, or the word "Copyright," or its abbreviation "Copr." is used if the notice goes on a copy, not a phonorecord, such as this book. If the notice goes on a phonorecord, use the symbol ℗.

Example: ℗ 1967 CBS Inc.

For many phonorecords, such as vinyl records and CDs, the label, packaging, container, or disc itself may contain original visual artwork, in which case it is all right to combine both symbols in one copyright notice.

Example: ℗© 1973 Grateful Dead Records.

The copyright notice should be affixed in such a way as to give reasonable notice of the claim of copyright. The three elements of the notice should ordinarily appear together on the copy or phonorecord or on its container or label. It is all right to abbreviate the name of the copyright owner to an abbreviation by which the name can be recognized, or a generally known alternative designation of the owner. On a phonorecord, if the producer of the sound recording is named on the phonorecord label or container, and if no other name appears in conjunction with the notice, the producer's name is considered part of the notice.

As we said, it is a very good idea to place a copyright notice on any un-published copies of your work that leave your control, beginning with your film treatment for *Hispaniola*.

Example: Unpublished work © 2012 [*Your Name Here*].

COPYRIGHT REGISTRATION

Registering your copyright with the Copyright Office is not a prerequisite to having a valid copyright, but there are several legal advantages to regis-tering that are always useful, and sometimes indispensable, in enforcing the copyright:

- Registration establishes a public record of your copyright, putting the world on notice of the basic facts of your copyright, such as who the owner is, what type of work it is, and when it was created.
- Registration is required before a copyright infringement lawsuit can be pursued in court, unless your work originates outside the United States.
- If your work is registered within three months after its first publication, or registered prior to its infringement, you can ask a court to award you statutory damages and attorneys' fees and costs against the infringer.
- If your work is registered within five years of its first publication, the registra-tion constitutes prima facie evidence of the validity of the copyright and of the facts stated in the registration certificate, putting the burden of proof on any challenger who tries to attack the validity of your copyright.
- Copyright registrations can be recorded with the U.S. Customs Service, to help deter imports of infringing copies from overseas.

Registration can be made at any time during the life of the copyright, but as we already mentioned, there are advantages to filing soon after creation or publication. When a work has been registered in unpublished form, it is not necessary to make another registration when the work becomes published, though you can register the published version if you wish.

For a full walk through how to register a copyright, see Appendix 1.

HOW LONG COPYRIGHTS LAST

Copyrights last a long time.

When you are the copyright owner, you want to know how long your rights last and when they expire. On other occasions, you need to figure out when somebody else's copyright expires. In our little hypothetical where we've thrown you in with Marlow, you'd like to know whether Bonnie Charlotte's copyright in her novel *Hispaniola* has expired. If it has, it's in the public domain and you won't have to hunt her down and get her permission to use it as the underlying work for the screenplay for your forthcoming movie *Hispaniola*. Nicest of all, you won't have to pay her for it. If her copyright hasn't expired, you will have to hunt her down and get her permission, and we'll be very surprised if you don't end up having to pay for it.

A couple of factors have made the computation of copyright terms in the United States a bit more complex than they ought to be. But if you're looking for someone to blame, don't blame us. Blame Congress.

For one thing, the Copyright Act of 1976 radically changed the way we compute copyright terms in this country, but it did not make the change retroactive. Since the law became effective on January 1, 1978, that date is a watershed. The method of computation for a given work depends on whether the work was created pre-1978 or post-1977.

For another thing, Congress lengthened copyright terms under the 1976 act, lengthened them again in 1998, and it made these changes retroactive, thereby postponing the day of reckoning when some of our most beloved authors, films, and cartoon characters shall at last enter the public domain to rub elbows with the likes of Shakespeare, Nosferatu, and Popeye.

Let's consider copyright terms for works first published in the United States.

Post-1977 Works

A work originally created by an author on or after January 1, 1978, not as a work for hire, is protected from the moment of its creation, and the term of the copyright lasts throughout the author's life plus an additional 70 years after the author's death. If the work is a joint work prepared by two or more authors, not as a work for hire, the term lasts for 70 years after the last surviving author's death. Copyright terms always run until December 31st of the year in which they are expiring. Based on current law, if an author died on July 4, 2010, his or her copyrights would expire on December 31, 2080.

A different rule applies to works made for hire. These gain a copyright term of 95 years from publication or 120 years from creation, whichever is shorter. If a movie produced as a work for hire in 2009 hit theaters July 4, 2010, its copyright would expire on December 31, 2105. If a script written as a work for hire in 2009 took a hundred years to produce, and the movie didn't hit theaters till 2109, copyright in the script would expire on December 31, 2129.

Pre-1978 Works

Under pre-1978 law, copyright started either on the date a work was published with a copyright notice or, if the work was registered in unpublished form, on the date of registration. The copyright lasted for an initial term of 28 years, starting from the date of publication or, if unpublished, the date of registration. During the final year of the initial term, the copyright was eligible for renewal for an additional 28 years, making for a total of 56 years of protection, provided the owner applied to renew. The one-year period within which the renewal had to be filed started on the 27th anniversary of the date of publication or, if unpublished, the date of registration, and ended on the 28th anniversary of that date. For example, if a work was published on March 1, 1930, it had to be renewed during the period starting March 1, 1957, and ending March 1, 1958.

That was pre-1978 law. Those terms have since been lengthened.

There are, of course, an enormous number of works created and published or registered before 1978. The copyrights in some of these works, especially in film, television, and music, are extremely valuable things that their owners would like to keep as long as they possibly can. Responding to successive waves of lobbying by such copyright owners, Congress has successively let copyright terms stretch and stretch, at a rate rivaling that of Pinocchio's nose when he's in storytelling mode.

The 1976 act extended the renewal term for copyrights existing on January 1, 1978, from 28 to 47 years, to make these works eligible for a total term of protection of 75 years. The Sonny Bono Copyright Term Extension Act, effective October 27, 1998, further extended the renewal term of copyrights existing on that date, and first copyrighted after January 1, 1923, by an additional 20 years. For instance, copyright in a work first published in 1923, and timely renewed, would have expired on December 31, 1998, but thanks to the Copyright Term Extension Act, its copyright will not expire until December 31, 2018.

The net result is that all works copyrighted between 1923 and 1977 and renewed on time have initial terms of 28 years and renewal terms of 67 years, for a total 95 years of protection, equaling that of post-1977 works made for hire. Copyrights in works first published in the United States before 1923 have expired, and such works are in the public domain.

Owners of works copyrighted between 1923 and 1963 had to file timely renewal applications in order to get a renewal term, and if they did not, they lost their copyright. Thinking this unfair, Congress in 1992 eliminated the renewal filing requirement for owners of all remaining pre-1978 copyrights that had not yet come up for renewal. The Copyright Amendments Act of 1992 made renewal automatic for copyrights obtained between 1964 and 1977.

Works created pre-1978, but not published or registered by January 1, 1978, receive special treatment. The copyright term for these is generally computed the same way as for post-1977 works, but the Copyright Act specifies that in no case does the copyright term for such works expire before December 31, 2002, and for such works published by December 31, 2002, the term of copyright will not expire before December 31, 2047.

DEALING IN COPYRIGHTS

Copyrights can be bought, sold, and licensed. People in entertainment and the arts do it all the time. It's the whole point of having copyrights. A copyright owner can license or sell the entire set of rights under a copyright or any subset of rights. The rights can be sliced and diced as the owner sees fit. Whenever you run across an existing work that you may want to use to create a derivative work of your own, you need to determine whether or not anyone owns copyright in the work.

COPYRIGHT RESEARCH

If the work contains a copyright notice, you start there, but you don't end there.

Copyright Office records can be searched to find information about registrations, including whether or not a renewal of a copyright was filed. To do a renewal search, you need to know the title of the work, the author name, the year the work was published, and the country in which it was first published.

The Copyright Office has put registration records from 1978 onward online. These include renewals filed from 1978 onward, so the online records include renewals for works copyrighted in 1950 and renewed during 1978 (but not for works that were copyrighted in 1950 and renewed in 1977), and all renewals for works copyrighted after 1950. These online renewal records can be searched for free at the Copyright Office's Web site.

Unfortunately, renewals of all pre-1950 works (and renewals for those 1950 works renewed during 1977) are not available online, so if you need to research such an older work, it has to be manually searched in the Copyright Office's *Catalog of Copyright Entries*. The catalog is available at the Copyright Office in Washington, D.C., and at most major metropolitan libraries and university libraries. But searching the paper catalog can be tedious. If you don't feel up to searching the catalog or don't have access to it, you can ask the Copyright Office to search for you, although this involves substantial fees and long turnaround times. You can get faster turnaround and less expensive service using a private search firm, the largest of these being Thomson CompuMark, but even these private search firms tend to take at least a week.

HISPANIOLA—THE SEARCH

You won't turn *Hispaniola* into a movie without a good deal of wheeling and dealing in copyrights. Before you wheel and deal with anybody, though, you had better size up whether anyone still owns copyright in the novel.

You start with the title page of the book:

HISPANIOLA

A Sequel to Treasure Island

by

Bonnie Charlotte

New York: Cutthroat Press

You flip to the copyright page, on the reverse of the title page, which says:

Copyright 1955 by Bonnie Charlotte. All rights reserved.

Not as old as you had hoped, yet still this book might be old enough to be in the public domain. It's time to do the math. Assuming its copyright notice is correct, the book was first published sometime in 1955, and the title page indicates it was first published in the United States. For pre-1978 works first published in the U.S., the initial term of copyright is twenty-eight years from the date of publication. If Bonnie renewed her copyright during the twenty-eighth year, between the twenty-seventh and twenty-eighth anniversaries of the publication date, its renewal term under current law would be sixty-seven years, making for a total term of ninety-five years, so that the copyright would not expire until December 31, 2050. If Bonnie failed to renew, the copyright has expired, *Hispaniola* is in the public domain, and you can use it for free.

Hispaniola's title page and copyright page tell you the title of the work, the author's name, the year the work was published, and the country it was first published in: all the information you need to do a renewal search. The good news is, you're in luck: the renewal search for this work from 1955 can be done online in a few minutes' time, for free. The bad news is, your luck's not perfect.

Bonnie Charlotte filed her renewal in 1982.

Her copyright will last until 2050.

Disappointed, you run to tell Marlow. You had your heart set on public domain but, whatever, *Hispaniola* is too good *not* to make into a movie. If the book is still under copyright, so be it. You'll just have to acquire the rights. You wonder whether Bonnie Charlotte is still alive, or whether you're going to have to deal with her children, grandchildren, or worse.

Oh, she's alive, all righ', replies Marlow, glottal stopping his t's this particular day in South London Cockney mode. If he starts calling you Luv, you're going to slug him.

She is?

A personal acquaintance of his, like everyone else in this town evidently.

Marlow gives you the backstory. Bonnie grew up the precocious daughter of a talented screenwriter, Jack Charlotte, acclaimed for scripting brisk sea adventures with a gentle proletarian undertow until he was blacklisted in the late 1940s. While still in her teens, to help make ends meet, Bonnie wrote and published *Hispaniola*. The book was well received, with one critic dubbing her the "Mary Shelley of Swashbucklers." Her publisher, Cutthroat Press, flourished in the 1950s, but wallowed in red ink in the '60s and tanked in '69. The book went out of print as rock 'n' roll eroded the reading habits of American youth, and the dawning of the Age of Aquarius hammered the last nail into the dead man's chest of nautical adventure fiction. Bonnie spent the next four decades teaching high school English, helping people like you learn to write, till her recent retirement.

Any studio ever option *Hispaniola?* you ask.

Oh, they tried, says Marlow. But Bonnie despises the studios, because of her dad.

Meaning she could be persuaded to entrust it to the right indie?

You know what the man says, Marlow grins wolfishly.

You nod.

Revenge is a dish best served cold.

So when do we meet her?

Not so fast, chuckles Marlow.

First you've got a thing or two to learn about buying and licensing copyrights.

BUYING AND LICENSING COPYRIGHTS

For each creative work going into the making of the movie *Hispaniola* that you don't create yourself, you're going to need a copyright. Each copyright you can get in only one of three ways, unless somebody dies and leaves it to you in their will. You can buy the copyright, getting a copyright assignment from the owner. You can pay for a copyright license from the owner, permitting you to use the work for your defined purposes. Or, for works created during the course of pre-production, production, and post-production, you can own the copyright in the first place by commissioning the artist to create the work for you as a work made for hire.

Copyright Assignments

When a copyright is bought outright, the buyer needs to insist that the seller sign a *copyright assignment* confirming the transfer. Copyright assignments are not valid unless put in writing and signed by the copyright owner or the owner's authorized agent.

A copyright assignment typically says that the owner sells, transfers, and assigns to the assignee specified rights under copyright and other applicable law in and to the work in perpetuity (that is, forever), either in the United States and worldwide or for specified territories, and either in all media or for specified media.

When Marlow takes you to meet Bonnie Charlotte, you're going to ask her for an assignment of the right to make a movie based on her novel. The right to make motion pictures based on her book is one of the derivative rights she holds as copyright owner, and you would like to own that right, together with all related rights you may need to make an artistic and financial success of the production and to profit from that success.

You need to make sure the words of the assignment are broad enough that Bonnie is selling you the rights to use the novel, including characters and everything else in it, to enable you, and whomever you collaborate with and whomever you hire, to write film treatments based on it, write screenplays based on it, make one or more movies based on it, produce sequels and other forms of entertainment in film and other media you care about, such as DVD, television, and Internet, and exploit, distribute, and sell the resulting works forever, as well as the perpetual right to produce, market, sell, and sublicense movie merchandise, on which you can guess Bonnie is going to want a piece of the action. The assignment must be specific. If it doesn't say in words that she has assigned you the right to produce and sell video games or action figures based on the book, movie, and characters, you won't be able to create and deal in *Hispaniola* video games and action figures. So start out with your wish list, and make sure the assignment includes everything you wish to make the production and its offshoots succeed.

You also need to be sure the copyright assignment won't conflict with any prior commitments Bonnie may have made to other folks. She once granted Cutthroat Press a license to reproduce, publish, distribute, and sell the book, but you need to know that she never assigned or licensed film rights to Cutthroat or anyone else. You can't have some other producer coming out of the woodwork claiming rights in the property while you're running around trying to get the film financed and made, or worse, after you release the film. For your peace of mind, the copyright assignment or a related document should include *representations and warranties,* things the copyright owner tells you are true and will stay true.

You will need Bonnie to represent and warrant that her novel is an original work of authorship of which she is the sole author and owner; that nobody else has any right, title, or interest in it, other than deals she has fully informed you about and you are okay with; that she has not sold, transferred, assigned, or licensed any of the same rights to anyone else, or allowed anyone else to use her work in a way inconsistent with your rights; that she has not granted any rights which might limit yours; and that she has not filed for or registered her work anywhere, except for the U.S. copyright registration you already know about and are depending on as the source of your rights.

To backstop these representations and warranties, you need Bonnie to give you in the copyright assignment or related document an *indemnity.* She should agree to indemnify you, that is, pay or reimburse your costs, for any damages or claims anyone makes against you in case any of her representations or warranties turn out to be untrue, and she should provide and pay your legal defense in that case.

COPYRIGHT LICENSES

You want an assignment of the film rights. Bonnie, on the other hand, may wish to cling to her ownership of the film rights and grant you just a *copyright license*. That's how she dealt with Cutthroat Press. She retained her ownership of the reproduction rights and distribution rights in the book, and granted the publisher an exclusive license to print, publish, and sell the book. Cutthroat had to pay her royalties under the license agreement, which also required them to keep the book in print, which Cutthroat eventually failed to do. You can bet Bonnie terminated the license when Cutthroat breached, and will be free to grant a new license to a new publisher, should one come along interested in reissuing the book under a new imprint. If your movie deal comes to fruition, you can bet publisher interest will be there, and you ought to factor that into your deal with Bonnie.

In granting a license, usually in exchange for royalties and sometimes other forms of payment, the copyright owner becomes a copyright licensor as well. The licensor typically grants a license to use the licensed property to create specific defined types of derivative works in specific defined media. A copyright license should include representations and warranties, and an indemnity, covering similar ground to that covered when a copyright is assigned.

The choice between a license and an assignment is negotiable. It's up to the parties which way to go. Authors, if they have the bargaining power, like to control the fate of their books, and they like to control the film rights in their books to the extent they can. *Hispaniola* may be Bonnie's book. But it's your film production. You need to control the film. You need an assignment of the film rights.

You will, however, enter into a number of copyright licenses in the course of producing and rolling out *Hispaniola* the movie and its offspring. For instance, on one hand, you will probably end up buying licenses and becoming a copyright licensee to acquire rights in some or all of the music to be used in the film. On the other hand, your production company will in due course also become a copyright licensor, for instance, when the time comes to strike deals for movie merchandise. Some of your licenses will be exclusive, some nonexclusive.

Exclusive copyright licenses, like copyright assignments, are not valid unless they are put in writing and signed by the copyright owner or the owner's authorized agent. A nonexclusive license is not required to be in writing, but under almost all circumstances it would be insane not to put a nonexclusive license in writing, since you don't want to have it come down to your word versus theirs, should there be a misunderstanding down the road, as there often is when you don't put it in writing.

OPTIONS

In any case, you're not going to buy an assignment of the film rights to Bonnie's book immediately. As producer, you will initially want to buy an *option* to acquire the rights. In a typical *option and purchase agreement,* in exchange for payment of a relatively small option price, the copyright owner grants the producer the option, within a limited period of time, to acquire the motion picture and related rights needed to make the film and commercialize it. This gives you the breathing space to put together the creative elements and the financing for the film, before having to commit to shell out substantial money. The option period for commercial film projects varies, but twelve to eighteen months is typical, and it is common for the producer also to have an opportunity to extend the option for an additional period, often a further twelve to eighteen months, upon payment of an additional fee or fees.

In the end, if all goes well before the option expires, the producer buys the copyright assignment for a pre-negotiated purchase price. That purchase price often consists of an up-front amount geared to a modest percentage of the final film budget, and typically also promises to pay the author contingent compensation geared to the producer's net profits, a bonus perhaps, if the film hits some specified performance benchmark, and usually a percentage royalty on movie merchandise. Often the producer will have the author sign a copyright assignment at the time the option and purchase agreement is signed, so the producer won't have to track down the author later on for a signature, it being understood, though, that the producer is not entitled to use or record the copyright assignment unless and until the producer pays the purchase price.

We mentioned recording. The Copyright Office has a system for *recordation* of copyright assignments, licenses, and other documents that affect copyright ownership, such as security agreements, where a lender takes a copyright as collateral to secure its loan. To record a document at the

Copyright Office, you file a Document Cover Sheet, downloadable from the Copyright Office Web site, an original of the document bearing the actual signature of the people who signed it, or a certified copy of the original, and the required fee. Though recordation is not required to make a copyright assignment or license valid, it provides legal advantages in some dealings in copyright, since it puts the world on notice of the assignment, license, security interest, or other matter covered in the document. Recordation of such documents is routinely used in entertainment and arts projects of any significant magnitude.

Although copyrights are created and protected under federal law, state law comes into play in several ways when dealing in copyright assignments and licenses. For one thing, copyright assignments and licenses involve contracts, so state contract law determines the validity of the contracts and the interpretation of their wording. For another, since copyrights are considered a type of personal property right, their disposition is subject to state laws governing ownership, inheritance, and transfer of personal property. For instance, minors can claim authorship and ownership of copyrights, but the laws of various states regulate dealings in personal property owned by minors, and typically require parental or guardian permission.

WORK-FOR-HIRE AGREEMENTS

You are thinking of writing the screenplay for *Hispaniola* yourself. But what if you meet with Bonnie, and she turns out to want to write the screenplay? If you let her write the screenplay, you need to have her sign a *work-for-hire agreement* making the screenplay a "work made for hire."

What if you and she hit it off so well that the two of you decide to co-write the screenplay? If you co-author a work outside the work-for-hire context, the authors of the *joint work* will be co-owners of the copyright, unless you make a specific agreement to the contrary. It is always best, before launching any such collaboration, to consider how you and the collaborator or collaborators should divide up copyright ownership and other rights, and you should put something in writing that reflects everyone's understanding and get everyone to sign it.

For *Hispaniola,* however, if you and Bonnie write the screenplay together, you don't want to be joint authors. You need your production company to be the author. If you and Bonnie both write, you and Bonnie both need to sign work-for-hire agreements confirming that the screenplay is a work made for hire belonging to the production company, not to you two jointly.

A work-for-hire agreement is sometimes set up as a separate agreement, but it is more often folded into one or more sections of the contract hiring a writer, director, actors, animators, or other talent signed to a film, television, video game, or other production. The heart of a work-for-hire agreement is the part stating that the work shall be considered a work made for hire.

The agreement will usually contain representations and warranties that address pitfalls similar to those a producer would want to avoid in taking a copyright assignment or license from the creator. A work-for-hire agreement typically will make the creator represent and warrant that the work commissioned is an original work of authorship of which he or she is the sole creator; that no other person co-authored it, worked on it, or has any right, title, or interest in it, other than people the producer specifically knows about; and that the creator hasn't granted anybody else any rights in the work. If any of this turns out to be false, the work-for-hire agreement usually makes the creator indemnify for damages. Employers and motion picture producers are extremely fond of such clauses, so before signing on to any work-for-hire project as creative talent, you need to read the fine print and feel confident your representations and warranties are true.

Work for hire is also a nifty way for employers and motion picture producers to avoid a major headache, from their viewpoint, known as *termination rights*. When an author assigns or licenses a copyright and says it's forever, it ain't necessarily forever. Authors have a special right to terminate any assignment or license after a certain number of years. If the author signed the assignment or license after 1977, the author can terminate it during a five-year window starting thirty-five years after the signing date (or, in case the assignment or license of rights includes the right to publish the work, starting the earlier of thirty-five years after the publication date or forty years after the signing date). If the author signed the assignment or license before 1978, the author can terminate it during a five-year window starting fifty-six years after the work was first published.

For example, suppose hypothetically that Cutthroat Press was still in business and had not breached its license agreement with Bonnie, so that the license agreement remained in effect. Bonnie signed the license in 1955. During a five-year window of opportunity starting in 2011, from the fifty-sixth anniversary of signing, Bonnie would be entitled to terminate the license, as long as she gave notice of termination within the window.

This termination right can be a dream come true for an author whose work becomes a hit only many years after its debut, and a nightmare from hell for publishers and producers. It enables the author or the author's heirs to unwind the original deal and renegotiate the terms, if the work has become much more commercially valuable with the passage of time. Just one main exception limits the termination right. Parties who make derivative works under license or assignment using the author's work as an underlying work, to the extent they create derivative works prior to termination of the license or assignment, can't have the rug pulled out from under them. They get to keep exploiting those derivative works created prior to a termination under the original license or assignment.

Termination rights are irrevocable. They can't be waived. They can't be signed away. Even if the author signs an assignment or license stating in big black print that the transfer of copyright is in perpetuity (that is, forever) and irrevocable, the author can ignore what he or she signed and unwind the deal within the termination rights window. If you are a publisher, producer, or anyone else paying to receive a copyright assignment or license, you need to factor in as you negotiate the deal the possibility that your supposedly immortal assignment or license may take a wooden stake through the heart if the author invokes his or her termination rights.

Works for hire, from the producer's viewpoint, sidestep the termination rights minefield. The creator of a work for hire never owns the copyright in the first place, and since there is no assignment or license of copyright, there's nothing to terminate. This is another major reason for employers' and motion picture producers' ongoing love affair with the work-for-hire exception.

ORPHAN WORKS

You got lucky when you stumbled across *Hispaniola* because it just so happens Bonnie Charlotte is still alive, and Marlow knows her and is willing to introduce you so you can negotiate for the film rights to her book. In the real world, though, when you try to research a work and track down the copyright owner, you may well draw a blank and end up with an orphan on your hands.

An orphan work is a copyrighted work for which it is difficult or impossible, after reasonable effort, to discover and locate the owner. Maybe the identity of the author was at one time known, but the contact details in the copyright registration are out of date and other sources don't reveal a current contact. Maybe the author is dead, and there is no way to determine his or her heirs, if any. Maybe the work was published anonymously and the author's identity can no longer be unraveled. Maybe the owner didn't register copyright in the work and you can't find other contact information. Maybe the owner assigned copyright but did not record the assignment.

Imagine discovering a great out-of-print book like *Hispaniola,* only to find out that neither you nor anyone else can safely reprint the book or create a derivative work from it, for fear some unknown copyright claimant who cannot be located after diligent search may come out of the woodwork after you release your work. Orphan work syndrome holds millions upon millions of literary, photographic, film, and musical works in limbo, with no safe way to share them with the rest of the world, and poses an enormous problem for documentary filmmakers and other creative media artists, museums, archives, and educational institutions around the globe.

Ironically, the orphan works problem in the United States is a retrograde blowback from two progressive moves Congress made to enable the United States to get in step with the international norms reflected in the Berne Convention, discussed later in this chapter. First, when the Copyright Act of 1976 eliminated the requirement that copyrighted works be registered with the Copyright Office, and instead declared that all original works of authorship fixed in any tangible medium of expression qualify for copyright, the copyright register ceased to serve as a definitive one-stop source to determine the existence of a copyright and identify its holder. Second, in 1989, when Congress eliminated the requirement that a copyright notice be placed on copies of a work for it to qualify for copyright, you could no longer presume that just because a copyright notice does not appear on a copy of a work, the author is not entitled to copyright protection.

To make matters worse, the 1976 act and later amendments dramatically revamped and lengthened the term of copyright, eliminating renewal registrations, and stretching the term for individual authors to life of the author plus seventy years and corporate work-for-hire authors to ninety-five years following publication. These ultra-terms turn the search for MIA parents of orphan works, including many films, photos, recordings, and texts of extraordinary historical, cultural, and artistic importance, into an attenuated Kafkaesque undertaking that makes perfectly sane creative artists and archivists want to tear their hair out.

So what's a mother to do?

Register of Copyrights Marybeth Peters appeared before Congress in support of an ill-fated Orphan Works Act of 2008. The bill would have created a safety net by limiting the damages awardable for infringement of copyright in an orphan work, as long as the infringer performed a good-faith reasonably diligent search to locate the owner before using the work, filed a notice of use with the Copyright Office before using the work, and attributed the work to the owner, if known. It would have allowed reasonable compensation for commercial uses, which would have been as mutually agreed by the owner and the user or, failing that, decided by a court based on objective market values for the work and the use. This approach would not have released orphan works into the public domain, but would have allowed users to go ahead with infringing projects, knowing up front their potential exposure was capped at a reasonable level. Under the bill, the Copyright Office would also have created a system to establish certified electronic image databases of pictorial, graphic, and sculptural works under copyright protection, to make it easier to locate copyright owners.

In response, a coalition of professional photographer, artist, writer, and art licensing organizations mounted a lobbying campaign against the Orphan Works Act of 2008. They argued that the legislation would negatively affect their members' ability to earn a living selling copies of their works, and that what started out as a bill to increase access for librarians, historians, and educators to vintage copyrighted works had turned into an attempt to dilute current copyright law. In the face of such opposition, the House and Senate failed to agree on a final version of the bill. Its parents skipped town for the winter recess, leaving one more abandoned baby in a basket on the doorstep of the Capitol building at Christmastime.

FIGHTING WITH COPYRIGHTS

Copyright owners aren't going to the trouble of protecting their copyrights for nothing. The value in a copyright depends on the fact that, if push comes to shove, you can deter people whom you perceive may be infringing your exclusive rights, and defend yourself against people who may perceive you to be infringing theirs. Sooner or later, you or your creative collaborators will sometimes play offense, sometimes play defense, whether you ever end up in court or not, because you aren't creating art in a vacuum. You need to know how to fight with copyrights.

COPYRIGHT INFRINGEMENT

Anybody who violates any of the exclusive rights of a copyright owner is an infringer. A copyright is infringed by reproducing, distributing, selling, publicly displaying, or performing the protected work, or by making a derivative work from it, without the permission of the owner. A copyright owner claiming infringement must prove that he or she owns a valid copyright in the work, that the alleged infringer copied the work or elements of it, and that the copying was legally unauthorized. Unless the alleged infringer admits copying, the copyright owner must prove copying by presenting sufficient evidence both that:

- the alleged infringer had *access* to the protected work, and
- *substantial similarity* exists between elements of the original work and elements of the infringing work, creating a reasonable inference that copying occurred.

Direct evidence that the alleged infringer had access to the copyrighted work is seldom available to the copyright owner unless the alleged infringer admits access or leaves a paper or electronic trail of access that the copyright owner can retrieve through investigation or discovery requests in litigation, or had a business relationship that facilitated or at least enabled access. Thus, access often has to be proved by circumstantial evidence. Increasingly, though, online access to works can readily be traced electronically.

Substantial similarity between two works exists if the ordinary observer would recognize the infringing work as copied from the copyrighted work. The spontaneous and immediate reaction of the ordinary observer, without aide or suggestion, is what counts. A court sometimes analyzes substantial similarity between two works compared in their entireties, including both protectable and unprotectable material. Other times it will dissect the original work and the alleged infringing work to determine individual points of similarity. Fragments of a work that are copied, even if small, can support an infringement claim. Infringement turns on the fragment's recognizability, not on its size. Copyright law protects any significant piece that the copyright owner can identify as taken from the copyrighted work. The presence of dissimilar material does not cure an otherwise infringing work.

Often the best defense against a copyright infringement claim is to prove you independently created the challenged work, thereby disproving the claimant's contention that the work was copied. That is one reason why it is so important to accurately document the chain of title of your work from initial development and acquisition of all underlying elements through preparation of the final work.

ANATOMY OF A CEASE AND DESIST

Let's reconsider that nasty letter you received at the beginning of this chapter. As scripted, the lawyer bragged about his client or clients and their copyrighted work, mentioned copyright registrations they own, if any, said your work infringes the client's work, said this was damaging the client, demanded you stop, insisted you comply with a bunch of other demands, and threatened to sue you if you didn't.

You may be able to do a bit of Internet sleuthing on your own in order to get a line on who these people are, and why they're rattling your cage. If they do own copyright registrations, it helps if the lawyer has enclosed with the letter copies of any registrations they claim, or at least stated registration numbers. This allows you to look up their claimed registrations in the Copyright Office records. But if you don't wish to cease and desist, or you don't like their other demands, you should find a lawyer to help. You will need to develop a strategy to defend yourself and your work. In developing a strategy, it will be helpful to consider a range of possible defenses, some of which you and your lawyer might include in a response letter, and some of which you might hold in reserve for a rainy day. The hierarchy of possible defenses normally runs something like this, in more or less the following order:

- Their work simply isn't copyrightable, so it's in the public domain.
- Their work could be copyrightable, but they failed to copyright it.
- Someone else may own copyright in the work, but they don't.
- They may have copyrighted it, but the copyright expired, so it's in the public domain.
- They may own copyright, but your use isn't infringing, because you did not in fact access the copyrighted work, and so could not have copied it.
- They may own copyright, but your use isn't infringing, because you created your work independently and copied no protected element from the copyrighted work.
- They may own copyright, but your use isn't infringing, because your use is fair use.

We take a closer look at some of these defenses, especially public domain and fair use, later in this chapter. But whatever defenses do apply, you should keep in mind that an early first response to a cease and desist letter, after analyzing potential defenses and strategizing at the front end with a qualified copyright lawyer, is usually key to achieving an early settlement of the matter, before things go ballistic.

COPYRIGHT LITIGATION
A Federal Case

Federal courts have jurisdiction of all copyright lawsuits. This jurisdiction is exclusive. You cannot pursue a copyright claim in state court, though there may be ways other than copyright, in some circumstances, to vindicate your rights in state court. Since copyrights in the United States stem from one and only one place, the Copyright Act, all copyright law in the U.S. is federal law. Any copyright dispute in this country that goes to court is bound to become, literally, a federal case.

Getting There

The owner of any of the exclusive rights under a copyright is entitled to sue in federal district court for any infringement of that right committed while he or she owns or owned it. However, a copyright owner cannot pursue a copyright suit until his or her copyright is registered with the Copyright Office. Filing a lawsuit to try to vindicate your copyright without registering it first is like bringing a knife to a gunfight.

But what if you apply to register your copyright, and the Copyright Office rejects your application? As we mentioned earlier, if that happens you can sue the Register of Copyrights, and ask the judge to compel the Register to register your copyright. Or you can sue the infringer in question, while at the same time serving notice on the Register, who can then opt either in or out of your lawsuit, depending on whether or not the Register sees any interest to be served by appearing in court. As you can imagine, though, you will face an uphill battle if you start off by fighting with the Copyright Office. So you'd rather not go there, except as a last resort.

Assuming you get past the registration hurdle, you are ready to file your complaint against the infringer. Your complaint will say a lot of the same stuff as a cease and desist letter, except that the sullen demands will be sweetened into respectful requests to the judge. The complaint will allege that you own one or more copyrighted works; will mention any relevant copyright registrations you own, attaching copies of same; will claim the defendant's work infringes or will infringe yours; will claim the defendant's actions are damaging you; will ask the judge to order the defendant to stop producing, distributing, or selling his or her work; and will demurely beg the judge to award you other remedies, like money damages.

You can't pursue a copyright lawsuit unless you file your complaint within three years after the infringement of which you complain, three years being the statute of limitations. You can sue only for infringing acts that occurred within three years of your filing of the complaint.

The court in a copyright infringement suit may require the copyright owner to serve written notice with a copy of the complaint on any person shown in the Copyright Office records to have, or otherwise shown to have, an interest or claim an interest in the copyright. This is one reason parties to copyright assignments, licenses, and security agreements like to record their documents with the Copyright Office. The court must require that notice be served upon any person whose interest is likely to be affected by a decision in the case, it must permit any person having an interest in the copyright to intervene in the suit if they wish to do so, and it may compel any person having an interest in the copyright to join the suit if the court considers it appropriate. So before you launch a copyright suit, you had better consider whether folks other than you and the defendant are going to be joining the party, and how any extra guests will impact your interests.

Remedies

Copyright plaintiffs usually go to court seeking some form of injunction to prevent the defendant from continuing to use the copyrighted work and also claiming money damages. In some cases the plaintiff really cares most about getting an injunction, in other cases the plaintiff cares most about getting money, and in a lot of cases the plaintiff wants both.

Injunctions

Any federal district court may grant temporary and permanent injunctions on such terms as it deems reasonable to prevent or restrain infringement of a copyright. An injunction can be served on the enjoined party anywhere in the United States, it operates throughout the U.S., and it is enforceable by any federal court having jurisdiction of the enjoined party.

Money Damages

A copyright infringer is liable for one of the following alternative measures of damages, at the copyright owner's option:

Actual Damages and Profits

As a copyright owner, you are entitled to recover your *actual damages* suffered as a result of the infringement, plus any *infringer's profits* that are attributable to the infringement but are not taken into account in computing the actual damages. In establishing the infringer's profits, the copyright owner is required to present proof only of the infringer's gross revenue, and the infringer bears the burden of proof of its deductible expenses and the elements of profit attributable to factors other than the copyrighted work.

Statutory Damages

As an alternative to actual damages and infringer's profits, if you registered your copyright within three months after the first publication of the work, or registered prior to infringement of the work, you can ask the court to award *statutory damages*. You can make the election to recover statutory damages instead of actual damages and profits at any time before final judgment in the suit. This flexibility gives the plaintiff a considerable tactical edge in the litigation.

Statutory damage amounts are in the court's discretion, generally within a range of not less than $750 or more than $30,000 per copyrighted work. But in a case where the copyright owner proves the infringement was willful, the court may increase the award of statutory damages to a sum of not more than $150,000. In a case where the infringer proves he or she was an "innocent infringer" not aware of the copyright and having no reason to believe his or her acts constituted an infringement, the court may reduce the award of statutory damages to a sum not less than $200. There is a special exception relieving nonprofit educational institutions, libraries, archives, and public broadcasting entities from payment of statutory damages when they infringed but believed and had reasonable grounds for believing their use of the copyrighted work was a fair use.

Attorneys' Fees and Costs

If you registered your copyright within three months after the first publication of the work or prior to infringement, you can ask the court to award attorneys' fees and costs. Since attorneys' fees and costs can be extremely high in copyright litigation, early registration within the time limit gives you another tactical edge in a lawsuit.

Impound and Destroy

The court can order the impounding of copies claimed to have been made or used in violation of the copyright owner's exclusive rights, and of plates, molds, masters, tapes, film negatives, and the like by means of which copies can be reproduced. As part of a final judgment or decree, the court can order that all offending copies, along with the means to produce them, be destroyed or disposed of in some other reasonable manner.

Downright Criminal

The most blatant form of copyright infringement is counterfeiting. Counterfeiters violate the copyright owner's reproduction rights when they duplicate copies of the copyrighted work as, for example, in the case of bootleg movie DVDs and music CDs. They violate the owner's distribution rights when they peddle their bootleg wares on the streets, at flea markets, and on the Internet. The copyright owner can sue the counterfeiter in a civil lawsuit for an injunction, damages, and attorneys' fees and costs, as just described, but criminal penalties also can be leveled against the counterfeiter, as you know if you ever actually bothered to read the FBI warning that appears at the beginning of commercial film DVDs, the one you can't fast forward away from. Anyone who imports counterfeit copies or phonorecords of a copyrighted work into the United States is also a criminal infringer. Criminal copyright proceedings have a five-year statute of limitations.

INFRINGEMENT DEFENSES

Never take a copyright claim at face value.

Ask yourself whether the things the claimant says are true, may be true, are false, or may be false. Try to see what you can confirm to be true or false using publicly available resources such as Copyright Office records, mainstream news reports, and other reliable online information. Don't take things you find on the Internet at face value either, of course, because there is plenty of misinformation, disinformation, and spun information in cyberspace, some of it likely planted there by the claimant, some of it often planted there by the claimant's enemies. But you may be able to learn a lot about the claimant online, provided you consider the sources of the information you find, and cautiously read between the lines. Run through the hierarchy of defenses we listed earlier. Ask yourself if any of the defenses apply, or might apply:

- Does the claimant's work seem uncopyrightable?
- Was the work copyrightable, but a notice requirement blown?
- Does someone else seem to own the copyright or an interest in it?
- Was the work copyrighted, but the copyright expired?
- Did you never access the work?
- Did you never copy any copyrighted element from the work?
- Did you use the claimant's work, but your use constitutes "fair use"?

Lawyers in the business of writing cease and desist letters aren't in the business of modestly understating their client's claims. Probe for overstatements, and we promise you'll find some. Question each element of the claim. Seek the advice of a seasoned lawyer to help you size up the quality of the claimant's case versus the quality of your defenses.

The Public Domain

The public domain is an enormous fountain of creative works not subject to copyright. You can drink from the fountain for free, but if somebody comes along and bottles the water, it's a safe guess he or she is going to want you to pay for the bottle, and will probably try to fool you into paying for the free water in it too. That's how the bottled water business works.

A work can be in the public domain for any of several reasons:

- It was not copyrightable to begin with.
- It was copyrightable, but the author deliberately chose to dedicate it to the public (altruism being a rare but beautiful thing).
- It was copyrightable, but when published, the author failed to use a proper copyright notice, back in the days when a copyright notice was required.
- It was copyrighted, but the author failed to renew the copyright, back in the days when an application for renewal was required.
- It was copyrighted, but the term of the copyright expired.

Copyright has expired for all works published in the United States in 1922 or earlier. They are in the public domain. If you have your eye on an old work published after 1922 and are biding your time till it enters the public domain, don't hold your breath. Post-1922 works published pre-1978, unless the owner blew a notice requirement or a renewal requirement, enjoy a term of ninety-five years. Works published in 1923 won't enter the public domain until 2019. Works published in 1924 won't enter the public domain until 2020. "But wait a minute, wait a minute, you ain't heard nothing yet"—*The Jazz Singer*, the world's first feature-length "talkie" to showcase synchronized dialogue scenes, starring Al Jolson and released by Warner Brothers in 1927, won't enter the public domain in the U.S. until 2023.

You can use a public domain work without asking anyone's permission. But no one owns the public domain work—including you. If you create a derivative work based on it, you gain a copyright to the extent of your own contribution of original authorship to the derivative work, but you don't capture any copyright in the underlying public domain work. For instance, a collective work might consist of a collection of silent films, stories, songs, comics, cartoons, or clip art graphics in the public domain. The underlying works remain in the public domain, but if the collection's creator uses at least a minimal bit of creativity in selecting and organizing those works, the collective work can be copyrighted. An application to register the collective work must limit the claim to what's original, and disclose and disclaim what elements of the collective work are public domain works. The public domain bottler can claim the bottle, but not the free water inside.

HISPANIOLA—THE DUE DILIGENCE

Speaking of public domain, says Marlow, have you forgotten something?

Huh? (You've been sitting on a footstool immersed in your copy of *The Creative Artist's Legal Guide* for the past hour, when Marlow kindly sidles up with a tea tray, an extra stool, and a box of books.)

Have you forgotten something? he persists.

What? We already searched *Hispaniola*. Renewed. Still under copyright.

Yes, Marlow nods indulgently, but *Hispaniola* is a sequel, derived at least in part from *Treasure Island*.

But, um, surely *Treasure Island* is in the public domain.

Surely? Marlow clears his throat. When was it first published, and where?

You dunno.

Rule One: Never take it for granted something is in the public domain.

Okay, wiseguy, when was it published?

First published in a children's magazine in the U.K. in 1881 and 1882, and first published as a book, simultaneously in London and New York, in 1883.

So it's in the public domain.

In *this country* it's in the public domain, says Marlow.

Ah. Okay, what about England?

Stevenson died in 1894. Over there Stevenson's works were generally protected under a standard rule of author's life plus 50 years, so in the U.K., the copyright in *Treasure Island* expired in 1944. You'll rest easier knowing *Treasure Island* was in the public domain here and there before Bonnie wrote her novel, and before you start your film.

Touché, smart ass.

Speaking of *Treasure Island*, you realize, of course, Bonnie's book isn't the only derivative work ever based on it. Within a few years after it entered the public domain, by no mere accident, the Walt Disney Company produced a movie of *Treasure Island*, released in 1950, Disney's first completely live-action film.

So?

So you had better make double sure Bonnie's *Hispaniola* doesn't infringe Disney's *Treasure Island*. After all, when she wrote her book in 1955, she obviously had access to the Disney film. Odds are she saw it before writing her book. You need to read the book with a fine-toothed comb and a magnifying glass and make certain none of the materials you'd like to use from the book have substantial similarity to the portions of the Disney film that are original to Disney. Portions of the Disney film lifted from Stevenson's book aren't a problem, because those are in the public domain.

Cool. You'll check whether the Disney film has any characters, scenes, or dialogue not in Stevenson's book that resemble characters, scenes, or dialogue in *Hispaniola*.

That's the ticket, smiles Marlow.

Good thing the only character from the original Bonnie brings forward in her sequel is Jim Hawkins.

True, but Bonnie's book isn't the only *Treasure Island* sequel ever written.

It's not?

Marlow rolls his eyes, dumping his box of books on the spare footstool.

All those?

These are the ones written prior to Bonnie's. You need to make sure her book doesn't potentially infringe any sequel published earlier than hers. Bonnie is as scrupulous as the day is long, but after all, she was a mere slip of a girl when she wrote *Hispaniola*, mistakes do happen, and you want to forewarn yourself if there are any accidental resemblances out there between her book and the others.

Scrupulous as the day is long? You make a mental note to be sure and get an ironclad set of representations and warranties from Bonnie when you come to terms with her.

Fair Use

A copyright grants the owner exclusive rights, such as reproduction rights, performance rights, display rights, and rights to create derivative works. But this does not mean you can never, ever use a copyrighted work without the owner's permission. Sometimes you can, thanks to the "fair use" exception.

The Copyright Act says the "fair use" of a copyrighted work, including fair use for purposes such as criticism, commentary, news reporting, teaching, scholarship and research, is not copyright infringement. This makes sense since the whole purpose behind the Constitution's grant of power allowing Congress to enact a copyright law in the first place is to "promote the Progress of Science and useful Arts." If nobody can criticize, comment, teach, or report news by quoting from a copyrighted work without permission, that ain't progress. That's a police state.

But what does Congress mean by "fair use"?

The best way to home in on this elusive question is to look at two cases, decided a hundred fifty years apart, which sandwich the Copyright Act like a pair of large, imposing bookends.

George Washington Slept Here

In the early days of the Republic, U.S. Supreme Court justices didn't confine themselves to hearing appeals. They used to "ride circuit," traveling around the country hearing federal trials. Justice Joseph Story, the youngest Supreme Court justice ever appointed, had thirty years on the job and had just finished writing the Court's landmark anti-slavery opinion in *The Amistad* (later to inspire the Steven Spielberg film *Amistad*—which itself became the subject of a rather acrimonious copyright lawsuit) when he rode circuit to Massachusetts in 1841 to hear *Folsom v. Marsh*. It would become another landmark, America's first "fair use" case, though not exactly what you could call a blow for freedom.

Jared Sparks, editor of *The Writings of George Washington*, a twelve-volume collection of—you guessed it—the writings of George Washington, sued the Reverend Charles Wentworth Upham, author of a two-volume *Life of Washington*, charging infringement because Upham had copied several hundred pages of Washington's letters from Sparks's twelve-volume page-turner. (Folsom and Marsh were competing publishers bankrolling the fight.) The borrowed letters amounted to four percent of Sparks's work, but over a third of Upham's, who spliced the letters into his G.W. bio to let the man who could not tell a lie tell the story of his life in his own words. Most of the letters were private ones Washington left in his will to his nephew, who had sold the rights to Sparks and the late Chief Justice John Marshall, their plan being that Sparks would edit and publish the letters.

Reverend Upham pleaded a fair use defense, arguing that his was a new and original work, and that he had selected only those letters suited to his limited purpose as a biographer, writing the book as one of a series adapted for school libraries.

With all due respect to the good reverend, Justice Story rejected the defense. It was not the fashion of the day to turn every federal case into a constitutional case, and since the U.S. Copyright Act had not long before been cribbed from Britain's Statute of Anne, he invoked time-honored English precedents. He said limited borrowing from the work of others is acceptable when the borrowing creates something "new and useful." A reviewer, for example, "may fairly cite largely from the original work, if his design be really and truly to use the passages for the purposes of fair and reasonable criticism. On the other hand, it is as clear, that if he thus cites the most important parts of the work, with a view, not to criticize, but to supersede the use of the original work, and substitute the review for it, such a use will be deemed in law a piracy."

You may say Upham had the deck stacked against him, since Sparks was a pal of the late chief justice, and Story was the best-known author of legal treatises of his day, partial to upholding a fellow author's copyright whenever he got a shot. Be that as it may, *Folsom v. Marsh* is the granddaddy of fair use cases in America, and Story is regarded as the patron saint of fair use, having set a rule of thumb, followed to this day, that "we must often, in deciding questions of this sort, look to the nature and objects of the selections made, the quantity and value of the materials used, and the degree in which the use may prejudice the sale, or diminish the profits, or supersede the objects, of the original work."

Story openly admitted "fair use" was darned subjective, saying that copyrights belong "to what may be called the metaphysics of the law, where the distinctions are, or at least may be, very subtle and refined, and, sometimes, almost evanescent." *Evanescent?* Great G.W.'s ghost! No wonder creative artists have been struggling to get a handle on fair use ever since.

Congress Gets in on the Act

One hundred twenty-five years and a crazy quilt of inconsistent judicial opinions later, Congress decided to add a section to the Copyright Act restating Story's guidance. The Copyright Act of 1976 says that in determining whether the use made of a copyrighted work in any particular case is a fair use, the factors to be considered include:

1. the purpose and character of the use, including whether such use is of a commercial nature or is for nonprofit educational purposes;
2. the nature of the copyrighted work;
3. the amount and substantiality of the portion used in relation to the copyrighted work as a whole; and
4. the effect of the use upon the potential market for or value of the copyrighted work.

If this still sounds subjective, it is. There is no specific formula, no set number of words, lines, or notes you can safely borrow without permission.

Can you hum a few bars on stage of a copyrighted song without paying a fee? It depends.

Some things are clearly okay according to the legislative history of the Copyright Act, the official backstory Congress wrote when it enshrined the fair use exception in the statute, but the list is a pretty conservative one:

- quotation of excerpts in a review or criticism for purposes of illustration or comment
- quotation of short passages in a scholarly or technical work, for illustration or clarification of the author's observations
- use in a parody of some of the content of the work parodied
- summary of an address or article, with brief quotations, in a news report
- reproduction by a library of a portion of a work to replace part of a damaged copy
- reproduction by a teacher or student of a small part of a work to illustrate a lesson
- reproduction of a work in legislative or judicial proceedings or reports
- incidental and fortuitous reproduction, in a newsreel or broadcast, of a work located in the scene of an event being reported.

Congress didn't answer all our questions about fair use by a long shot, and couldn't have even if they'd tried. Fair use is simply too situational. It takes a case-by-case approach. So, despite the statute, this puts us right back in Justice Story's realm, the realm of "judge-made law."

When a federal district court decides a copyright case, the decision can be appealed to the Court of Appeals for the federal circuit where the district court is located. There are twelve Courts of Appeals. Each has the power to overrule or affirm the judgment of the district courts under its wing. The two most influential in copyright matters are the Court of Appeals for the Second Circuit, whose turf comprises New York and a few other eastern states, and the Court of Appeals for the Ninth Circuit, whose turf comprises California and several other western states. The Courts of Appeals have written a number of opinions on fair use—some good, some bad—in a number of interesting cases.

They call the U.S. Supreme Court "supreme" because it has the power to affirm or overrule decisions the Courts of Appeals make. The Supreme Court doesn't have to take a case on appeal, and it usually doesn't, unless the justices feel the case raises legal issues interesting enough to turn their heads. In 1994, a fair use case interesting enough to turn their heads came walkin' down the street.

Pretty Woman Goes to Washington

Legendary Nashville music publisher Acuff-Rose sued members of the rap group 2 Live Crew and their record label, complaining that 2 Live Crew's song "Pretty Woman" infringed Acuff-Rose's copyright in Roy Orbison's rock ballad "Oh, Pretty Woman." The trial judge gave it up for the rappers, granting summary judgment. Summary judgment means that the facts essential to deciding the case are not disputed, so the court can decide simply by considering the undisputed facts and the parties' arguments, without holding a trial or hearing live witness testimony. The judge said 2 Live Crew's song was a parody that made fair use of the original. On appeal, the Court of Appeals reversed, saying the commercial nature of the parody rendered it presumptively unfair. The Supreme Court overturned the Court of Appeals, in *Campbell v. Acuff-Rose Music, Inc.*, holding that 2 Live Crew's parody, even though done for profit, could be a fair use of the copyrighted song for purposes of criticism or comment.

The Court said fair use situations require flexible case-by-case analysis of the four factors listed in the Copyright Act, not rigidly applied brightline rules. The factors have to be explored and weighed together in light of copyright's purpose of promoting science and the arts. You'll be relieved to hear that the Court didn't pen a set of rap lyrics to help us remember the four factors of fair use. They did, however, produce a pretty chill remix, which players embroiled in fair use fights keep coming back to, because it remains the Supreme Court's last major word on the subject.

Purpose and Character

The first factor helping or hurting your case for fair use is the use's purpose and character, including whether your motive is commercial or nonprofit. Commercialism alone doesn't sink a fair use defense. The Court said the commerciality of a derivative work claiming fair use is only one element to consider, and pointed out that nearly all the types of fair use listed in the Copyright Act, including news reporting, comment, criticism, teaching, scholarship, and research, are activities generally conducted for profit in this country. It's okay to engage in fair use and make money in the process.

The flip side is that the mere fact of a use being educational or nonprofit does not make it bulletproof against an infringement claim. Still, commercialism is a factor. Being commercial tilts against a fair use defense. Being nonprofit tilts in favor of one.

When you consider your work's purpose and character, you should ask if your work is just a substitute for the original that tries to fill the same market demand, or a similar one. Or does it add something new, with a different purpose or character than the original, thereby altering it with new expression, meaning, or message? In the magic of judge-made fair use jargon, a work that adds something new and different is called "transformative."

For example, 2 Live Crew's rap was a parody of Roy Orbison's classic. Parody transforms the original by making fun of it. Like other forms of comment and criticism, the Court said, parody can provide social benefit, by shedding light on an earlier work, and, in the process, creating a new one. The Court also said that the question of whether the parody is in good taste or bad is beside the point in a fair use determination. Reading between the lines of the Court's opinion, it turns out the parodists don't have to be pillars of the community, and vulgarity enjoys its place in the marketplace of ideas.

Parody has to copy to some extent from the original to make its point, or else your audience won't get it. The whole point of a parody is to use some elements of the prior work to create a new one that comments on the prior work. But you can't just copy for copying's sake. A parodist can justify quoting from an existing work in order to create a new one that, at least in part, comments on that author's work. But if your work doesn't take critical aim at the substance or style of the original, and you're just copying to avoid the drudgery of working up something "fresh" (the Court's word, not ours), the claim to fairness in borrowing from the other work diminishes, and other factors loom larger.

"Transformative" use isn't absolutely necessary to make a case for fair use, but the Court did emphasize that the goal of copyright—namely, to promote science and the arts—is furthered by the creation of transformative works. In other words, the more transformative the new work, the less significant other factors, like commercialism, are likely to be. So "transformative" is what you want your work to be if you're relying on fair use to defend it.

Nature of the Copyrighted Work

Because classic types of legitimate fair use for purposes like criticism, commentary, news reporting, teaching, scholarship, and research tend to deal in facts, it is often said that you normally have more leeway to copy from factual works than from fictional ones. But in the case of parody, the target of the parody is most often going to be fictional—we certainly hope Orbison's lyrics were—so it's fair to target fictional works in a parody.

Amount Taken

The less you take from the preexisting work, the more likely your copying will be excused as fair use. But taking a small portion of a work could get you in trouble, if the portion taken represents the heart of the work. That being said, the Court also recognized that in order to work, a parody sometimes has to rip the heart out of the original.

Even if 2 Live Crew's copying of Roy Orbison's first line of lyrics and characteristic opening bass riff went to the heart of the original, that heart is what most readily conjures up the song for parody, and it is the heart at which effective parody takes aim. The Court was favorably influenced by the fact that as soon as the rappers locked onto their target by copying the opening, 2 Live Crew's lyrics (which we dare not reprint here, even though the Court's opinion did) departed wildly from the Orbison lyrics, and their song produced distinctively different music.

Effect On Potential Market

The fourth factor in deciding whether a use counts as "fair" is its effect on the potential market for the copyrighted work. The Court said that if a use goes beyond mere duplication of the copyrighted work for commercial purposes, and is "transformative," it's not right to presume market harm. Copyright law protects a copyrighted work against a copycat horning in on the market for the original, and for potential markets for derivative uses that the owner of such an original generally might be expected to develop or to license others to develop, by putting cheap substitutes on the market. Copyright law does not protect a copyrighted work against criticism.

A parody isn't normally a substitute for the original. The two serve different markets, so this fourth factor weighs in favor of most parodies. A parody may diminish or even destroy the market value of the original work. A parody might be so funny the public can never take the original seriously again. This could cause the copyright owner loss of income, same as a lethal review can, but that's a risk you take whenever you put your work out there for the world to see.

On the other hand, if your use hurts the copyright owner not through criticism or comment, but rather by putting out there a substitute that deprives the copyright owner of income or undermines a new or potential market for the copyrighted work or derivatives, you're likely to get sued and your use probably won't be considered fair.

Interestingly, 2 Live Crew had requested permission from Acuff-Rose to use the Orbison original, and been denied. The Supreme Court said clearly that being denied permission to use a work does not weigh against a finding of fair use. If the use is fair, no permission need be sought or granted.

There could be times when you feel like asking permission even though your use is fair and you're not required to ask. There will be times, as we'll see later on, when someone else involved in your deal insists that you ask, even though it is not required. At all times, you should always think twice before asking permission, because asking permission often emboldens the ones you ask and gives them inflated notions of their rights. Whenever you do decide to ask, it is a good idea before you ask to think through what you are going to do if they say no. And, by the way, if you need permission because your use is not fair, then merely crediting the source of the copyrighted work won't convert your use into fair use or substitute for obtaining permission.

Fair use is called an "affirmative defense." In copyright litigation, the fair user bears the burden of proving that his or her use was "fair" and therefore not an infringement. You don't have to go through the defense unless the claimant first proves a "prima facie" case of infringement, by establishing that the claimant owns a valid copyright, that the term had not expired by the time of the alleged infringement, that the user had access to the work, and that the two works show substantial similarity.

You have to choose your battles. The cost of a fair use defense can be high, often prohibitive. At times you might have to decide whether paying a bully a fee for a license or permission you don't feel is legally required is less expensive than having a copyright suit on your hands or threat of suit hanging over your head or your production. If confronted by a situation raising a really, really interesting fair use issue, you may be able to enlist the support of one of the civil liberties groups, freedom of expression interest groups, law schools, universities or other organizations, such as the Stanford Center for Internet and Society's Fair Use Project, the Center for Social Media at American University, and the Berkman Center for Internet and Society at Harvard University, which sometimes take on fair use cases in order to help creative artists fight infringement suits brought by big copyright owners and thereby increase public awareness of the issues at stake. But that isn't going to be your day-to-day creative life. Your everyday life will involve a series of tough, not always pleasant decisions, and inevitable compromises. But if you keep in mind the four factors of fair use, you too can be like 2 Live Crew, and do your thing without compromising yourself or your art.

COPYRIGHTS ABROAD

There is no such thing as an international copyright.

Copyrights are territorial. An owner's rights are determined country by country. Bonnie Charlotte may own the U.S. copyright in *Hispaniola,* but her rights in the United Kingdom are a question of U.K. law. When Robert Louis Stevenson wrote *Treasure Island* in the U.K., his rights in the U.S. were a matter of U.S. law. Protection against infringement in any country depends on the laws of that country. Fortunately, nearly all countries nowadays with an audience or a market you want to reach protect foreign works under reciprocal ground rules set by international copyright treaties. But things were not always this way, and they were a long time coming.

A SMALL TOWN IN SWITZERLAND

Once upon a time, a beleaguered band of European diplomats whose governments had suffered years of heavy bombardment from the Association Littéraire et Artistique Internationale, an authors' and artists' lobbying organization founded by Victor Hugo of *Les Misérables* fame, holed up in a charming Alpine town to try to internationalize copyright protection. They met not only in the shadow of the Alps. They met in the shadow of literary greatness. Over two million fans had attended Hugo's funeral in Paris the previous spring. Failure was not an option, as Jean Valjean would have said. They got down to business and hammered out a treaty setting up a club of nations sworn to uphold authors' and artists' rights. They called it the Berne Convention for the Protection of Literary and Artistic Works. The year was 1886. Over the years, it has proved as sturdy, patient, and reliable as a Bernese Mountain Dog.

The Berne Convention creates a common framework among the members of the club for reciprocal treatment when it comes to copyrights. It has grown into a very big club, of 164 countries, including the United States, which finally joined in 1989. Its members form the Berne Union, and the Convention provides protection for the works of authors who are nationals of a member country, or whose works are first published in a member country.

The Convention upholds three basic principles.

"National treatment" says a work originating in one member country (whose author is a national of that country or which was first published in that country) must be given the same protection in each other member country as that country grants the works of its own nationals. This helps make sure you don't get picked on overseas just 'cause you're a foreigner.

"Automatic protection" says copyright in a member country can't be conditioned on compliance with formalities, such as copyright notice or copyright registration requirements. This notion, that copyright should arise automatically on creation of a work as soon as it is fixed in a physical medium, is one of several progressive ideas the Berne Convention pioneered that would take the United States a century to get with. As we have seen, for instance, the U.S. Copyright Act used to require notice. Among other changes in order to join Berne, Congress had to abolish the notice requirement, which it finally did in the Berne Convention Implementation Act of 1988, which took effect March 1, 1989.

"Independence" of protection says that copyright protection for a work in a Berne Union country is independent of whether the work is under copyright in its country of origin. This means that the term of copyright can differ from one country to another, copyright in a work can expire in different countries at different times, and the work may be in the public domain in one country but not in another. You have to check country to country to see where you stand in each.

The Berne Convention also sets minimum standards of protection regarding the types of works each member country must protect under its law (basically, "every production in the literary, scientific and artistic domain, whatever may be the mode or form of its expression"); the rights each member country must provide a copyright owner (including, among others, the right to translate, the right to make adaptations and arrangements, reproduction, performance, and broadcast rights, and the right to use the work as a basis for an audiovisual work); and the length of time copyrights in each member country must last.

In general, the term of copyright in each Berne Union country must last for the author's life plus a minimum of fifty years after the author's death, but there are a few special minimums for certain types of works. For cinematographic works, the minimum term of protection is fifty years after public release of the work or, if not released, fifty years after creation of the work. For works of applied art and photographic works, the minimum term is twenty-five years from the creation of the work.

The term of copyright in many Berne Union countries, including the United States, now exceeds these minimums by a long shot. For instance, for many years the term of copyright in the United Kingdom was author's life plus fifty years, as it still is in some Commonwealth jurisdictions, such as Canada, and in some jurisdictions with legal systems historically rooted in English law, such as Hong Kong. But in 1993, the European Community enacted a directive by which the copyright term in its member countries now extends to life of the author plus seventy years, matching the longer

German rule. Following this directive, the term of copyright in the U.K. is now author's life plus seventy years. Other Berne Union countries tend to fall somewhere along the fifty- to seventy-year spectrum. For instance, India provides for a copyright term of author's life plus sixty years, while Australia, which used to follow the traditional author's life plus fifty years, extended its term of copyright to author's life plus seventy years, upon enactment of the U.S.-Australia Free Trade Agreement in 2005.

One big wrinkle in all of this is the "rule of the shorter term." Under Berne, if a member country happens to provide under its law for a longer term than the Berne minimum and a foreign work protected in that member country ceases to be protected in its country of origin, the member country can, under its law, cut short the term of copyright so that it expires when protection in the country of origin expires. Countries of the European Union and most other countries follow the "rule of the shorter term," but the United States does not. If a work of U.S. origin enters the public domain in the U.S., it is going to automatically enter the public domain in those countries. The reverse is not true. A work of European origin that enters the public domain in Europe may be and often still is under copyright in the United States. A wrinkle within the wrinkle is that the rule of the shorter term is sometimes tinkered with in other bilateral or multilateral treaties. In North America, for example, the U.S. and Mexico don't follow the rule of the shorter term, but Canada does, except that Canada makes an exception for the U.S. and Mexico under the North American Free Trade Agreement, and does not apply the rule of the shorter term to works of U.S. or Mexican origin.

A final added wrinkle is the "work made for hire" exception, invented in the United States. Most Berne Union countries, including the countries of continental Europe, do not have a "work made for hire" exception, while others, such as the United Kingdom and Canada, recognize the concept only in the context of employer-employee relationships. Though the Berne Convention sets minimum terms, it does not prohibit "work made for hire" treatment. This made it possible for the U.S. to join the Berne Union without jettisoning work for hire. And it leaves Berne Union countries free in principle to adopt work-for-hire provisions along U.S. lines, for instance, by extending work for hire to independent contractors in motion picture productions. The most notable example of a country going that route is India. With the world's largest film industry, India has adopted a work-for-hire provision similar to that in the U.S. Copyright Act, a case of Bollywood taking a page out of Hollywood's playbook.

The moral of the story is that if you do wish to have copyright protection for your work abroad, you need to determine the extent of copyright protection available to works of foreign authors in each country of interest. If feasible, this should be done before the work is published in the United States or anywhere else, because protection will depend on the facts existing at the time of first publication, including where you first publish.

A NOT SO SMALL TOWN IN SWITZERLAND

The Berne Convention set up an official bureau in 1893 to handle administration of the treaty. Originally located in Berne, the bureau eventually moved to Geneva and morphed into the World Intellectual Property Organization (WIPO).

In addition to managing the Berne Convention and various intellectual property (IP) law treaties relating to trademarks, patents, and design rights, WIPO administers several other international copyright treaties that protect the rights of authors, performers, producers, and broadcasters. These treaties include the WIPO Copyright Treaty, adopted in 1996 among Berne Union members, which expands on the rights guaranteed by the Berne Convention.

Not under WIPO's wing, but reinforcing the Berne Convention, is the Agreement on Trade-Related Aspects of Intellectual Property Rights (TRIPs), one of several agreements that created the World Trade Organization (WTO). TRIPs requires all WTO members, among other things, to recognize intellectual property rights in ways largely in sync with the terms of the Berne Convention. Since most countries, at last count 147, are WTO members, and most of the rest would like to be, TRIPs helps shore up copyright protection overseas. The United States and the other developed countries that represent the lion's share of valuable copyrights globally like to fight their multilateral IP fights in the WTO arena, where they have greater clout than in the Berne Convention arena, where each member state, big or small, casts one vote. When trade disputes flare up between countries over IP issues, such as counterfeiting, TRIPs is often the weapon of choice.

One last wrinkle, just to show you that trade-talk horse trading can be a two-way street. When the United States joined the Berne Convention, the treaty required new members to extend copyright to works originating in other member countries if those works had not yet entered the public domain in their country of origin. Many foreign works had lost U.S. copyright protection in the past because they had failed to meet formalities such as copyright notice and renewal requirements. The U.S. stalled on this issue, but in 1996, following the Uruguay Round of trade talks that gave birth to the WTO and in order to meet obligations under TRIPs, Congress amended the Copyright Act to restore the remaining term of copyright protection for works that had entered the public domain in the United States due to failure to meet formalities. To qualify as a "restored work," the foreign work needs to have not yet entered the public domain in its source country, and at least one author had to be a national of or living in a Berne or WTO member country. Restored works were restored for all countries belonging to Berne or the WTO as of January 1, 1996, and were restored or will be restored for any country subsequently joining Berne or the WTO as of the date the country joined or joins. The restored work enjoys copyright protection for the remainder of the term the work would have enjoyed had it not entered the public domain. There are many such works, including many very valuable ones, so you need to take care if your creative path crosses one of them, lest you get attacked by a zombie copyright.

Way back when, in the 1950s, when the United States joining the Berne Convention was out of the question, UNESCO, the United Nations Educational, Scientific, and Cultural Organization—another Geneva outfit—developed a treaty called the Universal Copyright Convention, or UCC for short. The U.S. was reluctant to jump through the Berne Convention hoops by changing the way it computed copyright terms, by scrapping copyright registration and copyright notice requirements, and by providing for authors' moral rights as required under Berne. Developing countries were suspicious of Berne's rich-country orientation. And the Soviet Union was simply outside the capitalist copyright orbit. The UCC, the solution cooked up by UNESCO, served these odd bedfellows as a sort of Berne Convention surrogate. The treaty didn't dispense with formalities for copyright protection. Instead, it said that any formality in a national law could be satisfied by the use of a copyright notice in the form specified in the UCC, which was basically the same as the form of copyright notice specified under U.S. law. This enabled U.S. copyright owners to gain protection in other UCC member countries simply by placing a proper copyright notice on the copies sold there.

If you dabble in copyright of older works distributed internationally, sooner or later you may need to delve into the Universal Copyright Convention, but for newer works you can consider the UCC a dead letter. We're sure you're glad to hear this. You have your hands full as it is, as you set out to protect your creative works abroad.

THE OTHER FRENCH CONNECTION: MORAL RIGHTS

If you have worked in a film or other entertainment media production as a writer, director, actor, animator, artist, composer, or in just about any other creative capacity, chances are you have been made to sign paperwork containing a worldwide "waiver of moral rights"—most likely buried in the fine print just south of the "work for hire" clause.

Moral rights are traditionally alien to the American legal system. They originate in and are translated from a notion in French law called *droit moral*. Moral rights reflect the view that an author's rights should include not only transferable economic rights to exploit a work commercially, but also rights personal to the author to safeguard the artistic integrity of his or her work. Moral rights in continental European countries typically include a right of disclosure (empowering the author to decide when a work is complete and dictate when it may be displayed), a right of attribution (enabling the author to control the identification of his or her name with the work), a right of withdrawal (letting the author withdraw or modify the work following publication), and a right of integrity (empowering the author to prevent the work from being displayed in an altered, distorted, or mutilated form).

One hears loose talk in and around Hollywood about empowerment these days, but the day Hollywood studio execs put such moral rights in the hands of U.S. film directors will be the day Sunset Boulevard freezes over. With all respect to Monsieur Hugo, in American entertainment and media arts production, waivers of moral rights are here to stay.

Yet Berne Convention members are required to meet a minimum level of protection of moral rights. When the U.S. joined Berne, in order to meet that minimum, Congress enacted the Visual Artists Rights Act of 1990. The Visual Artists Rights Act covers only works of visual art in a decidedly highbrow fine arts vein, namely, paintings, sculptures, drawings, prints, and still photographs produced for exhibition only, limited to single copies or signed and numbered limited editions of two hundred or less. VARA grants no protection to things like motion pictures, books and other publications (print or electronic), applied art, or merchandise.

The only moral rights VARA recognizes are ones of attribution and integrity, specifically, a right to claim authorship of a work, a right to prevent attachment of the artist's name to a work he or she did not create, a right to disclaim authorship and prevent identification of the artist's name with a work where there has been a subsequent distortion, mutilation, or modification of it prejudicial to the artist's honor or reputation, and a right in some cases to prevent destruction of a work incorporated into a building. These moral rights last for the life of the author, or in the case of a joint work, until the death of the last surviving author, and they cannot be transferred, even though copyright in the same work can.

Because the Berne Convention neither sanctions nor forbids waivers of moral rights, each Berne Union member is left free to determine whether or not to allow parties to waive moral rights under its law. Some continental jurisdictions, notably France, make it difficult, if not impossible, for parties to waive moral rights, while jurisdictions that follow the Anglo-American common law tradition and foster a thriving film industry, such as the U.S., the U.K., Canada, and India, typically allow moral rights to be waived.

QUEEN ANNE'S SPANIEL

You have a right to know how we got here.

Copyright in America, like piracy, is a British import.

Merry old England under the "Merry Monarch" Charles II was not so merry for writers, when Parliament passed "An Act for preventing the frequent Abuses in printing seditious treasonable and unlicensed Bookes and Pamphlets and for regulating of Printing and Printing Presses." The writers' gripe about the Licensing Act of 1662 wasn't just that it imposed censorship, but that it shortchanged them when their books managed to squeak by the censors and break into print.

The law set up a register of licensed books, requiring a copy of every book published in the realm to be deposited with the Stationers' Company, a royally chartered old boys' club of commercial printers. In return for serving as censorship watchdogs for the Crown, company members held a monopoly on book and pamphlet printing. Members could buy out an author's manuscript for a song, and gain the permanent exclusive right to print and distribute the book. Authors earned no royalties when their books and pamphlets went best-seller, and since authors were barred from joining the Stationers' Company, they couldn't self-publish and cut out the middleman unless they went underground.

Eventually, thanks to a combination of inept lobbying by the old-school Stationers' Company and an artful letter-writing campaign by the new-school philosopher John Locke (whose interest, as an author, was more than philosophical), the House of Commons said "Nay" to renewing the

Her Highness The Lady Anne, the future Queen of Great Britain and Ireland, in 1683, at the time of her marriage to HRH Prince George of Denmark, by Jan van der Vaardt and Willem Wissing (National Galleries of Scotland)

Licensing Act in 1695. This wiped out the Stationers' Company monopoly, but as a result literary pirates leapt into the breach with a flood of bootleg editions that hurt legitimate authors and publishers alike.

When Queen Anne ascended the throne in the early eighteenth century, a more enlightened Parliament turned over a new leaf by passing "An Act for the Encouragement of Learning by Vesting the Copies of Printed Books in the Authors or purchasers of such Copies, during the Times therein mentioned." The Statute of Anne, which entered into force in 1710, was the first law of copyright. Later on—after some of those "seditious treasonable and unlicensed Bookes and Pamphlets" that made Charles II so paranoid took root in the colonies—the Statute of Anne became the model, in 1790, for the first Copyright Act of the United States of America.

Anne's Uncle Charles is best remembered for the canine breed bearing his name, and for the decree he issued that the King Charles Spaniel could not be forbidden entrance to any public place, especially Parliament. But Charles II's spaniel was a lapdog. Queen Anne's spaniel is the law of copyright. And this dog will hunt.

FURTHER READING

PRACTICAL GUIDE

A dizzying number of film finance and legal how-to guides are currently on the market. Too many of these guides are short on helpful, substantive advice and long on appendices filled with sample contracts. Far and away, the best of these guides is Michael C. Donaldson's *Clearance and Copyright: Everything You Need to Know for Film and Television,* 3rd ed. (Los Angeles: Silman-James Press, 2008). Donaldson provides a clear and comprehensive analysis of the legal considerations facing filmmakers and, to a lesser extent, television producers. For a book less about clearing rights and more about the legal side of independent film finance, see Schuyler M. Moore, *The Biz,* 3rd ed. (Los Angeles: Silman-James Press, 2007).

There are other guidebooks that focus on the creative side of film producing, but still emphasize the importance of legally controlling story material (through a twelve- or eighteen-month renewable "option" if not through an outright purchase). "Perhaps the single most important thing an aspiring producer can do is obtain motion picture rights to a property," writes Paul N. Lazarus III in *The Film Producer* (New York: St. Martin's Press, 1992), 3. Producer Larry Turman explains that "owning gives you power," and "without owning the projects you submit . . . you are vulnerable" to being cast aside for another producer. See Lawrence Turman, *So You Want to Be a Producer* (New York: Three Rivers Press, 2005), 75. These books are reminders of the ways copyright and contract law can assist, and not simply thwart, producers.

While many legal guidebooks have been written for aspiring filmmakers, very few have been published for aspiring new media, multimedia, or transmedia producers. This may change as more lawyers become experienced in these fields and more students come to identify broadly as media creators rather than as filmmakers. Standard legal guides do exist for many of the other long-standing commercial arts. Some titles that a Yale University Press reader recommended and we also find valuable are: Richard Curtis's *How to Be Your Own Literary Agent,* 4th ed. (New York: Mariner Books, 2003); Donald Passman's *All You Need to Know About the Music Business,* 7th ed. (New York: Free Press, 2009); and Donald Farber's *Producing Theatre,* 3d ed. (Pompton Plains, N.J.: Limelight Editions, 2006).

Regardless of what medium you are working in, you can freely take material from the public domain. We've covered some of the ways to identify public domain works, but for additional guidance, see Stephen Fishman, *The Public Domain: How to Find and Use Copyright-Free Writings, Music, Art, and More,* 5th ed. (Berkeley: Nolo Press, 2010).

FAIR USE AND CREATIVE COMMONS

Two of your most important tools as a media creator will be your understanding of fair use and your ability to make thoughtful judgments about what uses of copyrighted material qualify under this defense. Lee Wilson's *Fair Use, Free Use, and Use by Permission: How to Handle Copyrights in All Media* (New York: Allsworth Press, 2005) provides a cautious assessment of situations that would qualify as fair use for songwriters, graphic designers, and other media artists. Michael C. Donaldson's *Clearance and Copyright: Everything You Need to Know for Film and Television,* 3rd ed. (Los Angeles: Silman-James Press, 2008), 27, 41, also cautions that fair use is "a shield, not a sword" and provides a "safe harbor" set of criteria. Donaldson's "safe harbor" questions are useful for those seeking absolute certainty that a particular use is fair, but no checklist should replace your ability to make a deliberative judgment for yourself. Otherwise, you may censor yourself by eliminating uses that are fair but do not fit within the narrower "safe harbor."

For the past decade, Pat Aufderheide and Peter Jaszi at American University's Center for Social Media have studied and advocated fair use. The Center for Social Media collaborated with lawyers, teachers, and media practitioners to publish "Statements of Best Practices in Fair Use" for Documentary Filmmakers, Online Video Creators, and Media Literacy Educators, all of which can be downloaded from www.centerforsocialmedia.org/fair-use. Impressively, the Documentary Filmmakers' Statement prompted filmmakers to exercise more fair uses of copyrighted material and some distributors and errors-and-omissions insurers to consider adopting the statement. See Pat Aufderheide, "How Documentary Filmmakers Overcame Their Fear of Quoting and Learned to Employ Fair Use: A Tale of Scholarship in Action," *International Journal of Communication* 1 (2007): 26–32.

Sooner or later during your exploration of media and the law (perhaps after your eyes are burning from too much legal prose), you should crack open the witty, instructive, and engaging graphic novel *Bound by Law?* by Keith Aoki, James Boyle, and Jennifer Jenkins (Durham: Duke University Center for the Study of the Public Domain, 2006), www.law.duke.edu/cspd/comics/pdf/cspdcomicscreen.pdf. *Bound by Law?* explores fair use for documentary filmmakers, but also addresses some of the institutional barriers to implementing fair use in practice. Even with the fine work carried out by the Center for Social Media, your fair uses still run the risk of landing you in court and saddling you with legal costs you would rather direct toward your next project. For this reason, many critics have advocated reforming American copyright laws and, in the meantime, offered an alternative system through Creative Commons (you can find more on this in Chapter 6).

COPYRIGHT CRITIQUES

If you are unhappy about the way that copyright law limits your creativity, you are not alone. Several scholars, critics, and artists have called attention to the negative repercussions of the expansion of intellectual property law.

Lawrence Lessig is the most visible contemporary public intellectual in the United States to critically address our system of intellectual property law. In his writings on copyright, Lessig has powerfully shown how the current system of copyright has lost its social balance and ignored its constitutional mandate to serve the public. Lessig's most widely known book is *Free Culture: The Nature and Future of Creativity* (New York: Penguin,

2005), which sets out an agenda for copyright advocacy and reform. Lessig explains the title: "A free culture is not a culture without property, just as a free market is not a culture in which everything is free. The opposite of a free culture is a 'permission culture'—a culture in which creators get to create only with the permission of the powerful, or of creators from the past" (xiv). Lessig argues that for most of American history we have lived in such a free culture. Copyright protected commercial expression, but ordinary citizens could freely appropriate and adapt existing works into creations of their own, typically noncommercial expressions. But that commercial/noncommercial divide has faded as copyright owners (and the laws they have lobbied to pass) have become more aggressive. See also Lawrence Lessig, *The Future of Ideas: The Fate of the Commons in a Connected World* (New York: Vintage Books, 2002); Lawrence Lessig, *Code, Version 2.0* (New York: Basic Books, 2006); Lawrence Lessig, *Remix: Making Art and Commerce Thrive in the Hybrid Economy* (New York: Penguin Press, 2008).

James Boyle explores what the result of the expanded copyright laws has meant for a shrinking public domain. Boyle wisely uses the analogy of environmentalism to argue for the protection of the public domain. Much like our environment, a healthy public domain depends on recognizing and protecting cultural works that seem both big and small and ensuring their use for future generations. In his 1997 essay "A Politics of Intellectual Property: Environmentalism for the Net?" (www.law.duke.edu/boylesite/ip.htm), Boyle points out that a conceptual shift is necessary to prevent the public domain from eroding completely. If we don't teach the public domain, if we don't value it, and if we don't inspire future generations to use it, then the public domain will "disappear, first in concept and then, increasingly, as a reality." Boyle extends these arguments further in two books: James Boyle, *Shamans, Software, and Spleens: Law and the Construction of the Information Society* (Cambridge, Mass.: Harvard University Press, 1996), and James Boyle, *The Public Domain: Enclosing the Commons of the Mind* (New Haven: Yale University Press, 2008).

Neil Weinstock Netanel argues in *Copyright's Paradox* (New York: Oxford University Press, 2008) that today's copyright laws run afoul of the First Amendment protection of free speech. Creating works of expression requires authors to tap into preexisting, often copyright-protected cultural works. If those works are off limits, then individuals find their free speech limited and our society becomes a less diverse marketplace of ideas. If you are seeking additional confirmation for Netanel's argument, look no further than Kembrew McLeod, *Freedom of Expression®: Overzealous Copyright Bozos and Other Enemies of Creativity* (New York: Doubleday, 2005). The title of the book comes from a phrase—"freedom of expression"—that McLeod satirically yet successfully registered with the U.S. Patent and Trademark Office in 1998!

COPYRIGHT HISTORIES

If you want to learn more about copyright law's historical development, a good starting point is Paul Goldstein's *Copyright's Highway: From Gutenberg to the Celestial Jukebox,* rev. ed. (Stanford, Calif.: Stanford Law and Politics/Stanford University Press, 2003). Goldstein writes in a clear, lively, and concise style, though he problematically views copyright's main function as providing market signals to creators about audience demand (in contrast to, say, ensuring a vibrant culture that produces both commercial and noncommercial works). To provide balance against Goldstein's market research–oriented view, see Siva Vaidhyanathan, *Copyrights and Copywrongs: The Rise of Intellectual Property and How It Threatens Creativity* (New York: New York University Press, 2001). Boyle, Lessig, McLeod, and Netanel also critically scrutinize transformations in U.S. intellectual property law in their books cited above.

To understand more about the way in which Congress has historically passed copyright legislation, Jessica Litman's *Digital Copyright* (New York: Prometheus Books, 2001) provides an eye-opening account. Congress encourages the "stakeholders" (meaning successful artists and the copyright industries) to form a compromise and consensus about what is the appropriate course for copyright law. Once they reach an agreement, these stakeholding parties frequently draft the very legislation that Congress then passes into law (with some narrow exemptions carved out for smaller stakeholders, such as libraries, archives, and educators).

Some communication and media scholars, including Vaidhyanathan, have explored the interplay between copyright law, the media industries, and American culture. For film and video, see Jane M. Gaines, *Contested Culture: The Image, the Voice, and the Law* (Chapel Hill: University of North Carolina Press, 1991); Peter Decherney, "Copyright Dupes: Piracy and New Media in *Edison v. Lubin* (1903)," *Film History* 19, no. 2 (2007): 109–124; Lucas Hilderbrand, *Inherent Vice: Bootleg Histories of Videotape and Copyright* (Durham: Duke University Press, 2009). For music, see Joanna Demers, *Steal This Music: How Intellectual Property Law Affects*

Musical Creativity (Athens: University of Georgia Press, 2006), and Kembrew McLeod, *Owning Culture: Authorship, Ownership, and Intellectual Property Law* (New York: Peter Lang, 2001). And for an ambitious, engaging history that explores changing understandings and practices of piracy across multiple media forms, see Adrian Johns, *Piracy: The Intellectual Property Wars from Gutenberg to Gates* (Chicago: University of Chicago Press, 2009).

CHAPTER 2

Trademarks

"A dry martini," he said. "One. In a deep champagne goblet."

"*Oui, monsieur.*"

"Just a moment. Three measures of Gordon's, one of vodka, half a measure of Kina Lillet. Shake it very well until it's ice-cold, then add a large thin slice of lemon peel. Got it?"

"Certainly monsieur." The barman seemed pleased with the idea.

"Gosh, that's certainly a drink," said Leiter.

Bond laughed. "When I'm . . . er . . . concentrating," he explained, "I never have more than one drink before dinner. But I do like that one to be large and very strong and very cold, and very well-made. I hate small portions of anything, particularly when they taste bad. This drink's my own invention. I'm going to patent it when I think of a good name."

—*Casino Royale*, by Ian Fleming

Even James Bond, Hollywood's most valuable piece of intellectual property, wants to own his own piece of IP. We'll never know for sure whether he was joking about the patent, but he certainly does love his brands. An incorrigible name dropper, Bond is the epitome of what every trademark owner hopes every consumer aspires to be—a connoisseur.

Not just any gin will do for Bond, it has to be Gordon's. Not just any apéritif wine to flavor things up, it has to be Kina Lillet. The ultimate discerning customer, Bond would be at a loss without trademarks to identify the sources of the finer things in life, which construct his very identity.

But a funny thing happened to 007 on the way to the movies.

In the novels, aside from his Rolex, it's true James was a shade promiscuous with brands, driving a Bentley in *Casino Royale*, an Aston Martin in *Goldfinger*, and a Sunbeam Alpine in *Dr. No*, whilst hopping from bed to bed with Dom Pérignon, Veuve Clicquot, and Taittinger. In the films, though, he started sleeping around for money. Now the watch must be an Omega, the car a BMW, the champagne Bollinger, and the beer Heineken. It says so in his contracts. You may call him a tart, provided you recognize he's perhaps the best paid tart in entertainment history, thanks in considerable part to product placements, and he almost single-handedly saved MGM Studios from extinction when the roaring lion tanked in 2010 and had to claw its way out of Chapter 11 bankruptcy. James Bond has come a long way since his 1953 debut in Ian Fleming's *Casino Royale,* and so have trademarks.

In the world you live in today, trademarks impinge on nearly everything you produce as a creative artist in film or other media. Works of entertainment and the arts that get distributed and sold to the public, be they movies, TV shows, cartoons, graphic novels, video games, Web-based works, or the merchandise these spin off, inevitably come wrapped in an envelope of branding that deploys a constellation of trademarks, including those of studios, networks, publishers, and sponsors. Even if you choose to distribute and share an artistic work free on the Internet via a social networking site, such as Facebook, or user-generated content site, such as YouTube, your content will be embedded in a suavely trademarked Web interface. Even if you create works of fine art destined for display in the world's finest art galleries, your content will inhabit a trademarked installation, as a trip to the gift shop of your favorite art museum should readily convince you, because nonprofits also need to invoke the power of trademarks in an age of declining charitable endowments. Even if you create your work in the academic sanctum of a film school or other degree program in creative media, it is a safe bet your educational institution has trademarked itself and is merchandising the old alma mater to the hilt.

In your day-to-day life, trademarks are inescapable. As a first grader we once knew lamented over breakfast during an all too frequent commercial break in his favorite Nickelodeon cartoon: There are two people in this world you can't get away from—Ronald McDonald and Barbie.

But where did trademarks come from in the first place?

A BRAVE LITTLE TAILOR

Trademark law, like James Bond, is a British import.

Yet where copyright started as a statute, made by Parliament, trademark started as part of the common law, made by judges. Once upon a time, a year or so after Shakespeare wrapped up strutting and fretting his hour upon the stage, an up-and-coming clothier went to court, "whereas he had gained a great reputation for his making of his cloth by reason whereof he had great utterance to his benefit and profit, and that he used to set his mark upon his cloth whereby it should be known to be his cloth; and another clothier, observing it, used the same mark to his ill-made cloth on purpose to deceive . . ."

The tale of the brave little tailor of Gloucestershire was spun by one Justice Dodderidge, ad libbing from the bench years later while hearing a counterfeit jewelry case, *Southern v. How,* all according to a not necessarily reliable reporter who published an account of the case at a time when the court reporting biz was in its infancy. True or not, the supposed ruling in the tailor's case became part of the common law of England, such that the owner of a trademark can sue a knockoff artist for trademark piracy.

The common law of England became the common law of the American colonies, and morphed after independence into the common law of each state of the United States. *Southern v. How* became legal authority in America as well as Britain for the proposition that unauthorized use of someone else's trademark is unlawful trademark infringement.

Trademarks in this country were originally a matter of state law, but today federal and state trademark laws exist side by side. The federal Lanham Act of 1946, also known as the Trademark Act, came into effect in 1947. Congress based its authority to enact the law on the Commerce Clause of the U.S. Constitution, which gives Congress the power to "regulate commerce with foreign nations, and among the several states, and with the Indian tribes." Federal trademark rights cannot ultimately be obtained and kept unless the trademark owner can establish use of the mark in interstate commerce, which essentially means sales of goods or services under the mark have to cross state lines or U.S. territorial lines, or come in from overseas or from an Indian reservation.

Unlike federal jurisdiction over copyright matters, which is exclusive, federal jurisdiction over trademark matters is nonexclusive, because the Trademark Act does not preempt state law. State common law protection for trademarks and state trademark statutes still exist side by side with federal law. That being said, commercial development of artistic works these days rarely confines itself to a single state. Distribution of content on the Internet, for instance, is almost by its nature interstate. So most of the action in protecting trademarks in entertainment and the arts nowadays takes place at the federal level, and most cutting-edge legal developments impacting trademarks take place in Congress, in the federal courts, and at the U.S. Patent and Trademark Office.

Trademarks and copyrights share similarities in the way the legal system handles them and the ways people deal in them. Just as you can apply to register a copyright with the U.S. Copyright Office, search Copyright Office records, and assign or license a copyright to someone else, you can apply to register a trademark with the Trademark Office, search Trademark Office records, and assign or license a trademark. In substance, however, trademarks and copyrights are different rights meant to protect different things. The differences become clear once you know how to get trademark rights, how to protect trademarks, how to fight with trademarks, how to deal in trademarks, and how to handle trademarks abroad.

GETTING TRADEMARKS

A copyright you can get on your own. All you have to do is create an original work of authorship. The copyright springs to life the moment your work is put in fixed form. You can keep it a secret, tell no one, bury it in your backyard if you like. You've got a copyright.

Trademark rights you can't get all by yourself. They spring to life in this country in only one of two ways. One way is to venture into the outside world and use a mark to market and sell products or services, like the brave little tailor did. The other way, if you have not yet used the mark, is to file an application to register it, which becomes a matter of public record, stating that you intend to use the mark in commerce.

STRAIGHT FROM THE SOURCE

A trademark is a word, a name, a string of letters or numbers, a symbol, a logo, a design, a combination of these, or other indicator used to identify products or services as coming from a particular source. To qualify as a trademark, it has to be distinctive enough to distinguish the products or services it stands for from those of competitors, and consumers must perceive it not as a mere decoration, but as an indicator of source. This doesn't mean the public has to know the identity of the provider of the trademarked product or service. People seldom do. They just know it comes from a source that they can expect to produce more of the same.

To be able to distinguish the source's products and services, a trademark needs to stand out from others in the crowd, to be dissimilar enough in sight, sound, and meaning from competitors' marks that it does not confuse people about the source of the stuff bearing the mark. A mark that is not distinctive, or is confusingly similar to a competitor's mark, fails as a source indicator, and may be difficult or impossible to protect as a trademark.

A trademark is supposed to serve as a guaranty of quality. Not necessarily high quality, just a consistent level of quality people have come to expect of the mark. People tend to associate a given brand with a given trade-off between quality and price. If you buy stuff bearing a trademark and feel satisfied with the quality for the price, you will look for the same trademark next time out. Joe's Eatery ain't the Ritz, but you can count on decent eats at affordable prices. You don't need to know who Joe is, or even care whether Joe exists. The trademark Joe's Eatery guarantees a consistent level of quality that you, the customer, have come to expect. A pretty low one, maybe, but the price is right.

By signaling a reliable level of quality coming from a single source, a trademark can protect consumers against deception, as the brave little tailor's mark protected them against a sleazy competitor palming off sleazy cloth. The right to use a trademark means a right to exclude others from using the same or a similar mark for similar products or services. Trademark owners have a vested interest in clamping down on riffraff using confusing or deceptive marks to hustle competing stuff. This is thought to help police the marketplace, safeguarding customers against the unscrupulous. At its heart, trademark law is supposed to further a public policy of consumer protection, even though that goal often gets lost in the fray in today's trademark brawls.

Since a trademark identifies and distinguishes a supplier's products and services in the marketplace, trademarks have become key to brand identity and the centerpiece of most advertising and promotional campaigns. They can also generate substantial, steady streams of royalty income from licensing. Because of the power of trademarks, large brand owners plow millions upon millions of dollars into selecting, developing, registering, and protecting them.

Remember *Hispaniola*? You're going to have to get a grip on trademarks to make *Hispaniola* the movie happen. You will want to use them as source identifiers for three separate things. First, when you form a production company, the production company will need its own brand identity, a distinctive mark to identify it as a source of film production services. Second, you will want to trademark the title HISPANIOLA for the film itself, if possible, since it would be nice to be able to preempt competitors from releasing films with the title HISPANIOLA, though this is easier said than done. Third, you need to trademark the cornucopia of spin-offs and merchandise the movie has to generate in order to get the film financed and, hopefully, make everyone involved in the process very, very rich.

WHAT'S IN A NAME?

It will be easier to talk about trademarks if we first talk about names.

Related to trademarks, but not the same, are company names, trade names, and domain names. Each identifies something different from what a trademark identifies, though a name can also double as a trademark.

A *company name* or *corporate name* is the formal legal name of a business entity. Corporations, limited liability companies, and other business entities are formed under state law. Each state has a secretary of state's office or the equivalent where a start-up business can file articles of incorporation to form a corporation, articles of organization to form a limited liability company (LLC), a certificate of limited partnership to form a limited partnership, and so forth. Before accepting such a filing, the secretary of state's office checks its database to make sure no other entity of the same type has an identical name, because allowing two entities of the same type formed in the same state to have identical names could confuse or mislead business creditors, and sometimes facilitate business fraud.

A *trade name* is the name a business enterprise goes by in its dealings with customers and the general public to identify the enterprise. A company's trade name is often identical to its company name, but it doesn't have to be. Just as you have a personal legal name, but may prefer to use a nickname, a business may prefer to go by a nickname, or a name entirely different from its company name, which is okay, provided the management isn't out to defraud consumers or creditors. Such a trade name is known as a *fictitious business name*. Individuals running a business as a sole proprietorship or with partners in a general partnership are likewise allowed to operate under a fictitious business name, also known as a DBA (doing business as), usually by filing a fictitious business name statement or certificate of doing business at the state or local level.

The trade name of a business, or a similar name based on it, can also function as a trademark, if it is used as a source identifier for the goods or services the business deals in. But even when a trade name is not used as a trademark, unfair competition law at the federal and state level recognizes the right of the owner of a trade name to protect it against infringement by a competitor who comes along trying to divert business using the same or a confusingly similar trade name or trademark.

A domain name is obtained by registering it with a domain name registrar, such as Network Solutions or GoDaddy.com. A domain name serves as the Internet address for whatever Web site its owner chooses to upload to it, but the domain name can also serve as a trademark, if it is used as a source identifier for goods or services. Amazon.com is a domain name, but it is also a trademark and a trade name. Web site owners often display their domain name in prominent letters, usually stylized and often logoed, on the home page or the top banner of every page of a site, to create a source identifier for the Web site's products and services. Having a domain name is nice, but having a trademark is even better.

WHAT'S IN A MARK?

There are various kinds of trademarks composed of various kinds of elements.

A *word mark* consists of one or more words, names, or strings of letters, numbers, or other typographical symbols. Word marks include slogans. As we said in Chapter 1, you can't copyright a slogan, but you can trademark one. JUST DO IT® is a registered trademark of Nike, Inc. What makes it a trademark is that it is perceived by consumers as a source indicator. When people see this slogan used in connection with stuff, they assume the stuff comes from Nike.

A *design mark* consists of a logo or other design, graphic, or picture standing for a source of goods or services. When people see this one used in connection with stuff, they assume the stuff comes from Nike.

But a graphic or picture that is just for decoration, such as graphic art screenprinted on a t-shirt simply to make it look cool but not to indicate its source, is not a trademark. Purely decorative graphics can be copyrighted, but are not trademarkable. On the other hand, many design marks have sufficient artistic originality to be copyrighted as well as trademarked.

These two animals are trademarks of Disney Enterprises, Inc., but they show sufficient artistic originality to be copyrighted too, and we guess you know by now that you infringe Mickey's or Minnie's copyrights at your peril.

Composite marks combine word mark elements and design mark elements into a single mark. These include trademarks combining a company name and logo together in close enough proximity to create a unitary mark.

This one, owned by Paramount Pictures Corporation, is a composite mark combining the word mark element PARAMOUNT in stylized lettering above a mountain with an arc of stars surrounding them.

NON-TRADITIONAL MARKS

In addition to traditional word marks, design marks, and composite marks, the law has gradually come to recognize several types of non-traditional marks, gaining ever increasing ground with the proliferation of new media.

Color Marks

The color or colors of a product or its packaging can be trademarked if the public perceives the color or colors as a source indicator that has acquired distinctiveness in the marketplace. Tiffany and Company has registered the distinctive shade of robin's-egg blue used on its boxes and bags as a trademark for its jewelry and other products and retail services. But a color cannot be registered as a trademark if it is functional, since to do so would put competitors at an unfair disadvantage, as one manufacturer learned when it tried to register the color black for outboard motors, and was refused because black provides a competitive advantage, being compatible with a wider variety of boat colors.

Sound Marks

Sounds used consistently in promoting a product or service can become trademarks. Sounds that are unique, like musical melodies, are considered inherently distinctive, but a run-of-the-mill sound can also be trademarked if the owner establishes that the sound has acquired distinctiveness in the marketplace as a source indicator for its goods or services. Tetris Holding LLC, owner of the rights in the classic video game Tetris, has registered the word mark TETRIS, but it also registered as a trademark the sound of an electronic sine wave playing the game's musical theme, based on the traditional Russian folk song "Korobeiniki." An addictive tune it is, as you know if you've ever played Tetris.

Motion Marks

Moving pictures can also qualify as trademarks, with or without sound. The granddaddy of Hollywood motion marks is the MGM roaring lion, a registered trademark of Metro-Goldwyn-Mayer Lion Corp., first used in 1924, and still roaring fresh out of its Chapter 11 bankruptcy. These days, of course, you can hardly sit down to watch a movie, surf the Web, or turn on a mobile device without getting bombarded by at least half a dozen motion marks.

Scents and Flavors

The scent of a product may be registrable as a trademark if it is used in a non-functional way. One company managed to register a floral fragrance reminiscent of plumeria blossoms as a trademark for sewing thread and embroidery yarn. But scents that serve a useful purpose, such as the scent of perfume or an air freshener, are functional and not registrable. In theory, a flavor might be registrable as a trademark, but it is unclear how a flavor can function as a source indicator because flavor or taste generally performs a utilitarian function and consumers generally have no access to a product's flavor or taste prior to purchase.

Product Packaging and Product Design

Product packaging can be a trademark if sufficiently distinctive to identify to consumers the source of a product and distinguish it from its competitors. The iconic Coca-Cola bottle remains the classic example. Product configuration, the shape of a product itself, can also serve as a trademark, but to register a product configuration as a trademark, the brand owner must show the configuration has acquired distinctiveness and come to be associated exclusively with that brand. Apple Inc. went to considerable trouble to register the configuration of its iPod as a trademark in the U.S. and overseas.

STRONG MARKS AND WEAK MARKS

A trademark needs to identify its owner's products and services and distinguish them from others' products and services, but not all marks are created equal. Some are stronger than others. The more distinctive a mark, the stronger it is, and the greater degree of legal protection it receives. The Trademark Office and the courts traditionally like to analyze the level of distinctiveness of trademarks by arranging them along a spectrum.

Fanciful Marks

At the strong end of the spectrum are *fanciful marks,* also known as *coined marks.* These are invented words. For instance, the trademark XEROX was coined from the word "xerography" (from Greek *xeros* [dry] and *graphos* [writing]), itself a term coined in the 1940s to describe the dry photocopying technique that would make the Xerox Corporation rich and famous. The trademark ROLEX, Bond's timepiece of choice, back when he had a choice, was coined over a hundred years ago, when its owners wanted to make up a brand name that would be easy to pronounce in any language they wanted to market in (Japanese, evidently, was not on Swiss watchmakers' radar at the time). It's no accident many fanciful marks, like EXXON, include at least one X or another obscure letter, the point being to coin a mark that isn't already a real word.

Since a fanciful mark has no established meaning prior to brand launch, it functions purely to identify and distinguish the owner's stuff, and is exclusive to it. This makes fanciful marks the most distinctive and strongest marks. The downside is, it often takes lots of time and money to promote a fanciful mark, because prior to launch, no one has heard of it. The task of teaching an unsuspecting public the connection between a made-up mark and the stuff it brands can require a rather massive marketing budget.

Arbitrary Marks

Second in strength come *arbitrary marks,* composed of one or more real words with real world meaning, but used incongruously on stuff unrelated to that meaning. For instance, APPLE for computers and SPIKE for cable television broadcasting services are arbitrary marks. Because the semantic link between the trademark and the branded stuff is random or at least obscure, arbitrary marks also tend to require very considerable investment to indoctrinate consumers as to what they stand for, but arbitrary marks are on average a less steep marketing proposition than fanciful marks, because an arbitrary mark presents consumers with a real word they can sink their teeth into, making it easier to remember than a fanciful mark.

Suggestive Marks

We know what you're thinking, but no, *suggestive marks* do not have to include a dirty word, an off-color slogan, or a racy logo. A suggestive mark is one that includes one or more terms that hint at or evoke the branded products or services. DREAMWORKS for motion picture production services is a suggestive mark, melding creative artists' dreams with the works realized in film. Because they contain a hint about the branded products or services, suggestive marks often ease the expense and lead time to market to the public. The mark itself points the way to a connection between it and the stuff it signifies, so consumers "get it" more readily. On the flip side, suggestive marks are not given such extensive legal protection as fanciful or arbitrary marks are.

Descriptive Marks

Trademarks that directly describe a product or service or its attributes are *descriptive marks.* Words used in connection with products or services that are merely descriptive of them are not initially protectable as trademarks, since other competitors may use the same words to describe their stuff. However, descriptive wording, if used exclusively in connection with one source's products or services for a fairly long time, can develop *secondary meaning* as a mark associated with that single source, in addition to its primary descriptive meaning. UNITED ARTISTS, first used in 1923 for production and distribution of motion pictures, started life as a descriptive phrase, but acquired distinctiveness over the years as a trademark for these and other entertainment services brought to you by the company now known as United Artists Corporation.

The line between descriptive marks and suggestive marks is often a fine one, and drawing it is often a very subjective task. Yet the line is often a crucial one to draw, because a descriptive term cannot become a trademark unless it gains *acquired distinctiveness* in the marketplace by gaining a secondary meaning, whereas a suggestive mark automatically possesses *inherent distinctiveness* and can qualify as a trademark without showing that it has acquired distinctiveness. As a rule of thumb, to test whether a mark is suggestive, rather than merely descriptive, ask yourself whether the mark immediately conveys some attribute of the product or service, in which case it is descriptive, or whether some intervening mental step is needed to make the connection, in which case it is suggestive.

Generic Words

At the weak end of the spectrum come *generic words,* which are so weak in trademarkability that they aren't trademarkable at all. Generic words are the common name of a product or service. You can't claim PRODUCTIONS as a trademark for film production services, because competing producers need to use the generic word "productions" to refer to the things they produce. But you can combine PRODUCTIONS with one or more non-generic elements to form a trademark.

The spectrum of distinctiveness can be a slippery slope. A valid trademark, even a strong one, over time can slide into genericness, if the general public starts using it as the common word for the thing, and the owner doesn't manage or can't manage to stop it. Aspirin, cellophane, margarine, escalator, and videotape all started as trademarks, but ended up as unprotected generic terms, victims of their own success. If everyone starts using a trademark as the name of the thing branded, the mark loses its capacity to indicate source.

Brand owners facing this risk go to great lengths to attempt to stave off trademark genericide, because if your mark becomes generic your enemies can challenge and defeat your trademark rights. Xerox Corporation succeeded in staving off genericide for its mark XEROX with a public relations blitz encouraging users to talk about "photocopying" not "xeroxing" documents. GOOGLE is a fanciful mark for computer search services, coined in a misspelling of the word "googol" (meaning the number 10^{100}, itself a term coined in 1938 by nine-year-old Milton Sirotta and made popular in his uncle Edward Kasner's 1940 book *Mathematics and the Imagination*). Google Inc. has been grappling with potential concerns that GOOGLE may lose distinctiveness, as use of the term "googling" as a verb becomes ubiquitous and the word crops up in new editions of more and more mainstream dictionaries. Among other efforts, Google has issued detailed online guidelines for approved usage of GOOGLE and related marks (www.google.com/permissions/guidelines.html). How well is Google succeeding in its effort? Ask yourself this question: Can you google on yahoo? If the answer is still no, maybe Google is still doing all right.

Since the spectrum of distinctiveness is so subjective and fuzzy, it is typical in trademark disputes for each opponent to puff up its own mark, portraying it as far toward the strong end of the spectrum as possible, and to slam the adversary's mark, portraying it as far toward the weak end as possible. Because this form of arm wrestling is so prevalent, and because the Trademark Office and the courts dwell so much on the spectrum of distinctiveness, it makes sense when you create a new trademark to make it as strong as feasible, consistent with your branding strategy and your budget.

HISPANIOLA—THE TRADEMARK

Thinking up a clever trademark is the coolest part of launching a new venture, you tell yourself as you stride on in to Marlow's Collectibles, rattling the brass bells above the door with purpose. You need someone to brainstorm with. detect an eerie bluish glow emanating from the rear as you tiptoe down the shop's murky single aisle, sidestepping heaps of unshelved new arrivals piled land there on the floor. At his creaky oak desk Marlow hunches intently over top screen.

You didn't know Marlow had a computer, you remark.

My wireless, you mean? Marlow replies nonchalantly, his accent this ing grazing the green hills of Herefordshire and points west.

The advantages of a Starbucks® on every corner, free WiFi even at Marlow's Collectibles. You ask him: Think we can trademark . . . HISPANIOLA PRODUCTIONS?

Marlow casts you a blank look, his rimless specs reflecting back Google, in duplicate, spelled backward. He says: A shade redundant, isn't it?

How so?

Well, HISPANIOLA is already the name of your film.

Oh. True.

Besides—Marlow clicks a half dozen keystrokes and glances at the screen—as a trademark for a film production company, it's not available.

It's not?

Somebody else has already registered HISPANIOLA PICTURES.

How do you know?

It's called a trademark search, Marlow smiles indulgently.

Oh, you reply in a chastened whisper.

PROTECTING TRADEMARKS

The first step in protecting your trademark is to try to make sure your mark won't infringe someone else's. But the world of commerce is a big wide world. When you dream up a potential trademark, how can you know whether someone is already using the same or a similar mark for similar goods or services?

If your potential mark is a word mark or a composite mark with a word element, a good first-stage reality check that won't cost you a dime is to "google" your proposed wording (or perhaps we should say "utilize the Google® search engine to obtain information on the Internet"), and see what crops up. If anyone is marketing goods or services online using the mark you have in mind, odds are Google and other mainstream search engines will turn up at least some search results. It is also worthwhile to type in the address bar of your Web browser a domain name consisting of your proposed word mark plus .com, do the same for a few other common top-level domain names such as .net and .org, and repeat for obvious spelling variants of your proposed word mark, to see whether anyone is operating a Web site using your proposed word mark or a close variant to market similar goods or services. While you're at it, you can visit the Web sites of domain name registrars, such as Network Solutions and Go Daddy, to check the availability of domain names containing your proposed mark or variants, and you can conduct a WHOIS database search, which lists basic

contact information for the registrant of any domain name already registered. Keep in mind that registering a domain name, by itself, does not give
the domain name registrant any trademark rights in the wording contained
in the domain name, but the way the wording is used on a Web site may
give rise to trademark rights.

If your Internet search reveals a conflicting trademark, go back to the
drawing board and dream up a different candidate mark. If your Internet
search doesn't reveal a conflict, however, it doesn't mean you're out of the
woods yet, because you haven't yet conducted a trademark search.

TRADEMARK SEARCHES

The Trademark Office maintains a trademark register that is searchable
online. It gives details of all U.S. trademark registrations, live or dead. The
Trademark Office database also contains searchable online details of all
U.S. trademark applications, live or dead. On the Trademark Office's Web
site, you can search registrations and applications through the Trademark
Electronic Search System (TESS), a powerful search engine available free
to the public, which allows you to search based on various parameters.
You can search for all marks containing a certain word mark element or
a certain type of design mark element, you can search for marks within
a specific class of goods or services or naming a specific item of goods or
services in the application or registration, and so on. Each search generates
a result list, if there are any marks matching your search criteria. TESS
shows you for each mark on a search result list what the mark is, what
class or classes it covers, what specific goods or services it covers, the date
it was applied for, the date it registered, if it has registered, and who applied for it or owns it. The listings in TESS also link to a Trademark Applications and Registrations Retrieval (TARR) page, where you can view the
processing history of each application and registration. The office's Trademark Document Retrieval (TDR) function allows you to download copies
of any trademark application or registration and any other papers filed by
trademark applicants and registrants or issued by the Trademark Office.
When anyone files a U.S. trademark application, the details are available
to the public within a few days, free to access online, if you know how to
search and where to look.

Searching the Trademark Office database serves a different purpose from
searching the Copyright Office database of U.S. copyright registrations.
When you create an original work of authorship, you don't need to search

the Copyright Office's records to know you have created a copyright, and there is normally no reason to search those records before you apply to register your work. But when you think up a new trademark, you need to search the Trademark Office's records if you wish to be confident that no conflicting marks have already been applied for or registered.

How thoroughly you search depends on several factors. At a minimum, for a small business start-up, it is worthwhile making a "knock-out search" or "exact mark search" of TESS looking for any word marks identical to yours (or obvious variants, such as plural versus singular) in the class or classes of interest. You may be able to do this yourself if you familiarize yourself with TESS's search features. On the other hand, businesses in entertainment and the arts that plan to file a U.S. trademark application normally obtain, or should obtain, a full pre-filing federal trademark availability search covering the class or classes of goods or services of interest. A full word mark search requires very substantial trademark search experience, since it includes looking for possible phonetic or spelling variations, breaking down the word mark word by word and element by element, depending on the morphology of the word elements or other symbols contained in the word mark, possible ambiguous or alternative readings of those elements, and analysis of possible similarities in sound, sight, meaning, or connotation to other word elements.

Trademark search services such as Thompson CompuMark or CT Corsearch can conduct a full search, or you may prefer to ask an experienced trademark attorney to conduct the search. The search reports of trademark search services don't provide interpretation of the search results they generate, so you usually end up needing a lawyer anyway to interpret them. Either way the cost of the search will vary depending on how many classes of goods and services need to be searched, and on whether the mark is a word mark or a design mark, the latter being more expensive, since searching for design elements is normally more time consuming than searching for word mark elements.

In some instances, it is also advisable to conduct a search of state trademark registers and a common law search, which involves searching databases such as business directories and telephone directories to see what businesses turn up using a trademark or trade name similar to the proposed mark. State and common law trademark searches can be conducted only for word marks or the word element of a composite mark, because the search services lack the capability to search design marks at the state level or to search their common law business databases for design marks.

HISPANIOLA—THE TRADEMARK SEARCH

For now, you have your hands full with your federal trademark search.

Okay, you say, what should we call the production company?

Marlow shrugs. How about QUISQUEYA PRODUCTIONS?

QUESA what?

Quisqueya is the indigenous Taíno name for the island of Hispaniola.

Island? You thought Hispaniola was the name of a ship.

Marlow sighs. The ship was named after the island.

Never heard of it, you admit.

Marlow rolls his eyes. It's the second largest island in the Caribbean. Hispaniola is split between Haiti and the Dominican Republic. Quisqueya means "mother of the earth" in Taíno.

What's Taíno?

It was the language of the aboriginal people of Hispaniola, who had the singular misfortune of discovering Columbus in 1492. In any case, QUISQUEYA would make a strong mark.

Would it?

Taíno is an extinct language. QUISQUEYA is arguably tantamount to a fanciful mark. After all, you didn't even recognize it as a word when I said it.

True.

As an independent film producer you want a mark that sounds, well, inscrutable.

It's inscrutable, all right. But is it available?

That is the question, declares Marlow. He types www.uspto.gov and splashes of red, white, and blue light flash across his rimless specs like Fourth of July fireworks. In a flurry of keystrokes, he has his answer: QUISQUEYA PRODUCTIONS is available.

It is?

You're in luck. There are only a few live U.S. trademark filings that include the term QUISQUEYA, and they are things quite unrelated to film production, like prepaid calling cards, soft drinks, and sausages. So, you can adopt QUISQUEYA PRODUCTIONS as your film production trademark, and save HISPANIOLA as a trademark for the movies and the merchandise.

Are you saying we can trademark the movie title?

As a trademark for a single film, no. As a mark for a series of films, yes.

No kidding?

And don't forget the girls.

The girls?

Aye, the girl pirates. Marlow's accent starts drifting south along the rocky Cornish coastline. If he says Yar! you're going to slug him.

What about the girl pirates?

You'll want to trademark their names for dolls, toys, and whatnot.

Oh, you nod slowly, yes indeed. You open up Bonnie Charlotte's *Hispaniola* and flip pages. Okay, let's see: there's Lucia Bonaire, her sis Dominica, Martinique, the runaway Haitian slave, Montserrat, the French consul's rebellious daughter, Kitty, the indentured Irish maidservant, Guadeloupe, the renegade Puerto Rican sugar heiress, Jade, the Chinese short-order cook with culinary dreams . . . and Saba, the mysterious Taíno Indian princess.

That it? says Marlow.

That is it. So search already.

Marlow buries his noble aquiline nose in his laptop for a good quarter hour.

Well? You start tapping your foot.

Here we go, Marlow announces. I limited the search to dolls and toys, in Class 28. Dominica, Martinique, Montserrat, Kitty, and Guadeloupe are available. Lucia, Jade, and Saba are not. Various people have already applied for or registered them as trademarks for dolls.

Not bad, you say. We'll just change those three names.

Any candidates? asks Marlow, flexing his long, bony fingers.

LUCIA is out, you say. But can we try LUCIA BONAIRE?

Brilliant, says Marlow. LUCIA BONAIRE does seem distinctively different from just plain LUCIA, so not confusing, and . . . I see here no one has filed for BO-NAIRE. LUCIA BONAIRE it is. Next, you need a substitute for JADE.

What the hell, try JASMINE.

Taken.

Try LOTUS.

Taken.

Screw it, try BLOSSOM.

BLOSSOM . . . is a go. No live applications or registrations of record.

That leaves, um . . . what's a good name for a Taíno Indian princess?

Yahíma.

Where do you get this stuff?

Wikipedia. Marlow grins sheepishly.

Whatever, search it.

YAHÍMA . . . available.

Excellent, so much for the names. Can we trademark the dolls themselves?

Marlow stares at you and says: A doll can't function as a trademark for itself.

Oh.

But, not to worry. You can copyright each doll as a three-dimensional sculptural work. You can copyright two-dimensional artwork depicting each doll. And you can trademark the artwork for each doll, to the extent the artwork is used as a source indicator for the dolls, such as on product packaging.

Okay. You can picture Martinique, for instance, as trademarked art.

Martinique

Great, you say, we've got our crew:

LUCIA BONAIRE

DOMINICA

MARTINIQUE

MONTSERRAT

KITTY

GUADELOUPE

BLOSSOM

YAHÍMA.

Hmm, Marlow ruminates.

What?

Why not round out the line with a couple of evil pirate dolls?

Capital idea. Search JIM HAWKINS and RIPLEY.

JIM HAWKINS . . . available.

Super.

RIPLEY . . . no live application or registration, not for dolls or toys—

You can picture Ripley as trademarked art too.

Ripley

But . . .

But what?

RIPLEY might get a surname refusal.

What's a surname refusal?

I'll explain later. We can work it out.

Fine. Hey, when did you learn how to use a computer?

Marlow snorts. Before you were born, my dear.

Anyway, thanks for the free legal advice.

Advice? Marlow chuckles. This isn't legal advice. I'm merely imparting a bit of general legal information. If this were legal advice, rest assured, you'd be paying me a lot more than you are now. By the way—Marlow juts his noble aquiline nose pointedly at the faux parchment leatherette book tucked under your arm—are you returning that, or buying it?

You grumble, shell out $4.50, as penciled on the flyleaf of Bonnie Charlotte's *Hispaniola*, and make Marlow give you a receipt.

KEEPING TRACK

Whether or not you apply to register a trademark, as with copyrights, keeping clear paper or digital records of things you may need to prove someday is important. Keep track of when and how you thought up your trademark, what trademark searching or related research you did at the time, when and how you made plans to use your mark, the marketing, advertising, and promotional efforts made to publicize your mark, and the dates and circumstances of your first sales under the trademark. Proper paper or electronic record keeping of invoices, purchase orders, contracts, shipping documents, artwork, correspondence, and other documents evidencing your use of a trademark and preparations to use it can become key to being able to vindicate your rights in a mark.

And, yes, keep all of your receipts, starting with the one Marlow just gave you.

TRADEMARK SYMBOLS

Placing a trademark symbol in proximity to your trademark on branded products or product packaging, or in association with branded services (for instance, on a Web site banner) is not legally required, but is often a good idea. If the trademark is not applied for, or has been applied for but has not yet registered, you can use the TM symbol with the mark on your goods, and your choice of the TM symbol or the SM symbol (for "service mark") with the mark as used in connection with your services. The symbol ® stands for a registered trademark, and is legally not permitted to be used except with marks that have become registered.

Use of the TM or ® symbol helps protect your trademark, because it puts others on notice that you indeed claim the thing as a trademark. If later on your trademark is infringed, proper use of either symbol helps preclude the infringer from pleading "good faith" infringement of your mark. That being said, sometimes, especially in Internet usage or other electronic media, or in film credits, for instance, adding the TM or ® symbol may clutter the graphic presentation of a trademark. When that is the case, let your aesthetics be your guide. Omitting a TM or ® symbol does not imply that you do not claim trademark rights in a mark.

TRADEMARK REGISTRATION

Trademark rights arise in one of two ways, either by using a mark to market and sell products or services, or by filing an application to register a mark. As soon as you start using a trademark in commerce, you gain common law rights in the mark. The quality of those rights is another matter. Depending on the timing and extent of your use, you may gain rights in the mark prior to and superior to competing marks whose use would cause confusion among consumers as to source. One shortcoming of common law rights, though, is that they normally are confined to the geographic territory where the owner actually sells the branded goods or services, in contrast to rights under a federal trademark application or registration, which protect a mark nationwide. State trademark registration, which some local businesses find useful if their geographic horizons are truly limited to one state, has no interstate impact. Relying on common law rights or state trademark registration does not suffice in entertainment or media projects of any significant scope, in which case you would need the advantages of federal registration to protect the associated trademarks.

Trademarks used in the United States in interstate commerce are protected under federal law. A trademark can be registered with the U.S. Patent and Trademark Office to protect the owner's right to exclusive use of the mark for specified goods or services in one or more classes. The application to register the mark can be made either based on actual current use in the United States, or based on a good faith intention to use the mark in the future. The latter type, an *intent-to-use application,* cannot proceed to register until after the mark comes into actual commercial use in interstate commerce for the class or classes of goods or services listed in the application. For now, let's focus on U.S. trademark owners filing U.S. applications. We'll come around later in this chapter to look at international trademarks, inbound and outbound.

Although registering a trademark with the Trademark Office is not a prerequisite to having valid common law rights, there are distinct legal advantages to doing so. Among other benefits, a federal trademark registration:

- Is prima facie evidence of the registrant's ownership of the mark and of its exclusive right to use it in connection with the goods and services listed in the registration, shifting the burden of proof to any would-be opponent.
- Gives the public constructive notice of the registrant's claim of ownership, eliminating any potential "good faith" defense for a party making later use of a conflicting mark—*constructive notice* means third parties are treated as if they knew about your registration, whether or not they actually did know about it.
- Becomes *incontestable* after five years, making the registration conclusive evidence of the registrant's ownership of the mark, so that it cannot be challenged except on very limited grounds, such as fraud.
- Creates a right to sue in federal court for trademark infringement.
- Enables recovery in a federal court infringement action of infringer's profits, legal costs, attorneys' fees, and damages, including possible *treble damages*, an award of triple the amount of actual damages against especially egregious infringers.
- Can be recorded with U.S. Customs to help prevent the importation of counterfeit or unauthorized goods bearing infringing marks.
- Makes available criminal penalties against counterfeiting.
- Creates a basis for filing trademark applications in foreign countries.

Registration can be sought any time after you start using a mark, but you can also file on an intent-to-use basis before you start using the mark, and this has a crucial advantage. As soon as you file an intent-to-use application, you gain priority over anyone else in the United States who comes along after your filing date and either uses or files for the same or a similar mark for similar goods or services. By filing an intent-to-use application, you stake a claim to your intended mark and create the breathing space needed to develop and launch your business, without having to fear that someone else will come along and scoop the same or a similar mark for similar goods or services before you get your operation off the ground. Intent-to-use applications are so useful a tool that a majority of U.S. trademark applications are filed on an intent-to-use basis.

The right to a trademark normally depends on being first either to use the mark or to file an intent-to-use application. If you apply to register a mark prior to using it, but it turns out that another party has already used the same or a similar mark first in commerce, the party first to use is entitled to register the mark, not the party first to file. If you apply to register a mark prior to using it, and another party comes along after your filing date and uses the same or a similar mark in commerce, you are entitled to register the mark, even though the other party uses its mark before you use yours.

Suppose two marks used by two different parties are the same or confusingly similar. Which of the two enjoys priority? If Ahab started using QUEEQUEGS COFFEE on March 1, 2012, and Ishmael started using KWEE-KWEGS COFFEE on April 1, 2012, Ahab wins, because Ahab started using before Ishmael did. If Ahab started using his mark on March 1, 2012, and Ishmael filed an application to register his mark on April 1, 2012, and hadn't yet started using his mark, Ahab wins, because Ahab started using before Ishmael filed. But if Ahab started using QUEEQUEGS COFFEE on March 1, 2012, and Ishmael already filed for KWEEKWEGS COFFEE on an intent-to-use basis on February 1, 2012, Ishmael wins because Ishmael filed before Ahab started using. And if Ahab filed an intent-to-use application on March 1, 2012, but Ishmael already filed an intent-to-use application on February 1, 2012, Ishmael wins because he filed before Ahab filed. Whatever the scenario, odds are Ahab and Ishmael will each be hearing from Starbucks be-

---

HISPANIOLA—THE TRADEMARK FILINGS

Wait a sec, you say. $325 per class plus legal fees?

'Fraid so, says Marlow.

Just to file for QUISQUEYA PRODUCTIONS in one class?

Yes, International Class 41, entertainment services.

Plus we've gotta do HISPANIOLA, plus the ten pirate characters.

Mmm, says Marlow. For HISPANIOLA you'd like to file in Class 41 for the movie series and also pick up services such as providing information on the Internet

about the movies, video games, and other merchandise, production of videos, animated videos, video games, providing online computer games, arcade games, live theater productions, sporting and cultural events, fan club services, theme park services, that sort of thing. For HISPANIOLA and for your characters, you'd like to file in at least four classes of goods.

Go ahead, hit me.

In Class 9, covering electrical and scientific apparatus, you'll want to file for video game software and discs and pre-recorded movie DVDs, cartoon DVDs, and music CDs, but you can also pick up, if you intend to license them, DVD and CD players, karaoke players, radios, television sets, telephones, cell phones, cell phone covers and cases, mouse pads, decorative magnets, eyeglasses, and sunglasses.

Quite a mixed bag.

Indeed. Next, Class 16 covers paper goods and printed matter. You can file for a series of fiction books—Bonnie is sure to like that—and for trading cards, posters, art prints, picture books, address books, appointment books, coloring books, children's activity books, bookmarks, calendars, stickers, memo pads, coasters made of paper, greeting cards, stationery, maps, paper napkins, envelopes, paper party decorations, pens, pencils, paperweights, drawing rulers, pencil sharpeners, erasers, and staplers.

Gee whiz, all set for Back-to-School.

Precisely, nods Marlow with an avaricious chuckle. Next, Class 25 for clothing. I suggest you list t-shirts, shirts, tank tops, sweat shirts, sweat pants, sweat suits, jeans, pants, shorts, overalls, jumpsuits, skirts, dresses, blouses, jackets, sweaters, vests, swimwear, bathing suits, cover-ups, sleepwear, pajamas, robes, nightgowns, leotards, lingerie, panties, bras, boxer shorts, underwear, scarves, belts, socks, stockings, tights, leggings, gloves, coats and raincoats, hats, caps, headbands, visors and bandanas, shoes, slippers, boots, sandals, and flip-flops.

Hmm. Did eighteenth-century pirates have flip-flops?

I believe they invented flip-flops, says Marlow. Ditto sunglasses. Last but not least, Class 28, covering toys and sporting goods. You'll want to list dolls, obviously, and what are dolls without doll clothing, doll accessories, doll playsets, and dollhouses to go with them? You'll also want toy action figures and accessories, collectible toy figures, electric action toys, handheld video game units, playing cards, board games, chess sets, jigsaw puzzles, kites, party favors, party games, target games, toy building blocks, inflatable toys, balloons, beach balls, rubber balls, toy vehicles, toy banks, wind-up toys, yo-yos, baby multiple activity toys, bath toys, crib toys, inflatable bath toys, musical toys, toy mobiles, pet toys, plush toys, squeeze toys, talking toys, baby rattles, and a slew of gymnastic and sporting goods, and don't forget children's play cosmetics.

What if I want real cosmetics?

Class 3, with shampoos, soaps, lotions, and whatnot.

How about watches?

Class 14.

And jewelry?

Class 14 also.

In that case, we're up to seven classes for HISPANIOLA, six classes for each of the eight girl pirates, at least two or three for the two bad guys. This is going to cost a fortune. Where are we supposed to drum up the funds?

You need to find a deep pocket.

Roger that. Any ideas?

I'm working on it, drawls Marlow with a mysterious smile.

fore the dust settles, particularly if either of them uses the colors green and black or anything remotely resembling a circular logo.

For a walk-through on the trademark registration process, see Appendix 2.

Trademark Examination

Within a few months after filing, your application will be assigned to an examining attorney on the Trademark Office staff. Turnaround time varies depending on workload, but several days after filing, your application details are fully uploaded to the Trademark Office databases and you can track the progress of your application by looking it up in the Trademark Electronic Search System, clicking a link to Trademark Applications and Registrations Retrieval to view processing status, and downloading any items filed or issued regarding your application using Trademark Document Retrieval.

The examining attorney will review the application, check to see if it is complete, conduct a search of the Trademark Office TESS database to see if the same or a similar mark has been registered or applied for in the same class or related classes of goods and services, and decide whether, in his or her opinion, the mark you have applied to register is registrable.

If the examiner sees a problem, but it is a relatively minor one, you or your lawyer may receive a phone call or email from the examiner trying to iron out the issue. If the examiner sees a substantial problem with the application, you or your lawyer will receive from the Trademark Office an email notifying you that the examiner has issued an *Office Action,* and providing a link to download it. The Office Action will explain why the examiner is refusing to register the mark applied for, explaining the problem or problems, explaining what you may be able to do to address each problem, and occasionally asking for additional information. You will have six months to respond to the Office Action. When you receive an Office Action or other communication from the Trademark Office, it is imperative to mark the deadline on the calendar and put a surefire system of reminders in place. If you use a trademark lawyer to handle your application, your lawyer should note the deadline and send you reminders. If you miss the deadline, absent extenuating circumstances, you simply lose.

Here are some things that can go wrong during examination:

- *Form of Mark.* The examiner may object to the jpeg image of your mark, if it is not clear enough. This is normally an easy fix. The examiner may also ask you to tweak the wording of your description of the mark, if you are filing a design mark or a composite mark.
- *Identification of Goods and Services.* The examiner may object to your list of goods or services, saying your wording is vague, not specific enough, or not in line with the Acceptable Identification of Goods and Services Manual, trying to narrow your list of goods or services. Some examiners can be extremely picayune about this, and responding can be tedious, but normally this kind of objection can be hashed out by modifying your list.
- *Misclassification of Goods and Services.* The examiner may object to your list of goods or services, claiming that some items do not belong in the class or classes applied for, but rather should go in some other class or classes. This sort of objection ups the ante, because the examiner is angling to make you amend your application and add one or more new classes, at $325 a pop. If the goods or services the examiner picks on are key ones, your alternatives are to fork over additional fees, delete the questioned goods or services, or argue about it with the examiner.
- *Disclaimer.* If your mark contains one or more words the examiner considers to be generic words or merely descriptive words, the examiner will ask you to enter a disclaimer, which becomes part of your application and the resulting registration. For instance, when you apply for QUISQUEYA PRODUCTIONS, you can expect the examiner to ask you to enter a statement: "Applicant disclaims the exclusive right to use PRODUCTIONS apart from the mark as shown." Say yes to this, because you don't care if other film production com-

panies use the word PRODUCTIONS in their trademarks. It happens all the time.

- *Absolutely Not.* Some things just can't be registered. The examiner looks at the mark you apply for to see whether the Trademark Act allows it in the first place, because there are several grounds barring some types of things. If the examiner finds that one or more of these *absolute grounds* apply, the examiner will refuse to register your mark. The most common absolute grounds for refusal are:

  ○ *Generic Words.* A generic word, the common name of a product or service, isn't trademarkable at all for that product or service. It can't act as a trademark for that product or service, because it is incapable of distinguishing the source of the product or service it names. A trademark application for a generic word will be shot down in flames.

  ○ *Merely Descriptive.* The Trademark Act bars registration of a mark that, when used on or in connection with goods or services, is merely descriptive of an ingredient, quality, characteristic, function, feature, purpose, or use of the goods or services, unless the mark has acquired distinctiveness in the marketplace. This preserves up to a reasonable point the freedom of competitors and the public to use the descriptive wording. A trademark including descriptive wording combined with other terms can be registered, but as just mentioned, the examiner will probably ask for a disclaimer of the exclusive right to use the descriptive portion apart from the whole mark. One additional wrinkle here is that, aside from the Principal Register where most trademarks are registered, the Trademark Office maintains a Supplemental Register, where descriptive marks that have not yet acquired distinctiveness can be registered, awaiting the day when their owners hope they might acquire distinctiveness.

  ○ *Deceptively Misdescriptive Marks.* The Trademark Act bars deceptive marks, such as ones that falsely describe the contents of a product, or misdescribe the quality, character, function, composition, or use of a product, if buyers are likely to believe the misdescription, and the misdescription is likely to affect their purchase decision.

  ○ *Primarily Geographically Descriptive.* The Trademark Act bars registration of a mark if its primary significance is a generally known geographic location, the goods or services originate in that location, and a buyer would likely believe they originate there. You couldn't trademark HISPANIOLA PRODUCTIONS if your services consisted of producing travelogue DVDs about the island of Hispaniola.

  ○ *Geographically Deceptively Misdescriptive.* The Trademark Act also bars registration of a mark if its primary significance is a generally known geographic location, the goods or services do not originate in that location, buyers would likely believe they originate there, and the misrepresentation is a material factor in their decision to buy. You couldn't trademark HISPANIOLA CIGARS for cigars processed and rolled in South Carolina from South Carolina tobacco, if cigar aficionados would assume the cigars came from Haiti or the Dominican Republic, and this influenced their purchase.

○ *Primarily Merely Surname.* You can't register a mark that is primarily merely a surname unless it has acquired distinctiveness through use in the marketplace. Whether the primary significance of a mark is that of a surname depends on whether the surname is rare, whether the term is the surname of anyone connected with the applicant's business, whether the term has any recognized meaning other than as a surname, whether it has the "look and feel" of a surname, and whether its stylization is distinctive enough to create a separate commercial impression. Marlow couldn't succeed in registering MARLOW or MARLOW'S or MARLOW'S COLLECTIBLES unless he showed acquired distinctiveness, because Marlow isn't a rare surname, it is the surname of someone connected with him, namely Marlow, it has no other recognized meaning, and it has the "look and feel" of a surname.

○ *Functional Designs.* Product configurations or designs that are primarily functional are not capable of serving as source identifiers, and so are not registrable as trademarks, although they may be registrable under a design patent. If a product feature makes the product more useful to consumers or economical to produce it is primarily functional. Functionality includes the idea of aesthetic functionality. There is no trademark protection for aesthetically pleasing and visually attractive designs that are not source indicators. This means that in the United States competitors can imitate someone else's aesthetic design features to the extent that they are not copyrightable or patentable, something that happens all the time to fashion apparel designers, who have been calling for amendment of the U.S. Copyright Law to open up a window of copyright protection for fashion designs.

○ *Decorative Designs.* Given trademark law's take on aesthetic functionality, designs on products that are purely decorative or ornamental are not registrable. If a design feature is just decorative or ornamental, consumers won't see it as a source indicator. This doesn't mean that a design mark can't contain a lot of decorative elements; it simply means the mark must function to indicate the source of goods or services.

○ *False Connection and Disparagement.* The Trademark Act absolutely bars registration of a mark that, with regard to persons, institutions, beliefs, or national symbols, falsely suggests a connection, disparages them, or brings them into contempt or disrepute. The false connection bar didn't stop hundreds of misguided souls with no connection to Barack Obama except in their dreams from applying to register marks including the name OBAMA and many excruciating plays on words based on it, both before and after the 2008 presidential election. The Trademark Office refused them all, kept their fees, and laughed all the way to the bank. No one parts a fool and his money sooner than the USPTO. Don't try to register flags, coats of arms, and insignia of the United States or any state, municipality, or foreign country, either. You can't.

o   *Immoral or Scandalous.* The Trademark Act bars registration of "immoral or scandalous matter," defined as "shocking to the sense of propriety, offensive to the conscience of moral feeling, vulgar, lacking in taste or morally crude." This golden rule theoretically is measured in terms of a substantial portion of the general public, but in reality the Trademark Office and many of its examiners take a rather prissy view of what is immoral or scandalous, so don't throw $325 in the gutter trying to see whether you can get a really edgy trademark past the examiner. This isn't a First Amendment issue. It's not about free speech. It's just about what you can register.

• *Likelihood of Confusion.* So much for refusal on absolute grounds; now let's explore refusal on *relative grounds* and U.S. trademark law's biggest cottage industry. When examining an application for a mark, the Trademark Office examiner conducts a search of the TESS database to see if the same or a similar mark has been registered or applied for in the same class or related classes of goods and services. This part of the drill is called *relative examination*, since the examiner is comparing your mark relative to other marks filed before yours. If the examiner finds one or more conflicting earlier marks, and feels that your mark is likely to cause consumer confusion vis-à-vis the conflicting mark or marks, the examiner can refuse to register your mark on grounds of *likelihood of confusion.*

If the examiner finds a likelihood of confusion between your mark and a registered mark, he or she will refuse to register yours. If the examiner finds a likelihood of confusion between your mark and a mark for which an earlier application has been filed, the examiner will suspend your application until the earlier application either registers, in which case you will receive a refusal, or goes abandoned, in which case yours can proceed.

Likelihood of confusion between two marks is tested in a two-step analysis. First, the two marks, viewed in their entireties as the public would see them, are compared for similarities in appearance, sound, meaning, and commercial impression. The analysis shifts focus depending on the type of mark. For design marks, sight controls. If the overall visual impression created by two design marks is too close, the marks will be found confusingly similar. For word marks, on the other hand, sight, sound, and meaning interact in subtle ways. The impact in the consumer's mind of a similar semantic connotation between two word marks may outweigh visual and phonetic differences. Second, the goods and services of the two marks are compared to determine if they are related or if the activities surrounding their marketing are such that confusion as to source is likely.

For instance, suppose you made the mistake of ignoring Marlow's warning, and applied for HISPANIOLA PRODUCTIONS for "production and distribution of motion picture films" in Class 41. When conducting a search, the examiner would stumble upon an existing registration for HISPANIOLA PICTURES in Class 41 for "movie production services." The dominant portion of each mark is HISPANIOLA, the second portion of each mark is a descriptive word, and the two descriptive words are nearly synonyms. The two marks, viewed on the whole, are similar in sight, sound, meaning, and commercial impression. Comparing the services of the two marks, "production and distribution of motion picture films" overlaps with and is closely related to "movie production services." The examiner would refuse your application on the grounds that your mark HISPANIOLA PRODUCTIONS is likely to be confused with HISPANIOLA PICTURES.

Now suppose you are smart enough to take Marlow's suggestion, and apply for QUISQUEYA PRODUCTIONS for "production and distribution of motion picture films" in Class 41. When conducting a search, the examiner would find only one trademark registration or application containing the word QUISQUEYA, namely, ARROZ QUISQUEYA for "rice" in Class 30. The two marks QUISQUEYA PRODUCTIONS and ARROZ QUISQUEYA don't look much alike or sound much alike, don't mean the same thing, don't create similar commercial impressions, and are for utterly unrelated services and goods. Clearly, there is no likelihood of confusion between the two, and the examiner should not refuse to register QUISQUEYA PRODUCTIONS.

An examiner with a perverse sense of duty might issue an Office Action invoking the so-called *doctrine of foreign equivalents* to refuse your mark QUISQUEYA PRODUCTIONS on grounds of likelihood of confusion with HISPANIOLA PICTURES. Under this rule, words from foreign languages are translated into English to determine whether they are likely to be confused with other marks, and to determine whether they are merely descriptive or generic. But there is an exception for foreign words from dead or obscure languages that may be so unfamiliar to the U.S. public that they shouldn't be translated into English. You're in luck. Taíno is a dead language. You can argue this in response to an Office Action.

Trademark Office examiners aren't infallible. They sometimes make mistakes about what is and isn't trademarkable. If you feel a mistake has been made, the first step is to respond to the Office Action, trying to persuade the examiner of your legal point of view. After the examiner considers your response, if not persuaded, he or she will issue a final Office Action, to which you can respond within six months with a request for reconsideration, arguing the same or additional things. At the end of the day, if you cannot persuade the examiner to see things your way, you can appeal the decision to the Trademark Office's Trademark Trial and Appeal Board. If the board's decision on appeal is not in your favor, you can appeal it to federal court and ask a judge to decide whether your mark is registrable. But as with copyrights, you'd rather not go there.

Publication and Opposition

If you survive the examination process, the examiner will approve your mark for publication in the Trademark Office's *Official Gazette,* and the Office will email you a Notice of Publication. The *Official Gazette* is an electronic publication issued weekly and searchable online at the Trademark Office's Web site. Trademark search services and large brand owners monitor it weekly to check whether any newly approved and published marks potentially conflict with their marks. Anyone who wants to object to registration of your application must do so within thirty days of its publication date, by filing a Notice of Opposition with the Trademark Trial and Appeal Board or an extension of time to oppose. Unless an opposer or potential opposer comes out of the woodwork during that thirty-day period, your application can proceed to register.

Assuming your application makes it through the opposition period unopposed, as the vast majority of applications do, you should receive a Certificate of Registration within a couple of months if you filed based on use, or a Notice of Allowance if your application was based on intent to use. In an intent-to-use application, after you start using the mark in interstate commerce, you need to file a statement of use submitting a specimen of the mark as used and stating dates of first use. The Notice of Allowance gives you six months to file a statement of use. If you need additional time, you can obtain up to five back-to-back extensions of six months each, but these entail additional fees. All in all, on a straightforward application, if you have started using the mark, registration can be attained within about nine to ten months after the application date.

How Long Trademarks Last

A trademark registration is valid for ten years from the date the Trademark Office issues it, and can be renewed thereafter at ten-year intervals. To maintain the registration, a declaration of continuing use must be filed between the fifth and sixth anniversaries of the registration date, and between the ninth and tenth anniversaries. This requires marking several deadlines on the calendar and making timely filings to keep a registration alive, and all of these filings involve additional fees, so it is important when planning a brand to factor these maintenance costs into the equation. Unlike copyrights, which last a long time but must eventually expire, a trademark can in principle last forever, provided you keep on using it and keep putting coins in the USPTO meter.

FIGHTING WITH TRADEMARKS

Trademark battles share some procedural similarities with copyright battles, but there are also significant differences. First, nothing in the copyright arena is comparable to a trademark opposition, or to the other form of fighting conducted before the Trademark Trial and Appeal Board, a cancellation action, where the petitioner seeks to get a registered trademark kicked off the register. Second, state courts can hear trademark cases, but not copyright cases, since federal jurisdiction is nonexclusive for trademark, but exclusive for copyright.

One thing is for sure. There are a lot of trademarks out there. If you earn your daily bread in the realm of branded creative content, sooner or later you or your collaborators will bump into a dispute involving trademark infringement, and probably involving trademark infringement's big sister, trademark dilution, to boot. You need to know how to fight with trademarks.

TRADEMARK INFRINGEMENT

The owner of a trademark can claim infringement if a newcomer starts using the same or a similar mark for the same or related types of goods or services and such use is likely to cause confusion or deceive consumers as to the source of the goods or services. If the similarity is likely to confuse an appreciable number of ordinary consumers, then the "senior" user's claim of trademark infringement against the "junior" user prevails.

Sound similar to the "likelihood of confusion" standard the Trademark Office examiner used in reviewing your application? It is, with some huge differences. For one thing, the examiner looks only at what the trademark register says about registered marks he or she thinks may conflict with yours, whereas the aggrieved trademark owner may try to drag everything except the kitchen sink into evidence. For another, the examiner doesn't stand to win or lose money on the outcome, whereas for the aggrieved trademark owner, it is very much about the money.

Just as a copyright beef often kicks off with a cease and desist letter, the law firm you never heard of in Chapter 1 has a variation on a theme to send you if it thinks you're infringing its client's mark. A trademark cease and desist is a common prelude to a trademark opposition, a trademark cancellation, or a civil lawsuit. The lawyer will assert how great the client's brand is, will claim the client owns one or more trademark registrations or applications, will exaggerate how high the client's mark is on the spectrum of distinctiveness, will say your trademark infringes theirs, or the mark in your intent-to-use application is going to infringe theirs, will tell you to stop, and will probably demand money to boot.

As with a copyright cease and desist, you can do a bit of Internet research to get a line on these people. You don't want to take what they say at face value. You or your lawyer can search TESS online to find out whether they actually own any trademark filings, can check TARR to look at the processing history of filings they do own, which may reveal chinks in their shining armor, and can download from TDR documents in the Trademark Office files for their mark. If you don't think your mark is likely to be confused with theirs, and you don't want to cease and desist using your mark, you and your lawyer need to develop a defense strategy. If you can poke a hole in their priority claim by showing you used or filed your mark first, you can turn the tables and cease and desist them. If they happen to have screwed up in their filing, you might come up with a reason why theirs is invalid or vulnerable to cancellation. More often, your defense may simply be that, all things considered, you believe the two marks aren't likely to be confused.

If the two sides don't work things out privately, the attacker has two avenues for pursuing the claim, either a trademark opposition before the Trademark Trial and Appeal Board, or a civil lawsuit in federal or state court. Oppositions are much less expensive to prosecute or defend than civil litigation, but the board can't award either side money damages. All the board can do is refuse to register applications and cancel registrations, but often in the trademark world, having a trademark filing scuttled is enough to make its owner move on and choose a different mark.

If the opposer files against an application a Notice of Opposition, which is similar to a complaint in a lawsuit, the board emails it to the applicant, with notice of various deadlines in the case. The grounds for opposition will usually include likelihood of confusion, will tend to include trademark dilution if the opposer claims its mark is famous, and if the opposer thinks the examiner missed an absolute ground for refusal when examining the application, the opposer will throw that in the applicant's face too, provided the opposer's mark isn't vulnerable to attack on the same absolute ground.

Within forty days after receipt of the Notice of Opposition, the applicant needs to file and serve an answer or other response. The rules require the two sides to hold a conference, usually done by telephone, to discuss their claims and defenses, the possibility of settlement, and arrangements relating to discovery and trial evidence if they are not ready to settle. In fact, most oppositions do settle, and often settle before the legal fees on each side spiral out of control. If the applicant's case is weak, the settlement may involve the applicant abandoning its application and adopting a completely different mark. If the applicant's case is reasonably good, a settlement will more likely involve a *coexistence agreement,* under which the two sides agree, within certain negotiated parameters designed to avoid future confusion, sometimes with modifications in the form of the applicant's mark, to let each other's marks coexist on the Trademark Office register and in the marketplace.

The likelihood-of-confusion standard used by Trademark Office examiners when deciding whether to let an application through the turnstile is also the centerpiece of most trademark oppositions, because the examiner's decision isn't necessarily the last word on the subject. The opposer typically claims it owns one or more prior trademark registrations or applications, or that it would like to apply for a mark used earlier than the applicant's filing and use dates, but the applicant's trademark application is standing in the way of that. The opposer claims to be the senior user by virtue of prior filing or prior use, and puts the applicant in the role of the junior user. The board focuses in likelihood-of-confusion cases on whether the purchasing public would mistakenly assume the applicant's goods or services originate from the same source as, or are associated with, the opposer's goods or services. The determination is made on a case-by-case basis, applying a dozen factors that leave ample room for argument.

In a federal trademark lawsuit, whether the district court judge finds a likelihood of confusion between two marks depends on a comparison of the mark of the senior user and the later filed mark of the junior user, juggling mainly the following factors:

- the degree of similarity of the marks
- the relatedness of the goods or services
- the extent of their overlap in channels of trade
- the strength of the senior user's mark
- the likelihood of the two users expanding into each other's markets
- the likely level of buyer ability to discriminate between them
- evidence of actual confusion between the two
- the junior user's intent in selecting its mark.

The more directly competitive the goods or services, the less the degree of similarity of the two marks needed to establish likelihood of confusion. Comparison of the marks should not be a subjective question of whether the judge personally would be confused, but rather a question of whether the ordinary consumer would likely be confused, considering the impression each mark as a whole creates on buyers in the context in which they encounter the branded goods or services in the marketplace. When likelihood of confusion is a close call, doubts are resolved in favor of the senior user.

Evidence of actual confusion between two marks can consist of facts such as the senior user receiving phone calls or emails from prospective customers asking about the junior user's goods or services, but in big-budget lawsuits, the parties routinely commission consumer surveys conducted by specialist survey firms that formulate and go out with questionnaires to test the presence or absence of confusion. You may have the misfortune while cruising your local mall someday of being buttonholed by a fresh-faced young person with a clipboard trying to ferret out whether Zombie and Finch is easy to mix up with Abercrombie and Fitch. Trademark surveys can be very expensive, and can result in even more expensive legal bickering between the two sides as to whether the survey evidence should be admissible. They are one of the things tending to make full-blown trademark litigation prohibitively expensive, certainly for the little guy.

Trademark plaintiffs typically go to court seeking an injunction to prevent the defendant from using or registering the allegedly infringing mark, and claiming money damages. If the plaintiff owns a federal trademark registration, the plaintiff can ask the court to award in its discretion "treble damages" in an amount up to three times actual provable damages, and can ask the court to award attorneys' fees and costs. The court can also order the destruction of goods or materials bearing the infringing mark. The most blatant form of trademark infringement is, of course, counterfeiting. The trademark plaintiff can sue a counterfeiter in a civil lawsuit for all of the above, but criminal charges can also be brought against counterfeiters, because counterfeiting is a crime.

TRADE DRESS INFRINGEMENT

Related to trademarks is the concept of *trade dress*. Components of trade dress include the color, shape, design, size, and placement of images and words on product packaging and labels or on service marketing collateral. Trade dress comprises the total look of the product or service offering, and can include the design and shape of a product itself. The focus is on the gestalt, or whole picture, the trade dress presents to the ordinary consumer.

Unfair competition law protects the trade dress of an established maker against attempts by competitors to divert business by duplicating or simulating its trade dress. While trademark law protects specific marks used, applied for, or registered, the trade-dress concept encompasses the holistic appearance of a product, its labels, and packaging, including elements not protected or protectable by trademark. This makes trade dress infringement a more fluid and interpretive legal theory than trademark infringement, and the gray areas are abundant, but trade dress infringement generally turns on the following elements:

- close resemblance—the closer the overall resemblance of the rival packages, the more likely a finding of trade dress infringement.
- non-functionality—non-functional elements tend to be more strongly protected as trade dress than functional ones.
- directly competing products—an established user's claim of trade dress infringement is more likely to be upheld against a maker selling directly competing products or services.
- likelihood of confusion—a likelihood that a competitor's trade dress simulating an established user's may confuse consumers into thinking the products or services are from the same maker strongly supports a claim of trade dress infringement.
- intent—proof of a competitor's intent to trade on an established brand's goodwill, coupled with a likelihood of confusion, will usually make for a successful trade dress infringement claim.

- inherent distinctiveness—unless its trade dress is inherently distinctive, the established user must prove that its trade dress has acquired secondary meaning—gained consumer recognition as identifying the established user's products or services and distinguishing them from those of competitors.

Inherent distinctiveness of trade dress depends on factors such as:

- Is the trade dress more than just a common geometric shape or design?
- Is it more than a mere variation of a common form of ornamentation for a given type of product or service?
- Is it so unusual in its field that it is reasonable to presume consumers will perceive it as source-indicating?

Whereas a trademark case mainly concerns the exclusive right of the owner to use the protected mark to distinguish its product or service, a trade dress case takes a broader view and evaluates the consumer's likely level of confusion between two products based on the total impact of all aspects of product or service presentation. The courts have not yet ruled with consistency on whether the "look and feel" of a Web site qualifies as inherently distinctive trade dress, but a considerable volume of litigation is sure to continue to hover around the question.

TRADEMARK DILUTION

An aspect of trademark protection that is separate and distinct from trademark infringement is *trademark dilution*. While most trademark oppositions object to an application on likelihood-of-confusion grounds, if the opposer owns a famous mark, or claims to, you can expect the opposer to add dilution as a separate ground, and in a federal lawsuit to complain of dilution.

A federal Trademark Dilution Act, largely preempting earlier statutes adopted by several states, took effect in 1996 and was significantly beefed up by the Trademark Dilution Revision Act of 2006. These amend the Trademark Act to provide nationwide protection for "famous" marks against uses that "dilute" their distinctiveness, even in the absence of any likelihood of confusion as to the source of goods or services.

This protection entitles the owner of a famous mark to an injunction against anyone who commences use of a mark or trade name in commerce that is likely to cause dilution by blurring or dilution by tarnishment of the famous mark, regardless of the presence or absence of actual or likely confusion, of competition, or of actual economic injury.

"Dilution" means a lessening of the capacity of the famous mark to identify and distinguish its goods and services, and comprises both the notion of "blurring" of distinctiveness of a trademark, caused by its unauthorized use on products or services dissimilar to the famous mark's products and services, and the notion of "tarnishment" of a trademark, by unauthorized use of the mark that links it to products or services that are of poor quality or which cast the mark in an unwholesome or unsavory light that is likely to reflect adversely upon the famous mark.

Although only injunctive relief is ordinarily available under the Trademark Dilution Act, willfully intending to trade on a famous mark's reputation or to cause dilution can make a diluting party liable for damages, disgorgement of profits, and reimbursement of the injured party's attorneys' fees, and may result in an order for destruction of the diluting goods.

The law defines a "famous" mark as one that "is widely recognized by the general consuming public of the United States as a designation of source of the goods or services of the mark's owner." Factors taken into account in determining fame include:

- the duration, extent, and geographic reach of advertising and publicity of the mark
- the amount, volume, and geographic extent of sales under the mark
- the extent of actual recognition of the mark, and
- whether the mark is registered.

"Dilution by blurring" is defined as an association arising from the similarity between a famous mark and the diluting mark that impairs the distinctiveness of the famous mark. There are six nonexclusive factors a court or the Trademark Trial and Appeal Board may consider in determining whether a mark is likely to cause dilution by blurring:

- the degree of similarity between the diluting mark and the famous mark
- the degree of distinctiveness of the famous mark
- the extent to which the owner of the famous mark is engaged in substantially exclusive use of the mark
- the degree of recognition of the famous mark
- whether the user of the diluting mark intended to create an association between it and the famous mark
- any actual association between the diluting mark and the famous mark.

"Dilution by tarnishment" occurs when association arising from the similarity between a mark or trade name and a famous mark harms the reputation of the famous mark, such as when the defendant's use is unsavory or unwholesome, or the mark is used in connection with inferior products.

Importantly, the dilution provisions of the Trademark Act do not prohibit some uses of a mark, such as noncommercial trademark parody, protected by the First Amendment, as we turn to discuss in the next section.

TRADEMARK FAIR USE

Trademark fair use hovers around some of the same airspace as copyright fair use, but like most aspects of trademarks and copyrights, if you feel a temptation to analogize between the two, stifle it. Unlike the Copyright Act, which contains a full restatement of copyright fair use as developed in federal case law, the Trademark Act contains only a limited provision for a "descriptive fair use" defense to trademark infringement claims, and a relatively new provision specific to trademark dilution cases.

"Descriptive fair use" allows you to use descriptive wording or imagery to describe your product or service, even if the descriptive wording or imagery also happens to be someone else's trademark, as long as the wording or imagery is used fairly and in good faith only to describe your products or services, and not to fake out consumers into thinking your stuff is the trademark owner's stuff. This makes sense given the way trademark law treats descriptive terms. Earlier in this chapter we said a descriptive term can't gain trademark protection unless it has acquired secondary meaning in the marketplace as a distinctive identifier of source. If it does acquire distinctiveness as a source indicator for a particular brand owner, trademark law protects that secondary meaning, not the primary descriptive meaning. The brand owner can't preempt competitors from using the term truly descriptively, and the descriptive fair use defense essentially corroborates this.

Beyond descriptive fair use, federal courts throughout the land have laid out a smorgasbord of differing legal rules, some overlapping, some conflicting, to decide what else ought to be considered fair in trademark love and war. The U.S. Supreme Court hasn't tucked in to this all-you-can-eat feast yet in any serious way, but the Court of Appeals for the Ninth Circuit, hearing district court cases cropping up in California, and the Court of Appeals for the Second Circuit, which handles those coming out of New York, have set a reasonably consistent direction.

"Nominative fair use" allows certain nondeceptive uses of trademarks to refer to a brand owner's products or services or engage in comparative advertising. For instance, the Ninth Circuit Court of Appeals in *New Kids on the Block v. News America Publishing* held that the publishers of the newspaper *USA Today* could use the band's trademarked name to conduct an opinion poll. The court ruled that a trademark use qualifies as "nominative fair use" if it passes a three-pronged test. First, the product or service at issue must be one that is not readily identifiable without use of the trademark. Second, the user must use only so much of the trademark as is reasonably necessary to identify the product or service. Third, the user must not do anything that would suggest sponsorship or endorsement by the trademark owner. Since the *USA Today* pollsters could hardly ask their questions without using the name of the band, the polls refrained from using the band's logo or anything else more than necessary, and nothing in the write-up suggested the New Kids on the Block had sponsored the polls, *USA Today* made it all the way around the block without getting mugged, other than for legal fees.

Another handle for coming to grips with trademark fair use, a very big handle, is the First Amendment. The First Amendment provides more limited protection for "commercial speech"—defined as speech that does no more than propose a commercial transaction in a way removed from any exposition of ideas—than for other kinds of speech. But most creative works don't fall into the commercial speech pigeonhole because they go beyond merely proposing a commercial transaction.

In *Rogers v. Grimaldi*, Fred Astaire's famous dance partner Ginger Rogers sued to enjoin the U.S. release of Federico Fellini's film *Ginger and Fred* (*Ginger e Fred* en Italiano), starring Giulietta Masina and Marcello Mastroianni as aging hoofers Amelia and Pippo, who dust off their old music-hall act emulating Astaire and Rogers for a TV variety show. A merciless lampoon of Italian commercial television as an idiotic freak show, *Ginger e Fred* features a pretty typical array of, well, Fellini freaks. The Second Circuit Court of Appeals contributed its own juggling act, balancing the Trademark Act's governmental interest in protecting against consumer confusion and the First Amendment's constitutional interest in freedom of expression. The court decided the Trademark Act should be construed to apply to artistic works only where the public interest in avoiding consumer confusion outweighs the public interest in free expression, and that the interest in free expression should normally outweigh concerns about trademark infringement, as long as the use of a trademark bears some artistic relevance to the work at issue. Score one for the freaks.

If you're beginning to feel trademark fair use law is a bit Felliniesque, just wait. It gets better.

In *Mattel v. MCA Records,* the redoubtable maker of Barbie dolls sued MCA for trademark infringement over the release of the Danish band Aqua's Eurodance hit "Barbie Girl" on its album *Aquarius.* The lead vocalist in "Barbie Girl" sings in a high-pitched, doll-like voice, while in counterpoint her boyfriend Ken raps mildly suggestive lyrics, like "Come on Barbie, let's go party."

Endorsing the Second Circuit's *Rogers v. Grimaldi* rule, the Ninth Circuit Court of Appeals concluded that the use of Barbie in "Barbie Girl" is not an infringement of Mattel's trademark, and upheld the district court's summary judgment for MCA. The court reasoned that the use of Barbie in the song title is clearly relevant to the artistic work, namely, the song itself. The song is a commentary on Barbie and the values Aqua implies she represents. The title does not explicitly mislead consumers as to the source of the work, since it doesn't suggest the song was produced by Mattel.

The Ninth Circuit got another chance to take a walk on the wild side in *E.S.S. Entertainment 2000 v. Rock Star Videos,* when the proprietors of the Play Pen Gentlemen's Club in East Los Angeles took the producers of *Grand Theft Auto* to court charging trademark infringement. Each video game in the *Grand Theft Auto* series takes place in a fictional virtual city modeled on the less-than-model-city attractions of real U.S. cities. The *San Andreas* edition lets players savor the gritty underbelly of the charming "Los Santos" metropolitan area, replete with liquor stores, gun shops, tattoo parlors, bars, and strip clubs. These virtual establishments are inspired by photos taken by the game's map artists in real neighborhoods with the right ambience, but the business names, logos, and architecture are changed to protect the innocent. East Los Santos contains a virtual strip club called the PIG PEN, based loosely on E.S.S.'s PLAY PEN, including a risqué silhouette logo of a nude dancer inside the stem of the first "P." We hope we don't have to draw you a picture.

E.S.S. Entertainment claimed Rock Star's virtual PLAY PEN word mark and logo would cause consumers to believe E.S.S. endorsed or was associated with *Grand Theft Auto.* The trial judge called the bouncer, kicking E.S.S. out of court on summary judgment. The Court of Appeals affirmed, and reaffirmed *Rogers v. Grimaldi* and *Mattel v. MCA Records,* declaring an artistic work's use of a trademark that otherwise would violate the Trademark Act is shielded by the First Amendment unless the use has no artistic relevance to the underlying work, or, it has some artistic relevance, but it explicitly misleads as to the source or the content of the work.

The first prong of the test, whether the mark is artistically relevant to the work, is satisfied so long as the relevance is "above zero." Rock Star easily met this low threshold since its artistic goal was to develop a cartoonish parody of East L.A., and it was reasonable for Rock Star to re-create a critical mass of the businesses and buildings that constitute the city. Rock Star passed the second prong of the test as well, since its use of the mark PIG PEN did not explicitly mislead as to the source or content of the work. Observing that the brick-and-mortar strip club and the video game have nothing in common other than that both offer "a form of low brow entertainment" (the court's words, not ours), the Ninth Circuit saw nothing to indicate the public would reasonably believe that the strip club owner produced *Grand Theft Auto,* or that *Grand Theft Auto*'s producers run a strip club. Thus, Rock Star beat E.S.S.'s trademark infringement rap, but the map artists can probably forget about getting comped at the Play Pen Gentlemen's Club next time they visit the City of Angels.

If you're scratching your head at this point wondering why the four cases above dragged on through trial and appeal, when the correct outcome seems obvious, you're not alone. To call these defendants trademark infringers defies common sense. Like many trademark fair use cases, these four were easily decided by the district court, and rightly upheld on appeal. What's hair-raising is to think of the time and expense involved. The dilemma isn't that there are no defenses for trademark fair use. The problem is there are too many different defenses, differently stated, by different federal circuits. To post your creative work containing somebody's trademark on the Internet or otherwise distribute it nationally is to play Russian roulette, since you may end up hauled into court anywhere in the country. All this uncertainty fosters an environment where even cool-headed brand owners feel compelled to press strategic litigation in their perceived best interest, and the entertainment industry succumbs by further ratcheting up the hyperconservative clearance culture, where studios, distributors, and underwriters tend to insist that the producer obtain written permission every time a branded product appears on screen.

Moreover, if you are thinking of having a famous mark appear in a creative work, you not only need to worry about a trademark infringement claim, you also need to worry about trademark dilution. Here, the "fair use" defense is a creature of statute. Congress explicitly added a comprehensive fair use provision when the Trademark Dilution Revision Act of 2006 amended the Trademark Act. It says the following types of "fair use" do not constitute dilution by blurring or dilution by tarnishment:

(A) Any fair use, including a nominative or descriptive fair use, or facilitation of such fair use, of a famous mark by another person other than as a designation of source for the person's own goods or services, including use in connection with—

   (i) advertising or promotion that permits consumers to compare goods or services; or

   (ii) identifying and parodying, criticizing, or commenting upon the famous mark owner or the goods or services of the famous mark owner.

(B) All forms of news reporting and news commentary.

(C) Any noncommercial use of a mark.

If your proposed use fits one of the above pigeonholes, you have a defense against a trademark dilution claim. Notice how the pigeonholes line up with some of the trademark fair use theories we just looked at in the context of trademark infringement cases. While it would be nice to wish this statutory guideline will lend clarity to trademark fair use judgment calls in future dilution cases, if the future is like the past, you can expect to witness a pageant of colorful but expensive hammer-and-tong litigation probing the clauses above one by one, especially since owners of famous marks have the most at stake and the biggest war chests.

HISPANIOLA—THE PRODUCT PLACEMENT

You're lucky. You're making a movie about girl pirates in the late eighteenth century. Your characters don't need to eat, drink, shampoo their hair, and brush their teeth with brands that are registered trademarks and household names, if they brush their teeth at all, or wear designer clothes, drive luxury cars, or shoot luxury side arms like Bond. So you won't have a lot of trademark fair use issues of the sort you would run into in a contemporary story.

But if you're thinking of having the girls drink Captain Morgan® rum, don't go there. Aside from the anachronism, it'd cut into doll sales. If you're thinking they will sip Twinings® tea, that might help doll sales, but be advised, the mark has been in use since 1706 and R. Twining & Company Limited has the incontestable trademark registrations to prove it, so you would have to go to them ever so politely and ask their permission.

Better yet, says Marlow. Offer them a product placement.

First things first, say you. When are we going to see Bonnie?

First things first, replies Marlow. You haven't finished Chapter 2.

DEALING WITH TRADEMARKS

Trademarks can be bought and sold and frequently do change hands, for example, when a business is sold. When a trademark is bought outright, the buyer needs to have the seller sign a *trademark assignment* confirming the transfer. Since a trademark symbolizes the goodwill and consumer recognition its owner has built up in its products and services sold under the mark, trademark assignments are normally not valid unless they include an assignment of the goodwill of the business associated with the mark. A trademark assignment typically says the owner sells, transfers, and assigns to the assignee the specified trademark and all of the goodwill associated with it, either in the United States and worldwide or for specified territories. If there are U.S. or foreign trademark applications or registrations covering the mark, these should be identified by country and number in one or more assignments, so that the buyer can record the assignment in trademark office records. The buyer also usually needs to include in its purchase agreement some representations and warranties from the seller to ensure the trademark sale and assignment is not going to conflict with any prior deals, commitments, or assignments the seller may have made to others, and that the trademark is free and clear of any licenses, other than ones the buyer knows about and accepts, and an indemnity backstopping the representations and warranties is always a good thing to get.

Trademark licensing of entertainment, celebrity, fashion, and sports trademarks is an enormous global industry. The owner of the mark retains ownership and becomes a trademark licensor, granting a *trademark license* to a licensee, allowing the licensee to use the trademark for specified goods or services in exchange for royalty payments and perhaps other fees. Trademark licenses usually include representations and warranties, an indemnity, and other things you will delve into in Chapter 4 when you put together the Hispaniola deal, and some license agreements, especially of entertainment properties, consolidate trademark and copyright licenses in a single contract. As with copyrights, state law comes into play in dealing in trademark assignments and licenses, since state contract law determines the validity of the contracts and the interpretation of their wording.

Like the Copyright Office, the Trademark Office has a system for *recordation* of trademark assignments, licenses, and other documents that affect trademark ownership, such as security agreements, where a lender takes a trademark as collateral to secure its loan. These types of documents can be recorded online at the Trademark Office through its Electronic Trademark

Assignment System (ETAS). Although recordation is not required, it provides legal advantages in most trademark dealings, since it puts the world on notice of the assignment, license, security interest, or other matter covered in the document.

TRADEMARKS ABROAD

Trademarks are territorial. A U.S. trademark registration, or a common law right to use a trademark in the United States, does not give you the right to use a trademark in a foreign country, except for a limited degree of special protection given to famous and well-known marks against willful infringement in countries belonging to mainstream international trademark treaties. You are well on your way to snagging a U.S. trademark registration for HISPANIOLA, but gaining rights in the mark in the United Kingdom will be a question of U.K. and European Community law. Conversely, ownership of a trademark in a foreign country does not give the owner a right to use or register the mark in the United States, so foreign trademark owners have to take action under U.S. law to acquire trademark rights here. Both sides of the coin have ramifications for your ability to market, sell, distribute, and license *Hispaniola* the movie and all that movie merchandise at home and abroad, and to prevent overseas competitors and counterfeiters from using marks the same as or similar to your trademarks to manufacture and sell similar products, so you need to get the drift of international trademarks, both outbound and inbound.

OUTBOUND MARKS

The traditional way, and until a few years ago the only way, for the owner of a U.S. trademark to acquire rights in the same mark in a foreign country is to file a trademark application with the national trademark office of that country. The rules as to how the application is examined, how interested parties may oppose it, and so forth depend on the national trademark law of that country, and differ from country to country. In each country you apply in, you or your U.S. lawyer need to hire a local trademark lawyer qualified to practice there in order to represent you before the trademark office, navigate the examination process, and fend off oppositions or other objections. Often before filing in foreign countries, it is advisable to conduct a trademark search in those countries, either ordering a worldwide or regional search through a trademark search service such as Thomson

CompuMark or CT Corsearch, or ordering searches country by country to be conducted by your local counsel in each country.

Eurodance

The countries of the European Union each have a national trademark office, but there is also a union-wide system created in 1996 allowing for the filing of a single application at the Office of Harmonization for the Internal Market (OHIM) to obtain a registration, known as a Community Trade Mark, that protects a trademark throughout the EU. National trademark applications and registrations still exist side by side with the CTM, but the CTM has greatly reduced the cost of obtaining trademark protection in Europe. The EU members covered by the CTM include the United Kingdom, Ireland, France, Germany, the Netherlands, Belgium, Denmark, Italy, Spain, Greece, Austria, Finland, Luxembourg, Portugal, Sweden, Cyprus, Czech Republic, Estonia, Hungary, Latvia, Lithuania, Malta, Poland, Slovak Republic, Slovenia, Bulgaria, and Romania. Switzerland, Norway, and Russia are not members of the European Union and are not covered by the CTM, but they are members of the Madrid System, to which we now turn.

The Sun Also Rises

There is no such thing as an international copyright. But there is such a thing as an International Registration for a trademark. International Registrations are issued under a scheme known as the Madrid System, administered by the World Intellectual Property Organization and established under two international trademark treaties, the Madrid Agreement and the Madrid Protocol, which the United States joined in 2003 and the European Community joined in 2004. International filings under Madrid can reduce fees by as much as 50 percent in comparison to making individual direct filings country by country, so yes, indeed, the sun also rises.

The cornerstone for foreign protection of a U.S. mark under Madrid is an International Application, filed through WIPO, and based on one or more U.S. applications or registrations. (WIPO, you may recall, refers to the folks in Geneva who manage the Berne Convention and other international copyright treaties.) The International Application requests extension of trademark protection to selected countries of interest, with the official fees calculated based on which countries are selected. It is possible under Madrid to protect a mark throughout Europe and in many Asia-Pacific countries of key commercial interest, including China, Japan, Korea, Singapore, Australia, and, most recently, New Zealand. While most countries are members of the Madrid System, some have not yet joined. Canada, Hong Kong, and most Latin American countries have not, but several of them are considering joining. For countries outside the Madrid System, direct national trademark filings are the only way to go for now.

We'll Always Have Paris

The Paris Convention is another international intellectual property treaty, adopted by nearly all commercially significant countries. It also has a key favorable impact on international trademark filing strategy and budgeting. It allows a trademark applicant to use its first filing date in one country as the effective filing date in applications in other countries party to the convention, in a European Community Trade Mark application, and in an application for International Registration under the Madrid System, provided the applicant files these within six months of its first application date. For example, suppose you filed a U.S. application on April 30, 2012. A foreign application, a CTM application, or a Madrid filing for the same mark based on your U.S. application, if made on or before October 31, 2012, would be treated as if filed on April 30, 2012, and would enjoy priority over any application filed overseas for the same or a similar mark for similar goods or services anytime after May 1, 2012.

This six-month window of overseas protection for your U.S. filing date can be useful in planning and budgeting your foreign trademarks, especially if your international distribution and licensing plans are not very far along at the time you file in the United States. Since most U.S. applications are examined at the Trademark Office within three months or so, based on current turnaround, you gain the opportunity to see how the U.S. examination goes before committing where and how to file overseas. Just remember though: We'll always have Paris, Rick—but on any one application you'll only have Paris for six months.

INBOUND MARKS

Like other trademark treaties, the Paris Convention is a two-edged sword.

A non-U.S. applicant who files overseas in a country party to the Paris Convention is entitled to file in the United States within six months and enjoy treaty priority in the U.S. To assure your mark won't be trumped by a foreign party with the right to claim treaty priority, a well-tailored international search strategy can help zero in on what may lurk offshore. International searches can get expensive, but several of the better-heeled trademark offices, including those in the United Kingdom, Canada, Australia, New Zealand, and Hong Kong, among English-speaking jurisdictions, offer free online trademark search engines. OHIM maintains an excellent search engine, CTM-ONLINE, for searching its Community Trade Mark register and database of pending CTM applications on its Web site (www.oami.europa. eu). You or your U.S. lawyer may at least be able to perform a knock-out search for HISPANIOLA on these foreign search engines. Come to think of it, since you don't actually have a lawyer yet, you may as well ask Marlow.

As a U.S. applicant, you have only two bases on which to file a U.S. trademark application, either actual use in U.S. commerce or a bona fide intent to use. There are five bases, though, on which a non-U.S. applicant may file an application with the Trademark Office. In addition to the first two bases, a non-U.S. applicant can file based on a pending foreign trademark application, and register with the Trademark Office after the foreign registration issues, can file and register based on an existing foreign registration, or, if the foreign party holds an International Registration under the Madrid System, can file based on it, requesting extension of protection to the United States. These last three bases have the advantage that the non-U.S. filer can register without filing evidence of use in the United States, and doesn't have to start using the mark and file use evidence until the fifth to sixth anniversary of the registration date. This might sound unfair, until you keep in mind that when the shoe is on the other foot and you go to file overseas, in most foreign jurisdictions you don't need to start to use the mark until three to five years after registration.

HISPANIOLA—THE INTERNATIONAL TRADEMARK

Hullo, clucks Marlow, clicking keys: This I like.

What, what, what? you nag, tapping your foot impatiently.

HISPANIOLA, he announces, comes up clean on the knock-out searches. Not a soul has applied for a trademark containing the term HISPANIOLA, no Community Trade Mark, and not in Canada, Australia, New Zealand, or Hong Kong. How very promising. Of course, you'll want to order a full international search before you take the plunge.

This is going to cost a fortune, you complain.

O.P.M., my friend, replies Marlow.

O.P.M.?

Other People's Money, grins Marlow, as he powers down his wireless.

FURTHER READING

PRACTICAL TRADEMARK GUIDES

A book that helpfully guides beginners through the terrain of patents, trade secrets, and trademarks is *From Edison to ipod: Protect Your Ideas and Make Money,* by Frederick W. Mostert and Lawrence E. Apolzon (New York: DK Publishing, 2007). The authors discuss how to evaluate trademarks in terms of their debt load before you license them, advising careful research into mortgages obtained with trademarks as collateral. There is a volume of the handy Nolo series by Stephen Elias and Richard Stim, *Trademark: Legal Care for Your Business and Product Name* (Berkeley: Nolo Press, 2007). This book can provide further help on topics such as selecting a business name, dealing with cybersquatters (addressed in Chapter 6 in this book), and how to deal with trademarks internationally.

BRANDING FILM AND TELEVISION

Scholar Paul Grainge examines the development of media brands in the global marketplace in *Brand Hollywood: Selling Entertainment in a Global Media Age* (New York: Routledge, 2007). For the growing significance of branding in television, where channels are desperate to stand out from the hundreds of others like them, see Michael Curtin and Jane Shattuc, *American Television Industry* (New York: Palgrave Macmillan 2009). An interesting case study in cable channel rebranding is the switch from the Sci-Fi Channel to the odd-looking word "Syfy," to make it possible to register the name as a trademark; see Barbara Selznick, "Branding the Future: Syfy in the Post-Network Era," *Science Fiction Film and Television* 2, no. 2 (2009): 177–204.

BRANDED CHILDREN'S MEDIA AND TOYS

A classic discussion of the ways trademarks, in the form of characters in children's film and television, play a highly significant role in what gets made and what gets into toy stores; see Norma Pecora, *The Business of Children's Entertainment* (New York: Guilford, 1998). The giant troll in kids' brands is, of course, Disney. Walt Disney built an empire out of fairy-tale characters from nineteenth-century European works that were in the public domain, until he reinvented them, copyrighted them, and proceeded to torment the lowliest nursery school teacher who dared to put up a poster of Cinderella. For an account of how Disney raided European fairy tales and folktales in the public domain, see Richard Schickel's classic account *The Disney Version: The Life, Times, Art, and Commerce of Walt Disney* (New York: Simon and Schuster, 1968), now available in a third edition with an updated introduction (Chicago: Ivan R. Dee, 1997). For an update on Disney's contemporary business practices see Mike Budd, ed., *Rethinking Disney: Private Control, Public Dimensions* (Middletown, Conn.: Wesleyan University Press, 2005). To get a sense of how unmagical life can be for those unfortunate enough to play Disney characters, see *Inside the Mouse: Work and Play at Disney World* (Durham: Duke University Press, 1995), by a group of scholars identified as the Project on Disney (Jane Kuenz, Susan Willis, Sheldon Waldrep), who did undercover work at Walt Disney World.

For two decades, Ellen Seiter has been studying the flow of trademarked characters in children's toys and television programming, as brands from Barney to Bratz delight children, push up prices, and torment parents and policymakers. For a consideration of the children's cartoons "My Little Pony" and "Slimer and the Real Ghostbusters" and an analysis of licensed character toys at Toys "R" Us, see Ellen Seiter, *Sold Separately: Children and Parents in Consumer Culture* (New Brunswick, N.J.: Rutgers University Press, 1993). For an account of the Power Rangers phenomenon and the ways that the Internet unleashed a vast flow of fan activities, see Ellen Seiter, *Television and New Media Audiences* (Oxford: Clarendon, 1999). Finally, for a discussion of Pokemon and its handling by 4Kids Entertainment (a brand management firm that had its first success with Cabbage Patch dolls) as well as an analysis of how Neopets has sought to monetize online play through "immersive advertising" for famous candy, breakfast cereal, and movie brands, see Ellen Seiter, *The Internet Playground: Children's Access, Entertainment, and Mis-Education* (New York: Peter Lang, 2005).

CHAPTER 3

Terms and Conditions

Ethan and I have been making stories with movie cameras since we were kids. In the late '60s when Ethan was eleven or twelve, he got a suit and a briefcase and we went to the Minneapolis International Airport with a Super 8 camera and made a movie about shuttle diplomacy called "Henry Kissinger, Man on the Go." And honestly, what we do now doesn't feel that much different from what we were doing then. . . . We're very thankful to all of you out there for letting us continue to play in our corner of the sandbox, so thank you very much.

—Joel Coen, Coen Brothers' Best Director Acceptance Speech, 80th Annual Academy Awards, 2008

Most successful creative artists, even the Coen brothers, travel a long and winding road before they get an opportunity to play with other people's money in their corner of the sandbox. Joel Coen survived the undergraduate film program at New York University, then labored in the industrial film and music video vineyards as a production assistant before meeting director Sam Raimi and getting his break as an assistant editor.

You too should be so lucky, and then the day may come when you will wheel and deal with the likes of producer Scott Rudin, who bought the film rights to Cormac McCarthy's best-selling novel *No Country for Old Men,* which he had the brothers Coen transmute into a golden script, eight Academy Award nominations, and four Oscars, including Best Picture, Best Director, Best Adapted Screenplay, and Best Supporting Actor for Javier Bardem in the role of the ill-coiffed hit man Anton Chigurh. The day may come when you will ink actor's agreements with the likes of Tommy Lee Jones and Josh Brolin, and distribution deals with the likes of Miramax and Paramount. Before you ever get a chance to negotiate any contract at all, though, you will have entered into a lot more contracts than you probably realize.

THE BEST DEAL YOU'RE GONNA GET

Some things in life are non-negotiable.

If you stroll into a big-box consumer electronics store to buy a cell phone at a killer advertised price, the friendly, knowledgeable sales dude will probably tell you it requires a two-year service agreement. When you ask about your options, he'll probably offer you a choice of AT&T Wireless, Sprint, T-Mobile—glossy Catherine Zeta-Jones marketing collateral included at no added visible cost—and maybe one or two other service providers, if any still survive in your corner of the sandbox. When you pick a service provider, the sales dude will probably tell you about the cool menu of service plans available. When you pick a plan and tell him you actually want to read the service contract, he'll probably look at you funny. And chances are, if you tell him you want to negotiate Paragraph 9 of the contract, he's going to look at you like you're nuts.

The contract is non-negotiable, friendo.

AT&T Wireless, Sprint, and T-Mobile like you and would love to get your business, but they don't want to haggle with you over the terms and conditions. Their friendly, knowledgeable telephone customer service reps will explain the terms to you, up to a point, but they're not going to modify, amend, or delete Paragraph 9 for you just to get your business.

This kind of standard form contract is known in legal circles as an adhesion contract.

You either adhere to it as is, or not at all.

Take it or leave it.

The terms and conditions are non-negotiable.

As Anton Chigurh said: That's the best deal you're gonna get.

COOL SCHOOLS AND NOT SO COOL RULES

Stuff like the Coen brothers' Oscar acceptance speech is the stuff that dreams are made of, inspiring young people everywhere to envision a magical journey where school's traditional boring curriculum is abandoned in favor of filmmaking courses and a shot at a lifetime of play in a sandbox filled with cool toys, mostly digital. The easy availability and minimal cost of desktop media production and distribution through YouTube and Facebook have swelled the ranks of students aspiring to be Hollywood directors. Enrollments in film production courses and applications for film school are

An early film studio in Hollywood, 1916

skyrocketing. At the University of Southern California School of Cinematic Arts each fall, for every undergraduate slot available in production, there are at least two dozen applicants. The proliferation of computers in student life and the broader availability of desktop video, animation programs such as Flash, and nonlinear editing programs such as Final Cut Pro have multiplied the numbers of those aspiring to work in the entertainment industries. In fact, the rapid spread of digital media as communication technologies and expanded teen leisure time have encouraged legions of students—and often their parents—to dream of escaping the dull grind for a groovy job. Tales of the Wunderkind who starts out tinkering in the garage with Super 8 film and ends up a big Hollywood director have been around since the 1970s, thanks to the mind-blowing success of George Lucas and Steven Spielberg. Such dream scenarios gain renewed potency every time a widely admired director—or a widely admired pair of writer-directors—gives an acceptance speech like the Coen brothers' at the Oscars, Golden Globes, or Directors Guild of America Awards.

Most aspiring film school applicants want to direct, rather than work in media in other capacities, and most want to work in film, not television. In reality, it is far more likely you will end up working in television, not film, and in some role other than as writer-director. That is one of the few "realities" in "reality TV." In fact, the majority of growth in media-related jobs is on the marketing side of things. So you ought to be prepared for day jobs that may be a lot less creative than making your own student short films. Film school is also a place where you need to cope with the collective nature of most screen media production, and navigate, mediate, and juggle the respective rights of your classmates, crew members, and collaborators in creative work you may regard as essentially your baby.

Ever since 1910, when director D. W. Griffith headed for the West Coast and scouted out with Mary Pickford and Lionel Barrymore a film-crew-friendly neck of the woods northwest of downtown Los Angeles to shoot his pre-Zorro Zorro flick, *In Old California,* young folks have been heading to Hollywood with dreams of making it big. Today's Copyright Act ain't the Copyright Act of 1909, though, and especially since passage of the so-called Digital Millennium Copyright Act of 1998, which we drill down on in Chapter 6, the legal compliance policies of schools and other institutions and their impact on film students have become increasingly complex. It is imperative that you understand up front how copyright can affect your future schooling, employment, and ability to participate in the high-profile festivals and other competitions for showcasing your talent, as well as how it can affect your ability to control your own work and artistic destiny.

These days aspiring filmmakers have a tendency to give their work away for free too eagerly in hopes of being discovered. They give it away in part by posting it on the Internet at sites where, as a condition of participation, they have assigned away digital rights, often unwittingly. We shall return, with a large machete, in Chapter 6 to cut through some of the treacherous legal undergrowth of the Internet jungle floor that can trip you up on the path to film glory. In this chapter, you need to look under the hood at the sometimes not so cool rules of the game of the new blackboard jungle, where you might just feel the ones getting mugged are the students, as academic institutions often require some form of suspension or relinquishment of copyright in your creative work as a condition of playing in their sandboxes at all. Student complaints at all the major film schools—surpassing even the $64,000 question of whether copyright for creative work produced in class is held by the school or by the student—overwhelmingly zero in on schools' restrictions on posting creative work online.

Consider the institutional setting where you may find yourself embedded while nurturing your Oscar dreams. The first set of paws to lay claim to your creative work probably belongs to your dear old alma mater. Schools impose non-negotiable rules governing copyright in student media work for several reasons:

- Schools provide you access to costly equipment and facilities to create your media. These usually include cameras with superior lenses of superior resolution, more sensitive and complex sound recording gear, editing facilities with massive storage and retrieval capacity, the ability to generate and realize complex visual effects, and quite expensive screening facilities with large movie-style screens and sophisticated sound playback.

- Schools are brands. They license their names, trademarks, and colors on t-shirts, hoodies, coffee mugs, license plate holders, and tons of other branded merchandise available everywhere from college bookstores to Nike, Puma, and Adidas stores and online. Each of the schools discussed below employs in-house lawyers to manage and police their massive licensing programs, because the days when nonprofit institutions in education and the arts could sit aloof in their ivory tower are long gone. It takes an enormous amount of money to fuel an institution of higher learning. Licensing revenues are an essential part of the kitty, as are hiked tuitions from students, and sizable gifts from well-heeled alumni and sponsors, including some very big donations from some very wealthy media producers, directors, artists, and rights holders. A school benefits when a student's work does well in festivals or gets nominated for a Student Academy Award. Tales of errant student filmmakers violating copyright laws, holding up traffic, or trashing locations, on the other hand, damage the brand and hurt the school's ability to attract more students, donations, and prestige (not to mention ruling out your classmates' chances of ever using that location again!).

- Schools want to make sure they won't be held liable, as a sponsor or producer of your creative work, for any material in it that infringes or may infringe copyright, trademark, or rights of privacy and publicity. Universities and colleges are Internet service providers, running .edu servers for students and alums. Since under the Digital Millennium Copyright Act there are only limited circumstances where Internet service providers are insulated from liability for infringing media produced or distributed by their account holders, schools now occupy the vanguard of society's copyright compliance watchdogs. After all, their students are the prime demographic producing, sharing, and consuming audio-visual media, often with little regard or blatant disdain for the copyright laws the schools need to abide by.

- Schools often have special agreements with strategic partners who themselves hold direct interests in intellectual property. The more prestigious the school, the more likely its partners will include the large corporate entities that have lobbied most vigorously for expanded copyright and that see intellectual property as a primary profit source.

- Schools aim to instill in you a set of professional norms that include refraining from exhibiting your work in venues that either require you to consign copyright to the exhibitor or prevent you from a future exhibition or sale opportunities.

The strictness of a school's copyright policy depends on a variety of intertwining factors. If you are considering film schools to attend, you should understand these factors, because what might appear to you to be a prohibitive and anachronistic policy toward copyright might also tell you this school is an institution with a lot to lose. Having a lot to lose usually goes hand in hand with having resources, connections, power, and money. Resources, connections, power, and money pretty well round out the list of things you eventually need to get a film made in Hollywood.

On the other hand, there are many media artists, the majority in fact, whose dreams do not take the shape of mounting a major feature film production. For students pursuing the non-Hollywood dream, a more flexible school copyright policy may be exactly what you are looking for. This applies especially to media artists working in more ephemeral genres, or those whose intentions are more along such lines as improvisation, Web design, song lyrics, Flash animations, illustrations, musical scoring, political satire, or do-it-yourself (DIY) media.

A successful feature film script demands months or years of solitary work, normally after years of training and years of penning unsalable scripts consigned to some unlucky agent's slush pile. A video game requires design, programming, beta testing, and music, involving thousands of hours of labor by a large contingent of programmers to make it work. Cel animation, even for a cartoon as brief as one minute running time, requires hundreds of painstaking hours of drawing and frame-by-frame film capture. In contrast, a one-minute monologue performed before your computer's built-in camera that you concocted in a matter of hours for a class assignment, or as entertainment for your Facebook friends, does not warrant the same level of legal protection and caution. Neither does a casual musical composition made on GarageBand used as background music, or a set of homespun title cards put together with posterboard, ink, and paint. When you consider student work, and the types of copyright policies you would encounter in educational settings, you should weigh the advantages and drawbacks of these differing work styles, and consider whether your interests lie in a professionalized, Hollywood media world, or in a more academic, more artistic, or more viral kind of fame.

Ambitious media makers and performers, from an early age, dream of getting discovered overnight by posting their work on the Internet. We call this the YouTube fallacy. In selecting a school and evaluating its copyright policy, you want to make a realistic assessment of how likely it is that as an unknown artist, the work you create with your computer or camera will be stumbled across on the Web by an agent or a producer with the juice to give you or get you a paying job. All the top film schools face increasing pressure from students to alter their copyright policies to make all creative work the property of students, and to allow them to do whatever they want with it the moment it is finished—especially give it away for free. Digital media production has made this possible in a way that would have been unimaginable back in the days when students were shooting celluloid, sprocketed film that had to be processed at a lab and needed a physical film projector to be shown. But just because digital media production makes it possible to produce media as a one-man band, and post it overnight for the world to see, doesn't mean that is the best way to proceed if you want your creative work to flourish into more than a hobby.

Universities and colleges today face a special challenge in terms of copyright policy. A specter is haunting America—the specter of cease and desist letters—and it has spooked schools and teachers bad. Because the Digital Millennium Copyright Act makes those who operate servers potentially liable for illegal downloading and file sharing, any educational institution providing email accounts to students is potentially vulnerable. Fears of liability are often exaggerated or unwarranted, yet often schools are the first to try to indoctrinate young artists with conservative notions of copyright. As early as kindergarten, little kids are being sat down and made to read the fine print of "behavior" contracts that lay down strict rules constraining the use of copyrighted material, even for such purposes as a drama club assignment or an art class project, as well as hamstringing Internet usage on school PCs, with the threat of a trip to the principal's office to back it all up. The biggest bully on today's playground is the copyright owner. The threat of lawsuits, even groundless or frivolous ones, tends to turn schools chicken when it comes to defending one of the main values they are supposed to protect: fair use.

USC, UCLA, and NYU are widely regarded as the top three film schools in the United States, though there are also a number of other excellent ones, each with its own strengths. The three big schools cost serious bucks to attend and can be as hard to get your foot in the door as that med school, law school, or MBA program your parents, once upon a time, may have wished you would attend. If you get a grip on the copyright policies of these three film schools, which represent three contrasting templates, you will also be able to unravel the terms and conditions that would govern your creative life at other film schools. Each of the three reflects a set of trade-offs. It is up to you to decide for yourself, all things considered, which set of trade-offs suits you and serves you best.

USC

The University of Southern California School of Cinematic Arts has served as the training ground for many important Hollywood filmmakers, including Robert Zemeckis, John Singleton, and George Lucas. USC also has arguably the most conservative policy of any of the major film schools: it makes no bones about the school's ownership of student films. In exchange for assigning copyright to the school, though, the USC policy offers a very golden lining. You gain some or all of the following perks: production funds, equipment, insurance, guild agreements, assistance with festivals and distribution, and industry networking opportunities.

The insurance protection USC purchases covers a variety of nightmare risks. One is the chance of personal injury and property damage to equipment in the course of shooting a film, because stuff happens. Student filmmakers are notorious daredevils and typically protest having their creative impulses squelched by practical concerns over cracking lenses, dropping cameras, and running over tripods and mikes.

USC provides a special Screen Actors Guild agreement, protecting professionals who wish to collaborate on or appear in student films. Quite a few professional actors are more than pleased to work free or for nominal fees on USC student films simply for the exposure. But when actors join SAG, they sign on to the guild's set of terms and conditions. Among these, the guild prohibits its members from appearing in non-SAG productions. This means that SAG actors are normally precluded automatically from appearing in student films. But at USC, they can appear in student films because the School of Cinematic Arts worked out a special arrangement with SAG that has proved beneficial for all parties. For most of SAG's more than one hundred thousand members, the majority of days each year are spent between paid gigs—reading sides, going to auditions, and working day jobs unrelated to acting to pay that month's bills. By participating in a USC student film, they get to spend more days each year doing what they love— acting. Worst case scenario, they walk away with a DVD of a mediocre film that they can still use to show what they look like on-screen. Best case scenario, the film turns out exceptionally well and plays at USC's First Look Festival to an enthusiastic crowd, and attendees are mighty impressed by the lead actor. And hey, if you turn out to be the next Joel or Ethan Coen, maybe you'll bring that actor along to every subsequent set and make him your go-to character guy—your Steve Buscemi or John Turturro.

For you, the benefit of casting a member of SAG is clear: you get an experienced screen actor who will help distinguish your new work from run-of-the-mill student films. Or from the type of picture you were making just the previous year (remember that one where you had your fifteen-year-old cousin playing a seventy-three-year-old woman?).

Another key benefit offered by USC—and this is one protection racket aspiring filmmakers need in a world where the cease and desist business is alive and flourishing—is errors and omissions insurance. Distributors require E&O insurance before they will consider picking up a film. A few exhibition spaces, including some independent theaters, will on occasion screen uninsured works, but these make up a miniscule screening opportunity for budding filmmakers.

E&O insurance policies insulate within limits against copyright infringement claims. Policy premiums are very costly, and obtaining a policy, if the underwriters are willing to issue one at all, is a cumbersome exercise for a working filmmaker. Documentary media projects are especially sensitive because of the higher incidence of defamation claims and lawsuits than in fictional projects, and defamation risk is normally covered. Typical E&O policies also insure against trademark infringement claims, which can crop up whenever a branded product appears in your work, whether shown in an unfavorable light or in a setting where the trademark owner thinks your use of it adds cachet to your production, so you ought to pay for it, or dilutes the brand in a way the owner would rather squelch.

E&O insurance, though, does not relieve you of the responsibility of clearing rights in your projects. It is not enough to get releases from interview and on-camera subjects who might otherwise make right of privacy or publicity claims. A film producer must also pay scrupulous attention to the myriad elements that may appear in the camera frame, such as logos, signage, paintings or posters on a wall, and music playing in the background in a restaurant or on a car radio. Any of these can put the producer in a would-be plaintiff's line of fire, something you'd rather avoid even if you have E&O insurance, just like you prefer to avoid a car wreck even if you have auto insurance.

The USC School of Cinematic Arts handbook warns:

Rights and clearances may seem like a very burdensome requirement. However, they are critical. Every year we face potential litigation from people who believe that our students have infringed on their rights—music, literary, locations, etc. There are many examples of student films that were never seen outside of class because the rights were not properly cleared. When this happens it is heartbreaking for everyone. So follow the guidelines carefully. Rights and clearances will be important to you as a professional once you leave SCA. Now is time to begin learning about these issues.

USC has a point here (and we're not just saying that because the school keeps one of us gainfully employed). Although it may seem like the policy makes you jump through an endless series of hoops, those hoops are there for a reason—so you can develop the habit of anticipating rights problems and dealing with them before they become a problem. What it boils down to is assembling a production binder that contains all the actors' releases, location agreements, and copyright clearances you need for a film. When you finish the film, you submit the finished project and production binder to a staffer who double-checks all the clearances. If everything checks out, you can submit your film to festivals and, if you like, share it online. If there are problems, then you need to go back and fix them. And if you can't fix them, then you better cut your losses and move on to the next project where you will more diligently watch out for all rights issues. You may shoot on film and cut on digital, but paper and careful recordkeeping is what will make the difference between whether your film can go on to film festivals and play on the Web. This is true at USC and even truer in the media industry.

Whereas the NYU agreement, as you will see, requires you to indemnify the school for any blowback from claims and lawsuits arising from your films, USC falls on its sword and defends your film should anyone file a copyright infringement claim against it.

Fight on, as the Trojans say. And chances are, if you're reading this book, you already guessed that FIGHT ON® and TROJANS® are registered trademarks of the University of Southern California, a nonprofit California corporation, for a slew of merchandise and for educational, entertainment, and retail services.

The USC policy statement emphasizes that despite the school's ownership of your film, your assignment of copyright to the school does not interfere in principle with your ability to exploit the "underlying rights" of the work, defined as the underlying script, idea, treatment, concept, or other written work. As we saw in Chapter 1, though, ideas aren't copyrightable. So this emphasis, found in the NYU policy as well, may seem a bit disingenuous. Just as the Trojans need to beware of Greeks bearing gifts, you need to be wary of terms and conditions that appear generously to bestow on you something that never was the bestower's to give in the first place.

USC catches a lot of flak in Internet chat rooms, such as studentfilms. com, for its seemingly draconian copyright policy. From another vantage point, however, USC's system forces you to develop habits of thorough rights clearing and recordkeeping that—like it or not—you will need in today's litigious media environment. You may think it unfair that you cannot immediately hit "upload" after you finish your film in the editing bay at three in the morning. But those sobering weeks of waiting for the school to verify your rights clearances may save you the disappointment that results when months or years of work are hastily thrown away online for a fleeting fifteen minutes, or seconds, of overnight viral celebrity. Because of the burning desire of so many film students to post their work online for others to see, USC has relented up to a point, allowing clips of up to 10 percent of a student work to be distributed online.

UCLA

Meanwhile, across town at the University of California at Los Angeles School of Theater, Film, and Television, the understood policy is that copyright in student film belongs to the students. Many of the UCLA students we've talked to take pride in owning the copyrights of their films. Some see it as a key ingredient to the school's independent filmmaking sensibility. UCLA counts among its alums such indie luminaries as Charles Burnett, Alison Anders, and Alexander Payne, along with the godfather of the stylistically innovative New Hollywood directors, Francis Ford Coppola. Among the creative accomplishments of these same filmmakers, though, can also be found cautionary tales. For his MFA thesis, Charles Burnett directed the feature film *Killer of Sheep* (1977), a beautiful mosaic of the joys, sorrows, and everyday realities of adults and children living in L.A.'s Watts neighborhood. Burnett owned the copyright of his thesis film. What he did not own, and what he had not licensed, were the songs by Etta James, Dinah Washington, Earth, Wind, and Fire, and others that he included in the soundtrack. *Killer of Sheep* attracted critical praise in film festival and museum screenings, but the film was unable to secure wide distribution because of the expense of clearing all the copyrighted music. Finally, in 2007, some patrons ponied up the money to pay for the music rights, and *Killer of Sheep* received its first theatrical release, and can now be rented for public exhibition or purchased for home use on DVD. Burnett owned his masterpiece thesis project, but the film was tied up for thirty years because he hadn't cleared the music rights. If you were in his shoes, would you also have made the creative decisions you thought best despite the copyright liabilities? In the absence of the school taking copyright and clearance control, these tough decisions are in your hands.

UCLA still has no written copyright policy regarding ownership of student work, though implicitly students should be bound by the copyright policy that pertains to the UC system at large. Like all major research universities, the University of California has become more aggressive in asserting its rights in intellectual property created by faculty and students. But research universities herd techie cash cows like software, engineering, and medical patents more closely than they watch student film work. To give you a clue, in the UC system, the office that watchdogs its copyright interests is actually named "Technology Transfer."

Yet there are many other restrictions placed on films in the UCLA program, such as a maximum length of thirty minutes for dramatic films (Burnett's project wouldn't fly today) and fifty-two minutes for documentaries. UCLA imposes these and other types of rules to hold down costs and deter students from bogarting the choice equipment. Narrative and experimental thesis film projects are allowed a maximum of fourteen days for principal photography, and documentary thesis projects twenty-eight days, including the dates of check-out and check-in of equipment. Rules like these ensure that students monopolize neither the production facilities nor the school's public screening spaces. UCLA also imposes strict rules for the student filmmaker to secure insurance. Students must wait two weeks to secure insurance for on-location shooting, and everyone participating in a film must sign a University of California Release Agreement before shooting.

Wherever you go to film school, restrictions such as these will follow. They may be slightly less onerous at private universities with a single campus and enrollment under fifty thousand, as opposed to massive public educational institutions where enrollments number in the hundreds of thousands. Some of this is simply a matter of scale, with agreements hammered out by teams of lawyers defending against all manner of liabilities and lawsuits against the system as a whole, paid for in taxpayer dollars. When selecting a film school, have a look at the terms of the general liability insurance offered to students, and the costs associated with insuring a typical student thesis film—the kind of large-scale final project for which these three schools are famous.

UCLA lays out an explicit policy limiting the inclusion in student films of professionals, many of whom may be members of one of the creative guilds, such as SAG, the Writers Guild of America (WGA), the Directors Guild of America (DGA), the American Society of Cinematographers (ASC), the International Alliance of Theatrical Stage Employees, Moving Picture Technicians, Artists and Allied Crafts (IATSE), or the American Federation of Television and Radio Artists (AFTRA). This policy deserves your attention, because it points to the closeness of the production practices on student films at the top three institutions to those of Hollywood professionals. While many graduate students in film production classes are disappointed when they are relegated to a position of sound, cinematography, editing, or script supervisor on a student film, these roles are actually privileges of a sort, as the UCLA policy indicates by striving to keep production crews student-based:

Professionals in Creative Crew Positions not Permitted Except on Thesis Films

With the exception of the thesis project, Graduate and Undergraduate students are not permitted to use the services of a professional in a creative position on any project. Students, except those working on their thesis projects, are required to fill creative crew positions from their class and/or other students within the department (who will receive credit). If there is still a shortage on the creative crew, students will be permitted to engage students from other local film schools, providing that documentation of such student status is presented to the faculty instructor. Non-students can crew in any non-creative position.

Go Bears, as they say at Cal. We had better mention that GOLDEN BEARS® is a registered trademark of the Regents of the University of California for a whole bunch of goods and services. We suppose the Regents would like to register GO BEARS too, and have probably been saving up student tuitions to bankroll a very large trademark application for it.

NYU

We're not sure what New York University's mascot is, but it's a safe bet most creative artists don't go there for the football. That doesn't mean you don't have to look out for the occasional end run if you do go there.

The Kanbar Institute of Film and Television at NYU's Tisch School of the Arts, former stomping grounds of Spike Lee, Ang Lee, and Jim Jarmusch, proudly proclaims in its student handbook that any student work belongs to the student and any income made from student work belongs to the student. Like most things that sound too good to be true, there are a couple of catches.

Catch One is that you must agree not to exploit your work without the dean's permission except for entering it in festivals and competitions, and Catch Two is that you let the faculty and other students use your work for any "educational use" they see fit while you are still a student, as fleshed out in the NYU Student Handbook:

> To ensure that each student and faculty member has a meaningful opportunity to participate in the educational process occasioned by the production of each Student Work, the student(s) who owns each Student Work agrees not to distribute such Work in any manner, whether by sale or other transfer of the ownership or other rights, license, lease, loan, gift, or otherwise, except for entering such Work in festivals or competitions, and further agrees to make such Student Work available to other student[s] and to faculty members of the Tisch School of the Arts for any use relating to his or her education or to the education of such other students, until such student, or if more than one student owns such Student Work, until all such students have either graduated from New York University or are no longer matriculating at New York University. The dean of the Tisch School of the Arts may, in her sole discretion, waive these restrictions for any reason satisfactory to the dean.

Catch Three turns the school's claim on your work into a till-death-do-us-part sort of proposition:

> The interest of the Tisch School of the Arts in any Student Work extends only through the completion of the educational experience associated with such Work until its utility as an educational device or matrix has been exhausted.

Catch Four is designed to put the fear of God into you and your student artistic collaborators and make you do your rights clearance homework. Students must indemnify the school against any damages that ensue from producing the work. Consider this segment from a very lengthy stipulation contained in the NYU Student Handbook:

> All students who create or participate in the creation of a Student Work are jointly and severally responsible for such Student Work, including without being limited to, for determining and ensuring that such Student Work does not violate or infringe on any copyright, any right of privacy, or any other right of any per-

son, and that such Student Work is not libelous, obscene, or otherwise contrary to law. Such students shall also be jointly and severally responsible for obtaining any necessary permissions for the use of any copyrighted materials included in such Student Work.

Catch Five makes your grant back to the school a royalty-free copyright license to reproduce and display your work for any reason, and to honor the license in any deal you make with anyone else:

(5) The student(s) who owns each Student Work grants New York University: (a) the right to purchase prints or other copies of such Student Work at cost, whenever, in the University's sole discretion, such prints or other copies are needed for any University use; and (b) the right to reproduce, display, or perform such prints or other copies anywhere and for any reason, including, without being limited to, publicizing the Tisch School or the Arts or New York University, without any royalty or other payment of any kind to the student(s), provided that such prints or copies may not be rented or sold by the University. Such student(s) also agrees that he or she will not make any contract or commitment regarding the Student Work contrary to this policy or in derogation of the rights granted to the University by this policy, and that he or she will sign any document reasonably requested by the University to confirm or enforce any of the rights granted to the University by this policy.

The Lord giveth and the Lord taketh away. While giving you with one hand the feel-good consolation of owning copyright in your student work and being entitled theoretically to any income from the work, NYU sews up in a New York minute with the other hand a license back big enough to drive the Lexington Avenue subway through, maintaining the option of using your work to further the school's objectives. In practice, though, NYU filmmakers gain more immediate flexibility than USC students in sharing their work across festivals and the Web. NYU students don't have to wait for a staffer to clear their production binders and films. On the other hand, if one of those Internet audience members turns out to be a RIAA lawyer who hears the tune of copyright infringement, you hold all of the responsibility and the school holds none.

The three differing approaches to copyright and other legal issues raised by student films at USC, UCLA, and NYU simply reflect different ways of balancing the risks and rewards for the institution, the individual student, and the student body and faculty as a whole. Which balancing act works best depends on who you are. When weighing a decision among these three schools, or evaluating the policies of one of the many universities and colleges offering similar programs, you've got to ask yourself some questions:

What kind of creative work do I want to do?

What media and technologies am I interested in mastering?

Am I resolved to make films for the multiplex, or would I rather be measured, admired, and idolized based on a metric other than *Variety* box-office numbers?

Do I want to adapt to the norms of Hollywood here and now, or savor the free-floating academic and artistic freedom of festivals, curated shows, and online competitions?

Last but not least: Do I feel lucky?

Well, do ya, punk?

COOL JOBS AND MORE NOT SO COOL RULES

Terms and conditions are going to hang like a pesky albatross around your neck as long as you are in school, and they will keep coming back to haunt you wherever you may go once your student days come to an end. Because in creative media, good old-fashioned rule days are forever. But don't let them get you down.

Some things in life are non-negotiable. Other things are negotiable only through collective bargaining.

If your talents lie in screenwriting, you might join the Writers Guild of America. If you feel happier with a megaphone in your hand than a pen, maybe the Directors Guild of America is for you. If behind the camera is where you find the action is, the American Society of Cinematographers may beckon, and if it turns out, like Pinocchio, that it's the actor's life for you, before the camera or on the airwaves, you might even join the Screen Actors Guild or the American Federation of Television and Radio Artists.

But paying your dues doesn't give you the right to negotiate the rules of the game.

As we saw earlier, for instance, SAG forbids its members from working as performers for any producer who has not executed a basic minimum agreement with the guild. Every SAG member agrees to abide by this rule as a condition of membership in the guild. This is why the USC School of Cinematic Arts cut a specially tailored deal with the guild to let SAG members participate in USC student films. SAG members didn't individually bargain with USC, any more than they individually bargain with the studios. SAG bargains for them collectively.

Same goes for the Writers Guild of America. Consider its 2007–2008 strike over DVD and new media residuals, which targeted the Alliance of Motion Picture and Television Producers, a trade group representing several hundred U.S. film and television production companies. The guild's executive negotiated with AMPTP and at the end of the day—or a hundred days, as it turned out—the WGA East and WGA West membership got to vote an end to the strike by blessing a new three-year contract that the executive had hashed out with AMPTP.

Guilds and unions in the entertainment industry negotiate and enforce collective bargaining agreements to establish fair minimum "scale" levels of pay, overtime, and benefits, and to foster decent work hours and other working conditions for their members. They collect residuals for broadcasts, exhibitions, and sales of their members' recorded performances, and establish health and pension plans for creative artists who would otherwise have none. To a limited extent, they try to protect the artist's rights of their members, for instance, in Directors Guild of America rules defining the director's role, protecting the sanctity of "one director to a picture," waived only rarely for special cases, such as the Coen brothers.

Some things in life are non-negotiable.

Other things are negotiable only if you happen to be senior management.

Should your creative drive lead you into the loving embrace of a film studio, a television producer, a video game publisher, or even a toy company, you will run into a tangled nest of terms and conditions. You may be a salaried employee of some big TV network, or a freelancer frolicking at a creative distance from the nine-to-five grind. But you're gonna have to serve somebody, as Bob Dylan advised. And it's a safe bet you're gonna run into "work for hire" provisions buried approximately halfway deep in the devil or the Lord's boilerplate.

From Chapter 1 you will recall that creative artists in motion picture and other audiovisual productions are either employees, preparing works within the scope of their employment that automatically belong to the employer, or independent contractors made to sign work-for-hire agreements by the producer or other party ordering the work. Studio employers and independent producers coordinating any kind of audiovisual work with their head screwed on right will resort to "work for hire" in the terms and conditions you will be asked to sign, and while they are at it, they will make you say you waive artist's moral rights, to the extent you have any, to boot. There is simply no percentage in quarrelling with you after the fact over who owns copyright and who controls the destiny of the finished product. Those are the rules of the game when they and you play with other people's money. About the best you can do is to read and understand what those terms and conditions say.

As Anton Chigurh said: That's the best deal you're gonna get.

If you are a member of one of the entertainment guilds, however, instead of a freelancer or an intern or a production assistant or an extra working for a day rate, your deal will provide for residual payments. Residuals are the consolation prize that the unions representing creative workers in Hollywood bargained for in exchange for work-for-hire arrangements: fractions of the profit that a film or television program makes that accrue back to you. Residuals are the concession for those years of unremunerated work as an aspiring director or writer, or actor. Residuals are the payoff for all those scripts and pilots and unfinished films that never make it to the multiplex or to broadcast or cable, and provide an assurance that revenue-sharing will happen when you land a hit. In an industry notorious for its inability to reliably predict successes, residuals enforce some level of profit-sharing when a blockbuster happens. When residuals work as they are supposed to, they help you recuperate the costs you have incurred in your career before your work is finally produced and you score a hit. For actors, residuals compensate you for the potential career risk of overexposure, when a popular show is repeated in reruns and syndication and you become so associated with a particular role that your future casting gets limited. Residuals can make you rich, especially if your film or television program is broadcast on television over a period of many years, in syndication, and in many different markets around the world. There is lots of money to be made in television, and critics increasingly see the artistic value of many television programs as easily meeting the standards of feature film production. So don't rule out the small screen as a good entry point for your dream career. There is lots of steady, quality work in television, and it is easier to break into than feature filmmaking.

In 2008, the writers represented by the WGA took real risks in the strike over the issue of residual pay for television episodes streamed online or sold per download. Going on strike is risky in a business where thousands of aspirants are dying for a chance to take your place, where you risk infuriating other segments of the Hollywood labor market (such as DGA and SAG members) who have less choice and power than the writers, and when you can make your bosses mad if you expose the economics of media conglomerate profiteering. The years since the strike was settled, however, have shown that the writers were correct to worry about the vast increase in streaming of television programs. Three of the biggest media conglomerates—NBC Universal, Disney-ABC, and Fox—joined forces to buy a piece of hulu.com, and despite the protests of the producers during the strike that no one made any money on television showed online, Hulu currently offers paid monthly subscriber rates and collects online advertising revenue. The formulas for remuneration in the form of residuals are a gigantic bookkeeping nightmare, and the devising of new formulas for digital distribution is the most hotly contested issue in creative labor negotiations today.

The WGA negotiations over residuals for work shown online point to the unremunerated nature of so much media production for the Internet—all the videos, photos, and blogs posted on the Web (and thereafter the property of the Web site owners). It brings the concerns of the middle aged, such as health insurance and mortgages, to spoil the party of Web 2.0 as a dazzling route to self-expression unfettered by material or economic constraints. The digital divide as it separates creative workers along generational lines is not merely a matter of ability and innovation with new technologies, but also a matter of experiences in the labor market. Hollywood has had unions for ninety years, and there is a collective memory of how badly the studios can behave toward their workers when they do not have collective bargaining. By contrast, the model of "entrepreneurial labor" common to the Web, online video, and video gaming is risky, hyper-competitive, and ultimately exploitive compared with working in Hollywood. Sure, if you lucked into stock options at Google ten years ago, you are now sitting pretty. But most Silicon Valley talent has less rosy stories to tell.

Some things in life are non-negotiable. Sometimes you get bound by contracts you didn't have a chance to negotiate. Eventually though, if you stay the course in the creative arts, you will get a shot at negotiating some terms and conditions of your own. And when you do, you might just find it's easier said than done.

FURTHER READING

CHOOSING SCHOOLS

There are dozens of excellent film and media programs across the United States. When selecting a school, look for programs that offer a well-rounded education from permanent faculty. This way, you can rely on your instructors for long-term career advice, for guidance about internships, and for letters of recommendation to help you land your first job. An entertaining

guide to U.S. film programs that categorizes them according to their orientation to industry, experimental work (usually avant-garde or art films),
and independent films has been written by two NYU graduates, Karin Kelly
and Tom Edgar, titled *Film School Confidential: The Insider's Guide to Film
Schools* (New York: Perigee Trade, 2007). The authors rate schools in terms
of equipment quality, equipment access, and tuition costs. Be sure to get the
revised edition. The main professional organization for college teachers of
media production is the University Film and Video Association. The association includes more than a thousand members and holds an annual conference, and its Web site can be a good way to research student filmmaking
opportunities and the faculty at schools of interest to you: www.ufva.org.

If you feel lucky and want to skip school altogether and try your luck in
film, some explanation of the different types of employment to go after and
how to contact the guilds can be found in Jane Bone and Ana Fernandez,
Opportunities in Film Careers (New York: McGraw-Hill, 2004), and *Fer-
guson's Careers in Focus: Film* (New York: Infobase Publishing, 2007).

PRECARIOUS WORK IN NEW MEDIA

Andrew Ross has written two books analyzing the uncertainty of employ-
ment in "new media" industries from Silicon Valley (California) to Silicon
Alley (New York). For a sobering account of life at the hip advertising firm
Razorfish and the strain of freelance and casual employment see Ross's *No-
Collar: The Humane Workplace and Its Hidden Costs* (Philadelphia: Temple
University Press, 2004). Ross portrays the growing class of the "precariat"
and the global rise of aggressive "rent-seeking" tactics in *Nice Work If You
Can Get It: Life and Labor in Precarious Times* (New York: NYU Press,
2009). Another important warning about the uncertain status of the non-
union creative worker can be found in Gina Neff, Elizabeth Wissinger, and
Sharon Zukin, "Entrepreneurial Labor Among Cultural Producers: 'Cool'
Jobs in 'Hot' Industries," *Social Semiotics* 15 (2005): 307–334. UCLA professor John Thornton Caldwell examines the lifestyles of "below-the-line"
artists (camera operators, editors, cinematographers) in film and television
production in his entertaining book *Production Culture: Industrial Reflex-
ivity and Critical Practice in Film and Television* (Durham: Duke University
Press, 2008).

There are a few signs that Silicon Valley might learn something from
the WGA. Jaron Lanier has defected from the "Internet idealist" position
because, he argues, business opportunities for writers and artists have de-

creased, and "the only business plan in sight is ever more advertising. One might ask what will be left to advertise once everyone is aggregated." Lanier explores the notion that designing the Internet so that content is always free might have been a mistake in his book *You Are Not a Gadget: A Manifesto* (New York: Knopf, 2010). For an upbeat account of the rise of creative work in urban areas see Richard Florida's books, *The Rise of the Creative Class: And How It's Transforming Work, Leisure, Community, and Everyday Life* (New York: Basic Books, 2003) and *Who's Your City?: How the Creative Economy Is Making Where to Live the Most Important Decision of Your Life* (New York: Basic Books, 2009).

WORK FOR HIRE

A fascinating history of the judicial development of the work-for-hire doctrine can be found in Catherine L. Fisk, *Working Knowledge: Employee Innovation and the Rise of Corporate Intellectual Property, 1800–1930* (Chapel Hill: University of North Carolina Press, 2009). Fisk notes the importance of cases emanating from popular stage plays, often themselves pirated from Europe, in the gradual erasure of employees' rights to their own work. The theme of Michael Perelman's *Steal This Idea: Intellectual Property Rights and the Corporate Confiscation of Creativity* (New York: Palgrave, 2002) is the increasing greed of corporations in aggrandizing copyright in work created by employees.

CHAPTER 4

Contracts

It was written I should be loyal to the nightmare of my choice.

—*Heart of Darkness*, by Joseph Conrad

HISPANIOLA—THE DEAL

That wasn't so bad, was it? says Marlow.

You groan. Contract negotiations with a retired English teacher really stink.

Bonnie Charlotte laughs, seated beside Marlow in the front of his vintage Aston Martin DB5.

Miss Bonnie, Marlow hams up a fake Southern accent, you sure drive a hard bargain.

You hold your tongue, scrunched up in the back seat, wondering where he jacked the car.

It seems like years since that fateful afternoon you dusted off *Hispaniola* the novel on a chance visit to Marlow's Collectibles. Over time you've learned a thing or two about contracts. You've negotiated your share, and lost a friend or two along the way over creative deals gone wrong. But all in all contracts helped you cement solid relationships with valued collaborators. The exercise of putting to paper their expectations and yours in a given media arts project, even if only a one-page term sheet, has helped clear up at the front end misunderstandings that would otherwise have derailed your collective vision and left a bad taste in everybody's mouth.

Creative arts are subjective. So are copyright and trademark law. You are never going to eliminate the subjective elements in your art, or in the law that glues cooperative artistic projects together. By putting in writing each person's responsibility in a project and what each person stands to gain or lose, contracts help you cope with the subjectivity, and they form enduring ties that bind despite the uncertainties life throws at us all.

Marlow's right.

Bonnie drives a hard bargain.

Even so, you've got her signed option and purchase agreement in your hot little hand.

Option and Purchase Agreements

Your plan from Day 1 was to avoid having to buy a copyright assignment of the film rights to Bonnie's book immediately. Instead, you wanted initially to buy an option to acquire those rights. As we discussed in Chapter 1, in a typical *option and purchase agreement*, in exchange for payment of a relatively small option price, the copyright owner grants the producer the option, within a limited period of time, typically twelve to eighteen months, often with an available further extension of twelve to eighteen months, to acquire the motion picture and related rights needed to make the film and commercialize it. This gives you the breathing space to put together the film's creative elements and financing, before having to commit really substantial money. If all goes well before the option expires, the producer buys the copyright assignment for a pre-negotiated purchase price.

Today you offered Bonnie $500 for the option to acquire the motion picture and related rights in her novel. She pressed for $2,000. The dust settled at $1,250. Upon exercise of the option, she wanted to license you the rights, but you wisely insisted she give you a copyright assignment. The initial option period is twelve months, and you arm-wrestled from her the right to extend the option for a further twelve months on payment of a further $1,250. If you fail to get your other ducks in line and exercise the option within two years, Bonnie will walk away with your $2,500 and be free to sell the film rights elsewhere. Two years sounds like a lot of time. But it isn't.

If all goes well, you'll exercise the option and purchase the copyright assignment for a small specified percentage of the final film budget. You also promise to pay her contingent compensation of 2 percent of producer's net profits and a bonus if the movie hits a specified box-office benchmark. You offered her a 5 percent royalty on movie merchandise, she countered at 15 percent, and you ended up at 10 percent.

You wanted to write the script, but Bonnie insisted her son Bobby be attached to the film as sole screenwriter with sole "written by" credit. Nothing like a little nepotism, yet you warmed to the idea when you learned Bobby Charlotte has two Oscar nominations under his belt, even if he is still living at home at age forty.

Bonnie expressly reserves the right to write a new novel series based on *Hispaniola* and publish with a publisher of her choice. You also give her a right of first negotiation to author any spin-off books derived from your movie or movie sequels. In turn, she gives you a right of first refusal to option the film rights for each new novel, on the same terms as the first.

She signed a copyright assignment when you signed the option and purchase agreement, but made you promise not to record it at the Copyright Office unless and until you pay her the purchase price. You and Bonnie put everything in writing in the agreement, which expressly states there are no oral promises between you.

Producing a movie is more work that you thought. Whether the whole of *Hispaniola* adds up to more, or less, than the sum of its parts depends in large part on the contracts underpinning the production. Each with its own pitfalls, together they form a web of interdependent legal relationships, a tangled web at that, but one you must nonetheless weave. For as Marlow says, entertainment contracts are the stuff that dreams are made of.

Going Upriver

Where're we headed? you ask.

The Marina, says Marlow.

The Marina? I thought you said we're going to Hollywood.

Kid, replies Marlow, all roads in this town lead to Hollywood.

Sorry you asked.

Marlow nods. We're looking for a yacht.

The *Nellie* lies in its slip without a flutter of sails. The wind is calm. The Marina stretches before you like the beginning of an interminable waterway. A waterway awash with Other People's Money.

The Director of Companies, as Marlow calls him, is your captain and your host. You watch his back as he stands looking to sea. He resembles a pilot, in his meticulously weathered Greek fisherman's cap. It is difficult to realize his work is not out there in the luminous estuary, but behind him, within the brooding gloom of the entertainment biz. The Lawyer mixes herself a martini, generous in size as James Bond's, if less discriminating in choice of ingredients. The Accountant has brought out a box of dominoes and absent-mindedly arranges them in rows and columns resembling an ivory Excel spreadsheet.

Marlow sits cross-legged, back straight, palms outward, in the pose of a hawk-faced Buddha with tinted specs. The Director of Companies makes his way aft into the cabin and sits down. You exchange a few words. Afterward there is silence on board the yacht. The day is ending in a serenity of still and exquisite brilliance. The water shines pacifically. The sun sets, dusk falls on the Marina, and lights begin to appear along the shore.

Let's get down to business, says Marlow suddenly.

His remark does not seem at all surprising. It is accepted in silence. And presently he says, very slowly—

My friend here just optioned Bonnie's *Hispaniola*.

The Director of Companies grunts.

Marlow already told you the guy's been angling to option the book for decades.

Let's hear about it, says the Director of Companies.

You stand and deliver your pitch.

The Director of Companies nods appraisingly. Have you got a treatment?

You hand it over.

You took the precaution beforehand of registering your treatment, for a modest fee, with the Writers Guild of America.

The Director of Companies starts reading.

A quarter hour later he looks up and remarks: Wow.

Told you you'd like it, says Marlow.

The Director of Companies turns to you and says: This is one of those rare projects that deserve loads of tender loving care. I propose we take you and Bobby Charlotte under our wing. Our studio will finance the film, you produce *Hispaniola* in-house, you'll be attached to the film as producer and director, and Bobby will be attached as writer.

Over my dead body, says Bonnie, still nursing a grudge over Dad's blacklisting.

Very well, the Director of Companies smiles equably. There are other ways we can structure the deal.

Film Financing and Distribution Agreements

Marlow forecast your host's next couple of moves on the ride over, and explained the trade-offs. Since he can't persuade you to produce the film in-house, the Director of Companies proposes a *production/finance and distribution agreement* (or *PFD agreement* for short). His studio would hire Quisqueya Productions to produce the film in exchange for a specified contractual fee. The studio would undertake directly to finance the production and distribute the film, and would own worldwide perpetual distribution rights. In addition to the flat fee, QP would receive a participation in net profits, if any, though you wouldn't want to hold your breath waiting for the participation to pay off, after the Accountant and the Lawyer get through tooling the definition of "net profits." The artistic downside to a PFD agreement is that, while QP in theory would be an independent contractor, in practice it would become a vassal of the studio, subject to studio control of the production, which could be very heavy-handed.

Bonnie speaks up for both of you: We're not doing a PFD agreement.

The Director of Companies says: Fine. How about a negative pickup?

In a *negative pickup agreement* the studio agrees to pay an independent film producer a fixed price for delivery of a completed film, but does not finance production costs. The producer has to line up a loan to fund production. The studio exerts less control over the production than under a PFD agreement, leaving the producer greater creative discretion, but on the other hand financing becomes the producer's headache. Negative pickups usually convey film rights for the United States and Canada to the studio in perpetuity, and sometimes, but not always, convey worldwide rights.

In tandem with a negative pickup limited to the United States and Canada, the producer may seek to line up pre-sales with foreign distributors to help finance production costs, perhaps with the help of a sales agent working the major film markets. A *pre-sale agreement* is a distribution agreement for a specific foreign territory signed before completion of the film. The distributor commits to pay, upon delivery of the film, a fixed advance or minimum guarantee in exchange for film distribution rights in the territory for a fixed term, and usually also agrees to make contingent payments to the producer if the film achieves specified sales benchmarks in the territory.

Since negative pickups and pre-sales, at heart, are copyright licenses to distribute and display a motion picture, you need to focus on the scope of the licenses granted. When does each license start, and how long does it last? What languages are licensed to whom for dubbing and/or subtitling? Aside from theatrical display rights, what other media are covered, such as DVD, video-on-demand, basic and premium cable and satellite television, broadcast television, and what ancillary rights, such as soundtrack rights and music publishing rights? What sorts of events, including nonpayment, bankruptcy, and infringement problems, can constitute a default and potentially trigger an early termination?

QP in this deal format will become an air traffic controller among its distributors, orchestrating the film's take-off in the various territories and various media. The U.S. theatrical release will be cued up before overseas theatrical releases, and distributors with theatrical rights will insist QP put into place holdback clauses to ensure QP's other licensees don't release the film in downstream media, such as DVD, video-on-demand, cable, satellite or broadcast TV, until the theatrical distributors enjoy a decent interval, typically three months, to profit from theatrical sales without competition from downstream.

Production Loan and Security Agreements

The whole point of signing the negative pickup and pre-sales agreements is for you the producer to hold assured contract rights to payment that are triggered by delivery of the completed film. These contract rights will serve as collateral for a production loan. You aren't going to guarantee repayment of the loan with your personal assets, and no lender in his right mind is going to give you an unsecured loan. A lender in his right mind is going to want as much security as possible if he's going to bankroll you in this very risky business.

Speak of the devil, up the *Nellie*'s gangplank approaches the inexorable click of a well-heeled pair of Bruno Magli loafers. Into the cabin strides the Banker, a bit peaked, having come from a late meeting in the whited sepulcher of Century City, but sleek as a seal in a pearl-gray suit of tailored Shantung silk. He glad-hands everyone and takes a seat.

Any lender who steps up to the plate to finance your production is going to want to earn interest on the production loan, and fees, lots and lots of them. Of course you are going to end up paying the lender's legal expenses to boot out of the loan proceeds. The only way the Banker is going to be willing to make the loan in the first place, though, is if it is fully secured by very good collateral, chiefly, QP's contract rights to receive the negative pickup payment from the studio and receive the pre-sale advances from the distributors. The Banker will insist that the studio and the distributors acknowledge their obligation to pay upon delivery of the completed film, whether they like the finished product or not, as long as it is based on the script, is directed by the named director, the key named actors appear in it, the film's run-time is as stipulated in their contracts, and the film receives the Motion Picture Association of America rating it is supposed to receive.

Completion Bonds, LCs, E&O Insurance, and Due Diligence

In addition, the Banker will require you to obtain and pay for a *completion bond* to guarantee that even if you screw up the production, the film will get completed and delivered without you, because the Banker is depending on the studio and the foreign distributors paying for delivery of the film as the source of funds to repay your loan. The completion guarantor will keep track of your progress on the production, and if worse comes to worst will take over the production if the schedule or budget gets too far out of whack.

Moreover, although the Banker may trust the studio's credit if it is good enough, he is likely to require from the foreign distributors the added security blanket of a *letter of credit*. An LC is a direct commitment from the distributor's bank to pay the producer, as beneficiary, the amount of the pre-sale advance, automatically upon the producer's presentation to the bank of a draft requesting payment and stating that the film has been delivered. The distributor must agree to reimburse the issuing bank, and this reimbursement obligation is normally secured by a cash deposit made by the distributor with the issuing bank.

The distributors, especially since they're committing and often depositing money before you've made your film, will demand security blankets of their own, as will the studio. They will make QP represent and warrant that it has good title to the film and that there are no infringement or other claims against it, or security interests encumbering it. They will make QP promise that the film will be based on a specific script, that it will be produced for a specified budget, and that the director, writer, and principal actors or actresses are attached to the film, and they will insist QP provide signed letters of intent and other documentation corroborating those promises.

The studio and the distributors are going to scrutinize your chain of title, as is the Banker, so it's a good thing Bonnie's copyright registration for her novel is valid, and that you are holding her copyright assignment of film rights to the novel, ready to record at the Copyright Office as soon as you exercise your option. Rights in the screenplay for the movie will be sewn up by the work-for-hire provision in the writer's agreement you and Bobby are going to hammer out, and the remainder of the production agreements will provide the needed comfort that no one involved in the production claims a piece of the intellectual property. The studio, the distributors, and the Banker will order searches of Copyright Office records to check whether any security agreements or other conflicting documents are filed against the copyrights in the book or the screenplay, they will run searches at the state level of recorded security interests, to make sure QP hasn't hocked the same rights as collateral for any loans they don't know about, and they will run litigation checks to make sure QP isn't embroiled in any lawsuits or subject to any court judgments clouding its rights.

The studio, the distributors, and the Banker are also going to insist you go out and buy *errors-and-omissions insurance*, a contract insuring against the risk that your film infringes someone else's copyright, or someone else's rights of privacy or publicity, trademark, or other relevant rights. They will make you name them as additional insureds under the policy. In turn, the E&O insurance underwriter is going to troubleshoot your chain of title even more closely, and insist that you obtain all third-party permissions and clear all rights needed, in their lawyers' opinion, to release your film.

You're willing to jump through all these hoops if this will enable you to avoid giving a percentage of the equity in QP to a private equity investor, who might become a pest poking his or her nose into the company's affairs, and enable you to avoid ending up under the studio's thumb creatively, as you would under a PFD agreement, and provided also the Banker can finance the entire production in one loan, so you don't have to go around town hat in hand begging for gap or bridge loans at extortionate rates.

You are adamant that the studio and the foreign distributors who will prime the pump for your production loan should not get a share of the ancillary rights that will form the backbone of your transmedia storytelling colossus, such as rights for a television series, animated TV shows and feature films, stage plays and live musicals, music, merchandise, video games, and books. The book rights will remain Bonnie's preserve, and the remainder must be left for QP to exploit and profit from as you see fit.

The Color of Other People's Money

The Director of Companies offers you a cigar, which you wisely decline. It's a bit early in the game to start celebrating.

All we need now, the Director of Companies muses with a flick of his vintage gunmetal Dunhill lighter, is a pair of bankable stars in the two lead roles.

Any suggestions? Marlow asks.

Ashleigh Somerset is ready for anything, according to her agent.

Anything?

Anything but another Jane Austen flick.

We can't afford to hire her, can we? you ask hopefully.

The Director of Companies chuckles. You can't afford not to.

You wince.

He says: She's less of a prima donna than the tabloids make out.

How much less?

A bit less. Her agent is on his way over as we speak.

You sigh.

Like System of a Down warned: You should have never trusted Hollywood.

Humor me on this, pleads the Director of Companies.

Whatever, you grumble. Pencil her in as Lucia Bonaire.

And opposite her, in the role of Hawkins? asks Marlow.

I'm thinking Vic Ronson, playing against type, says the Director of Companies.

Against type? snorts Bonnie. I thought Ronson was back in rehab.

Hey, says the Director of Companies, this role cries out for a degenerate.

You have a point there.

So are we on? he smiles, taking a drag on his Montecristo A.

Let's run the numbers, shrugs Bonnie.

Well? the Director of Companies barks at his team. What're you waiting for?

The Accountant shunts his dominoes to the far edge of the table with a croupier's efficient grace, flips open his laptop, and starts a real Excel spreadsheet. The Lawyer downs her martini, sits down beside him, opens her briefcase, and pulls out a sheaf of deal memos.

Looks like another all-nighter, mutters the Lawyer to the Accountant.

He rolls his sympathetic brown eyes at her.

You begin to suspect there's a thing between the two of them.

I'll put on the teapot, Marlow says helpfully, and tiptoes off to the galley.

You contemplate the big picture in silence, traversing in your head the places the rivers of intellectual property and contract rights watering Hispaniola the Franchise must flow in order for each party's garden to grow. There are quite a few properties to irrigate and cultivate, and quite a few types of agreements you need to build in order to produce, market, and distribute to an adoring public the fruits of everyone's creative labors. Though they differ in some ways, all of these agreements are built of the same essential set of building blocks used in the contracts we discussed earlier: grants of rights, and waivers of rights, promises of performance, and promises to pay, conditions, representations and warranties, guarantees and indemnities.

Hispaniola—The Book

When she wrote *Hispaniola* as a teen, Bonnie was fortunate in that her father had a loyal literary agent willing to pitch and sell her manuscript to Cutthroat Press. That agent, like Cutthroat, is long dead, may they rest in peace. Bonnie will need a new literary agent to pitch her new Hispaniola book series, and a new publisher to make it flourish.

Agency Agreements

In a typical literary agency agreement, the author, who may be a novelist, poet, nonfiction writer, or screenwriter, appoints the agent to represent him or her to pitch, negotiate, and sell a specific literary work, or to provide representation for all of the author's works of authorship. To stay in the driver's seat, the author should insist that any proposed sale be approved and signed by the author. The agent will make the author represent and warrant that he or she is the sole author of any represented work and the owner of all literary rights in the work, much as you made Bonnie represent and warrant that she is the sole author and owner of *Hispaniola*.

If the appointment is an exclusive one, as the agent will usually insist, the author agrees during the term of the agreement not to employ any other agent to represent the author for the work or works covered, but exclusivity as to various media can be negotiable, depending on the author's bargaining power. The agent normally wants the exclusive right to negotiate U.S. book sales, foreign book sales, and sales of subsidiary rights for audiobooks, electronic publishing, film, television, recording, theatrical and other dramatic media, and sometimes for merchandise, in the United States and worldwide. However, the author is better off not granting the agent an exclusive right for subsidiary sales in any medium other than print, unless the agent has a proven track record for that medium.

In Bonnie's case, you're not going to let her empower her agent to negotiate any subsidiary rights deals for film, television, recorded or live musical, theatrical, or other dramatic media, or for merchandise. You make Bonnie promise in your option and purchase agreement to stipulate in any agency agreement she makes for the book series that the agent is confined to print, audiobooks, and electronic publishing in the U.S. and overseas.

Agents do love books, but they aren't agenting authors merely for the psychic income. The agreement will entitle the agent to a commission equal to a percentage of author's royalties on domestic book sales, a percentage of foreign book sales, and varying percentages of other subsidiary sales. Though negotiable to an extent, commissions of 15 percent for domestic book sales and 20 percent to 25 percent for foreign book sales are common. Padding the foreign commission rate enables the agent to recruit and pay foreign subagents or co-agents to make foreign sales happen. Since the author pays the agent a higher commission on foreign sales, the agent is responsible to pay all commissions earned by foreign agents. If the author does care about international sales, it is advisable to corroborate who the agent uses overseas in key markets of interest, and how well they've done in recent years in these markets.

The agent normally insists on having the authority to receive royalties and other payments on the author's behalf. The agent wants to take earned commissions off the top, lest the author spend it all on a wild spree, or get wrapped up writing his or her next work and neglect to answer the phone for a couple of years. On the other hand, when the agent collects royalties or other payments due to the author from a publisher, the author should insist on receiving these, net of agent's commissions and pre-approved reimbursable expenses, within ten business days. The agreement should state clearly what types of expenses are reimbursable. If the agent wants to recoup costs like photocopying, postage, and courier service fees, the author should ask what these are likely to run, and impose a cap not to be exceeded without author's approval. The agent should promise to send the author annual or semi-annual statements showing all royalties and other author payments, commissions, and deductions for the period, and if the author is a U.S. taxpayer, the agent should prepare and send the author promptly after each year end an IRS Form 1099 or other tax documentation identifying total payments and total commissions.

The agent usually promises to use "best efforts" or "reasonable best efforts" to promote the work or works covered, but at the end of the day, the agent either succeeds in selling the work or not. If the author isn't satisfied, he or she needs to have the right to vote with his or her feet by terminating the contract. Many agency agreements provide for termination by either side on thirty days' prior written notice, but the agent normally insists on a right, after termination, to continue to manage book contracts the agent already negotiated while the agency agreement was in effect, and retain commissions on those. The agent also often insists that if the author, within a specified period of months after termination, signs a book deal with a publisher to whom the agent presented the same book proposal before termination, the agent receives commission and other compensation equivalent to what the agent would have received had no termination occurred.

The author should see to it that the agency agreement provides a right to inspect and audit the agent's books, a requirement that the agent notify the author if the agent files for bankruptcy, and a provision empowering the author to direct payments from publishers directly to the author, bypassing the agent, in the event of the agent's bankruptcy, disability, or death, to avoid royalties getting entangled in bankruptcy or probate proceedings.

Publishing Agreements

While you keep busy signing up the talent for *Hispaniola* the movie, Bonnie and her literary agent will be working to line up a publisher for the *Hispaniola* book series. She plans first to put the original novel back in print, then follow with at least three newly written sequels, a year or so apart.

The publisher would prefer to publish the first book and gain options to publish each sequel, but Bonnie insists on a four-book deal committing the publisher to publish the first book and three sequels. The publisher would prefer she give it outright copyright assignments of all of the rights within the scope of the book deal and let it register copyright in its name, but she insists on retaining ownership of copyright in each book and registering the copyright in her name, and is only willing to grant the publisher a copyright license. It all comes down to Bonnie's bargaining power, and that's largely a function of how much buzz you and she manage to generate about *Hispaniola*.

When the dust settles, Bonnie will grant the publisher an exclusive license, during the term of copyright of each book, to publish, reproduce, distribute, sell, and sublicense the book in hardcover, trade paperback, mass market paperback, book club edition, books on tape, electronic books, as well as other new media now known or later developed, worldwide, in all languages. Bonnie will not grant the publisher any film rights or other rights to create derivative works based on the novels, except for translations into foreign languages. Expressly excluded from the publishing agreement will be film, television, radio, Webcast, podcast and other broadcast rights, dramatic rights, and merchandising rights, all of which she has already optioned to you.

The publisher will insist on a noncompetition clause, in which Bonnie promises not to write and sell any competing book to another publisher during the term of the publishing agreement. What if, down the road, Bonnie writes a nonfiction book about real eighteenth-century girl pirates of the Caribbean? She should have her agent make sure the publishing agreement defines "competing books" relatively narrowly, in terms of nonillustrated book-length works of fiction, leaving her free to negotiate a separate deal with this publisher or any other publisher of her choice for anything nonfiction, for graphic novels, or for picture books.

Bonnie will agree to deliver each book manuscript by a specified date, with a specified minimum word count, agree to proofread the publisher's proofs of each book, and otherwise agree to cooperate in the publishing process. The agreement will contain clauses addressing what happens if the publisher doesn't like one of her manuscripts, or if the market for these books goes south. The publisher will angle for a right to terminate under certain such conditions, defined as broadly as possible, while her agent will skirmish to define those conditions as narrowly as possible.

The publisher will agree to pay Bonnie royalties based on specified percentages of sales. The rates may vary depending on the medium, and may increase after certain benchmark sales levels are hit, while lesser royalty rates will apply to book club, deep discount, and foreign sales. Bonnie and her agent will scrutinize the agreement's wording to see whether her royalties are based on retail prices, wholesale prices, or net prices, how sales are defined, and what exclusions from sales apply, such as for returns.

On the strength of expected demand for the book series, thanks to *Hispaniola* the movie, Bonnie hopes to negotiate hefty advances against royalties, payable on signing of the agreement and on delivery of each manuscript. She will also make her agent negotiate a healthy best-seller bonus, just as she socked you for a performance bonus in your option and purchase agreement. If the publisher licenses any subsidiary rights, it is going to have to pay Bonnie a specified percentage of the publisher's net receipts from licenses, such as for book club special editions, foreign-language editions, e-books, and books on tape. The agreement will require the publisher to provide her and her agent annual or semi-annual royalty reports, and Bonnie will have the right to audit the publisher's accounting books.

Just as you insisted on representations and warranties from Bonnie in your option and purchase agreement, the publisher will insist she represent and warrant that each book is an original work of authorship of which Bonnie is the sole creator, that it has not previously been published (other than the first *Hispaniola* novel), that it doesn't infringe anyone else's copyright or right of publicity, invade anyone's right of privacy, or defame anyone. Like you, the publisher will insist she give it an indemnity backstopping these reps and warranties. The publishing agreement will contain provisions addressing how Bonnie and the publisher would handle things in the event a copyright infringement or other legal claim or lawsuit were to rear its ugly head.

The contract will require the publisher to publish each book within a specified time after delivery of Bonnie's accepted manuscript, and to keep each book in print throughout the term, failing which, Bonnie can terminate, as she did with Cutthroat Press many years ago. Bonnie also will insist on detailed provisions regarding advertising and promotion of the series, and do her best to make these dovetail with QP's advertising and promotion of the *Hispaniola* movies, merchandise, and whatnot. The publisher will get the right, subject to Bonnie's approval, to use her name, likeness, and biography in promoting the books. Bonnie will insist on the right to approve the book jacket and marketing and advertising materials promoting the series.

Based on your recent experience negotiating your option and purchase agreement, you feel fully confident that Bonnie will make her literary agent earn his or her commissions, and that when they sit down to sign her publishing agreement they will leave a rather large pool of publisher's blood on the floor.

Hispaniola—The Movie

Now that Quisqueya Productions is slated to produce *Hispaniola* the movie, it is up to you to negotiate the talent agreements, so you can know where QP stands with the key creative people contributing to the film and you can start fleshing out your production budget. You had better start with Bobby. Let's see how large a pool of blood Bonnie's son makes you leave on the floor.

Writer's Agreements

Bobby Charlotte is attached to your film as screenwriter, so QP needs him to sign a writer's agreement. You've got to get it in writing, otherwise the studio won't sign the negative pickup agreement, the distributors won't sign their pre-sales agreements, the Banker won't issue a commitment to lend, and QP won't own copyright in the screenplay as a work made for hire.

Bobby's not an employee, he's an independent contractor. So without a written work-for-hire provision in line with the Copyright Act, no work for hire. You need to have him acknowledge in the work-for-hire provision that the screenplay and all results and proceeds of his services as screenwriter constitute a "work made for hire" specially commissioned by QP for use as a part of a motion picture, such that QP is the author and owner of copyright in the screenplay, lock, stock, and barrel, with the right to exploit the results and proceeds of his services in all media, now known or later devised, throughout the universe in perpetuity. You will also make him expressly waive any author's moral rights, even though the waiver may not be enforceable in some jurisdictions, especially in continental Europe.

Bobby is a member of the Writers Guild of America. Even though QP is not a member of the Alliance of Motion Picture and Television Producers or other big-shot producer bound through collective bargaining by the WGA Theatrical and Television Basic Agreement, Bobby will insist on having the Basic Agreement apply to his writer's agreement, as a matter of contract between QP and him by mutual agreement. Among other protections, he wants the Basic Agreement minimums to govern as a floor in negotiating compensation.

You already wrote a treatment, so you just have to pay for the screenplay. You will pay him installments on delivery of the first draft screenplay, and the final draft screenplay. He will insist that QP bring in no other writer to do rewrites or polish the script—not even Mom—so you'll have to pay him for rewrites and polish, as well, at least in line with WGA minimums. When you commence principal photography, he will also be entitled as writer to a final payment equal to a modest percentage of the production budget, but from this you will deduct installments previously advanced. He's also going to insist as screenwriter on 5 percent of the film's net profits, and Mom has already warned you, you better say yes, or Bobby's going to have a hissy fit.

A promise is a promise, and you have every honest intention of paying for the screenplay, but you must make Bobby agree that if QP breaches the writer's agreement, his sole remedy is to go after QP for money damages, and that he can't terminate the agreement or seek a court injunction, as this might hold up production or release of the film, causing the studio, your distributors, and the Banker to have their own hissy fits.

Credits matter to writers. Bobby as screenwriter gets sole "written by" credit in the film. His mom the novelist gets the source-material credit: "Based on the novel by Bonnie Charlotte." You guess the both of them will also want to be an executive producer, with a separate contract, a separate fee, and a separate credit. And you're fairly sure they'll dream up a few more fees and credits before the dust settles.

You need to make Bobby represent and warrant that he is free to enter into the writer's agreement, that no third-party rights will be violated by his doing so, that he has no conflicting obligations, and that he hasn't made and won't make any third-party agreement that could interfere with his working as screen-writer or interfere with QP's rights. He should also represent and warrant that the screenplay doesn't violate anyone's copyright or rights of privacy or publicity, or defame anyone. Most important, he must rep and warrant that the screenplay is written solely by him and is a wholly original work of authorship, other than elements from Mom's underlying novel. Make Bobby promise to sign and deliver to QP a certificate of authorship, when the time comes and the screenplay is completed, to shore up your chain of title and satisfy studio, distributor, and lender documentation requirements.

You'll put his hand to the fire, requiring him to indemnify QP in regard to his representations and warranties. On the flip side, Bobby will require QP to indemnify him, if he gets caught up in a claim or lawsuit resulting from the way QP develops, produces, distributes, or exploits the film.

What if QP fails to bring it all together and produce the film by a specified date? In that case, Bobby will insist on *turnaround*, meaning that the rights in the script revert to him. If Bobby does turn around at that point and get a film made with another film company, then as soon as principal photography based on the screenplay commences, Bobby will have to repay QP its costs paid on the screenplay. QP should take a security interest in the screenplay and record it at the Copyright Office, to make sure he actually does pay you back if this worst-case scenario comes to pass.

What if Bobby screws up, and doesn't write a screenplay you can shoot the film with? To address this possibility, you will propose that Bobby be *pay or play* under his writer's agreement. This will mean QP must pay him whether or not it ever uses his screenplay, but you can remove him as writer at your discretion, provided you pay him.

Bobby may ask for a right of first negotiation to write the screenplay for each film sequel, but you plan to stand this on its head, and make him commit to write the screenplay for each sequel on the same terms as the first. He will probably argue that if the film series is doing well, his services as screenwriter become more essential than ever, and press you for escalating compensation with each successive sequel. Moreover, since he has sole "written by" credit, it would be normal for Bobby to ask for a right of first negotiation to write any television spin-off that QP may later decide to produce.

Bobby should have a reasonable degree of creative input into the film production process, provided he doesn't get in your face as director. He will probably require that he be invited to view a cut of the film sufficiently early in the process that any editing suggestions he makes, if accepted by you, could actually be implemented, and he may insist on being invited to other screenings, which isn't a bad idea.

You presumably have to go out of town to shoot, so the writer's agreement will have to cover Bobby's travel, accommodations, and incidental expenses on location. He'll also want you to provide him and a guest with invitations to each film premiere, plus travel and accommodations on a par with yours as director. You have a funny feeling he's going to want to bring Mom. Bobby will probably insist on a few additional miscellaneous perks, which you and the Accountant will have to grind out in the budget.

Director's Agreements

At least drafting your own director's agreement with Quisqueya Productions, you guess, ought to be a piece of cake. Guess again. You can't always get what you want when you use other people's money to produce your film. This contract will be between you and QP, but you need it approved by the studio, the foreign distributors, and the Banker, and they're going to rake each clause over with a fine-toothed comb to make sure you're not self-dealing with QP at their expense. Bobby and the key actors will also be curious to see how you as director treat yourself. So don't get greedy, but do get what you need to direct the film right and be fairly paid.

Like Bobby in his writer's agreement, you must provide your services on a work-for-hire basis. You will have to acknowledge that all results and proceeds of your services as director constitute a work made for hire specially commissioned by QP for use as a part of a motion picture. You will also have to see to it, in another work-for-hire contract or a copyright assignment, that QP ends up owning copyright in the treatment you wrote, and you will need to sign a certificate of authorship of the treatment to connect the dots in QP's chain of title. If you'd like to be paid something for the treatment, you'd better ask the Director of Companies tonight, nicely, while he's in a good mood. Of course, as writer of the treatment and as director, you'll also have to give QP a waiver of moral rights.

Since Bobby held you to the WGA Basic Agreement as a floor in his writer's agreement, you should join the Directors Guild of America and insist that your director's agreement conform to the DGA Basic Agreement. The money parties you're about to crawl into bed with can't very well beef about that.

Creatively speaking, there are a couple of provisions you would like to try to get in your director's agreement, though getting them won't be easy. You'd like to be *pay and play*. This would ensure your right to direct the film, not just your right to be paid to direct. Forget it, the money parties will reply, you're not an established feature film director. But at a minimum they should let you be pay or play, on a par with Bobby. You may as well try for a right of *final cut*, to control the final pre-release edit of the film, though again, ordinarily only well-established directors get this. Final cut would give you the discretion and creative freedom to make the movie as you see fit, subject to a few objective conditions such as following the approved script, bringing the film in within stipulated theatrical film run-time, and getting the anticipated Motion Picture Association of America rating.

Since you own and control QP, you might think that you as director don't have to worry about QP as producer pushing you around. Think again. In the tangled web of contracts you weave with the money parties, the completion guarantor will insist on a right of *takeover*. This entitles the completion guarantor, if QP fails to produce and deliver the film in accord with the approved budget, script, and other delivery requirements, or if the completion guarantor sees a reasonable risk of failure, to step in as production manager, act as QP's legal agent in all matters relating to the production, and control the production bank account. Your director's agreement and the other talent agreements must acknowledge that the completion guarantor can replace the producer in that case, stepping into QP's contractual shoes.

Although takeovers are rare, if your production started to go haywire, the threat of takeover would be real enough. To stave it off, you would have to toe the completion guarantor's line at the expense of your creative vision, since otherwise your days as a director would be over, at least your days as a director spending other people's money. Some of your contract terms as director might have to be compromised, but for that very reason, it is a good idea to try at the front end of the deal to negotiate yourself as director the strongest contractual hand you can.

While you're at it, nail down for yourself a right of first refusal to edit the movie for television or for dubbed or subtitled versions for foreign markets, and a right of first refusal to direct sequels. If the Director of Companies presses you for a commitment to direct sequels, make sure you negotiate a heavy escalation in base and contingent compensation. You can bet Bobby will do the same.

Actor's Agreements

Just like Bobby as writer and you as director, Ashleigh Somerset will have to provide her services on a work-for-hire basis. Her performance will be the property of QP, which will have the unlimited right to exhibit the film containing her performance in all media throughout the universe in perpetuity. Like Bobby and you, Ms. Somerset must also waive moral rights.

Marlow already warned you, her agent is going to insist that Ashleigh be pay or play, but her pay or play will be superior to Bobby's and yours. Bobby as screenwriter and you as director will get paid whether or not QP ends up using your services to make the film, but if QP doesn't end up actually making the film, Bobby and you won't get paid at all. Ms. Somerset, on the other hand, shall receive her guarantee whether or not the film gets made, and whether or not you end up using her in it. Her agent is going to require QP to deposit funds in escrow covering the guarantee, so that QP can't squeak out of its promise to pay or play.

As a member of the Screen Actors Guild, Ashleigh will make her actor's agreement incorporate the SAG Basic Agreement, but her guarantee will be huge. The studio and the foreign distributors don't mind the impact on the production budget, even though it jacks up the price of the negative pickup and the pre-sales, because box-office-friendly Ms. Somerset will be the proverbial tide that lifts all boats, boosting the return on their investment. If for any reason you sign with her and then replace her with another actress, though, she'll pocket her guarantee and cry all the way to the bank, and you will have dug a fatally deep hole in your production budget. So do try to get along with Ms. Somerset, and show her plenty of consideration and respect on the set. After all, movie fans will be lining up around the block to see her, not you.

Credits matter to actors, and you'll have to hash them out in plenty of detail with the Agent, ensuring Ashleigh top billing. Then you'll have to turn around and diplomatically hash out Vic Ronson's credits with his people, and finally cram smaller credits down the throats of the ingénues you rope in to play Lucia Bonaire's pirate gang and Jim Hawkins's nefarious first mate Ripley.

The other thing that matters most, as a practical concern for the actors, will be your scheduled start and stop dates for filming. Yours is not the only film project Ashleigh is attached to, and you will have to juggle your schedule around her other commitments, then make sure the other actors are available when you need them.

The Five People You Meet in Hollywood

Heads up, mutters Marlow, as he swings by and pours you another cup of tea.

Welcome aboard, Stu, bellows the Director of Companies, as a well-tanned silver fox in a pink alpaca golf sweater enters the cabin and gives the assembled crew the once-over. The Agent has arrived.

The Director of Companies brings him up to speed on the project, then throws out a proposed figure for Ashleigh's guarantee that sounds astronomical to you.

The Agent counters with an even more astronomical figure.

Done. The Director of Companies doesn't even blink.

The Agent says: Ashleigh has to have the right to approve the other actors.

No problemo, Señor, replies the Director of Companies.

The Agent says: Ashleigh has to have the right to approve the choice of director.

Uh-uh. *That's* the director. Your host jerks a peremptory thumb at you.

The Agent says: Ashleigh has to have the right to approve the script.

Then you woke up, Stu, the Director of Companies sneers.

The Agent shifts ground, and reels off a list of required perks. Ashleigh's travel and accommodations are going to cost a small fortune, and you have to let Ashleigh's executive assistant and her hair, makeup, and wardrobe people accompany her on location, all at QP's expense. If you film on location in a foreign country, the Agent says, QP has to give Ashleigh a tax indemnity to make up any differential between foreign and U.S. taxes.

The Director of Companies turns to you and says: You're filming in Puerto Rico. You wag your head obediently.

That will help, pipes up the Accountant, patiently rerunning his spreadsheet.

One last thing, says the Agent: Ashleigh's pop singing career could use a boost.

That's an understatement, you remark.

How about let her sing the title song? Maybe something with a little reggae beat?

You pretend to stick a finger down your throat.

So, says the Agent, you won't let her sing?

Not on my watch, you reply.

Okay, no biggie, the Agent backs down.

The Director of Companies gazes at you for the first time with a look bordering on respect. The Lawyer, the Accountant, the Banker, and the Agent follow suit. You've done it. You've met the five people you meet in Hollywood, and survived the encounter with more dignity intact than you could have anticipated in your wildest dreams.

As soon as the Agent takes his leave, the Accountant emits a low moan.

Problem? you ask.

Yes. After budgeting in the actors, there's no money left for the music.

That's no good. You need to fill two-plus hours of soundtrack.

QP will just have to raise some equity, says the Accountant.

Perhaps you could use eighteenth-century period music? suggests Marlow.

Say *what?* you reply.

A bit of baroque, throw in a few sea shanties. Public domain, free for the taking.

You look at Marlow like he's nuts.

Just a thought, sniffs Marlow.

Wait a second, Bonnie says. Do you remember Roland Kurzweil?

There's a blast from the past, grunts the Director of Companies.

Indeed, says Marlow. He wrote the music for some of those swashbucklers your father scripted, did he not?

Bonnie nods. Not the world's greatest flicks, but the scores were masterpieces.

That they were, the Director of Companies nods.

You might recall, Bonnie turns and says acidly, your studio blacklisted Roland along with my father.

Before my time. The Director of Companies spreads his plump hands helplessly.

We'll let bygones be bygones, snorts Bonnie. The point is, Roland was working freelance on a score for *A Pirate's Life* at the time, but your back office neglected to draw up the contract. When they blacklisted him, he couldn't sell the completed score under his name, and he wasn't willing to let a front take credit, so he kept the score and kept the rights for himself.

You mean, Roland still owns a never-before-heard Kurzweil score? asks Marlow.

Never heard publicly, says Bonnie. He played it for me privately.

Good stuff?

To die for.

What ever happened to Kurzweil?

He and his grandson were running a piano store in the Valley, last I heard.

Do you think he'd part with the score on the cheap? you ask.

Better yet, just flip him a fair share of the movie merchandise, Bonnie shrugs.

Let's track down Kurzweil, says the Director of Companies.

I'll go make a few calls, Marlow volunteers.

He borrows your iPhone and steps out onto the upper deck.

Hispaniola—The Cartoon

As the Lawyer massages her deal memos, and the Accountant his spreadsheet, the Director of Companies turns to you and asks what you plan to do with the animation rights.

You allude vaguely to a few irons in the fire you supposedly have.

How about licensing us for an animated series? he asks.

Us?

Yeah, us. Our latest merger saddled me, as you must know, with that god-damned kids' cable channel which shall remain unnamed. Their content, pardon my French, is—

Crap?

To put it politely. We need a hot new series. Help me out.

Possibly.

This'd be a real a win-win.

How so?

You'd get to concentrate on moviemaking, and think how many dolls we'd sell.

We? You remind him you're retaining the merchandising rights.

Sure, sure. I only had in mind a modest participation.

How would a cartoon deal work?

Basically, you license us the rights to create an animated TV series based on your movie, its story, and characters. Our network hand picks an up-and-coming young animator, someone with a promising track record, but no pretensions about pay. Matter of fact, I have just the young lady in mind.

We engage her as creative director and co-producer to make a short based on your film. She signs on to create and deliver character designs, storyboards, and script. Once the animator delivers the completed pre-production materials, we farm those out to an independent studio of our choice to produce the short. The animator also has to provide a week or so post-production services. We pay her a flat fee, one third on starting pre-production, which should take a couple months, one third on our acceptance of the pre-production materials, and one third on acceptance of the final short.

Sounds a lot easier than making a live action show, you remark.

Sure, says the Director of Companies, and the best part is, we reduce the actors to voices.

You nod.

The actors come in and record on a relatively flexible schedule, and we own the tapes as work for hire. Now, says the Director of Companies, the animator gives us an option to engage her as co-producer on an initial television series cycle based on the short. If we don't like the short, we start from scratch with another fresh young face till we get it right. It's pay or play, of course. We're not obligated to produce the show or use the animator's services or materials. If we do use them, we have the right to revise and change the stuff any way we like.

If we do like the short, we air it a couple of times to see how it plays, and if everything clicks with the kiddies we exercise the option. If we exercise the option, the animator receives sole or shared "created by" credit, and is locked as co-producer for the first series cycle on a pay-or-play basis for a specified fee per episode. We also take five additional exclusive, successive options to engage the animator as co-producer on up to five more series cycles. If we go the whole hog, we end up with enough episodes to syndicate later on down the road. The animator is tied for all episodes produced for the life of the series as a co-producer on a pay-or-play basis, unless we fire her for cause.

Assuming we produce the show based substantially on her materials, she gets a "created by" credit and, assuming she fulfills her work, a co-producer credit. But we keep the unqualified right at all times to engage other individual producers, directors, writers, and consultants to work on the show. Say, would you like to be an executive producer on this one?

Why not?

You got it, the Director of Companies beams expansively. Since the animator's going to get sole or shared "created by" credit on the series, we'll toss her a per episode creator royalty, reducible by up to half if she ends up sharing with other credited writers or creators. We'll also give her a back-end participation of 2.5 percent of adjusted gross receipts as an advance against 5 percent of net proceeds derived from ancillary uses of the series, reducible again by up to half if she ends up sharing with other credited writers or creators. All this is non-negotiable of course.

Of course, you smile.

We'll also give her, long as she doesn't screw up on the series, a right of first opportunity to co-produce the initial TV spin-off, prequel, sequel, or remake based on the series, the initial direct-to-video based on the series, and the initial feature-length animated motion picture, on terms to be negotiated in good faith, with the first series deal as a floor, and if we don't agree on a deal on any of these within thirty days, we only have to throw her a one-time passive payment, and she's out of our hair.

During pre-production and production, the animator's services have to be exclusive to us, and during post-production, they can be on a nonexclusive, first priority basis. Her storyboard, character design, script writing, and animation direction services, unfortunately, are subject to a collective bargaining agreement between our network and the Animation Guild, but it is what it is. We receive, at no additional cost, a perpetual nonexclusive right to use the animator's name, voice, likeness, approved photos, and approved biographical info in the show and for advertising, publicity, and promotion of the show, including promotional "behind the scenes" footage. This one cries out for a "Making of" special, don't you think?

You give him a thumbs up.

The animator has to sign a very lengthy work-for-hire provision in favor of the network, and a certificate of authorship for chain of title, acknowledging the network as sole and exclusive author and owner of copyright in her work on the project, including pre-existing concepts and pitch materials, drawings, literary or dramatic material written by her, ideas, gags, plots, logos, titles, themes, stories, and new characters she thinks up, if any, whether or not reduced to drawing or writing, and whether or not actually used in the show. The rights are ours throughout the universe in perpetuity in all media, forms, and formats, including television, motion picture, DVD, videocassette, videodisc, sound recording, publishing, music publishing, theme park, legitimate stage, electronic, interactive, digital, computer-assisted media, and other new technologies known or hereafter devised, and so are all ancillary rights, including merchandising rights—

Yeah, you interject, which the network has to turn around and assign to QP.

Could we do a license back instead? the Director of Companies asks sheepishly.

You shake your head. QP's taking an assignment.

If you insist, says he. You really think you're going to like the toy business that much?

Why not?

The Director of Companies grins jadedly. Talk to me when your first holiday season is late to ship, then tell me how much you like the toy business.

Does the network get reps and warranties from the animator?

And how. More or less like the ones Bobby'll have to give you on the movie screenplay.

And backstop them with an indemnity?

Say, you *are* a fast study.

Thanks, chief.

Now, the Director of Companies says, rubbing his hands, the animator is in "default" under her contract if she breaches any rep or warranty or anything else in it, or refuses or fails or neglects to perform to the full extent of her ability as, when, and where reasonably required by us, or if she's convicted of a felony.

A felony?

This is a kids' network, for Christ's sake. If the animator commits a criminal offense or any act bringing her into public disrepute, scandal, contempt, or ridicule, or which shocks, insults, or offends a substantial portion or group of the community, or reflects unfavorably on the animator, on us, or on any affiliate or sponsor, we may, among other things, terminate or suspend the agreement.

We can terminate the agreement for any reason or no reason. Since we're engaging her on a pay-or-play basis, if we fire her for any reason other than for "cause," we'll pay her the unpaid portion of the guaranteed fixed compensation and vested contingent compensation per our deal memo in connection with series options exercised so far prior to the date of termination. But if she renders services for a third party during what would have constituted the term of her services under our agreement if we hadn't fired her, all monies she earns for such services shall be applied against and shall reduce any unpaid guaranteed fixed compensation payable to her.

On the other hand, if we breach the deal, the animator's sole remedy is an action for money damages. We make her agree she has no right to go into court seeking an injunction to hold up release of the cartoon or anything of the sort. We can assign this agreement to anyone we like, but of course the animator can't.

Nothing like covering all the bases, you say.

That's why they pay us the big bucks, amigo.

Okay, I'll get back to you on the animated series.

While we're at it, the Director of Companies says, we ought to talk interactive.

You're beginning to understand why Marlow calls him the Director of Companies.

Hispaniola—The Merchandise

By the time you're done paying off your production loan, who knows how much you'll make on the movie beyond your director's fees? Bonnie has effectively cordoned off book sales for her sweet self. Where you stand to unearth treasure on *Hispaniola*, if at all, may be digging in the mundane but lucrative field of licensed merchandise.

Quisqueya Productions will set up a merchandising division to roll out and manage your licensing program for the various categories of products, from dolls to lunchboxes to video games, that you want to bring to market under the HISPANIOLA brand and related trademarks like LUCIA BONAIRE and the rest of her crew, JIM HAWKINS and RIPLEY. You will have your lawyer, as soon as you can afford to hire one and let Marlow off the hook, draft a standard form license agreement to use with each domestic U.S. licensee, and a second form of agreement to use with each foreign licensee. Some of your U.S. and foreign licensees may be allowed to sublicense rights to selected sublicensees, to the extent this makes business sense, but no sublicensing will be allowed without your permission. When you get down to negotiating the licensing deals one by one, you may modify the standard agreement to fit the circumstances of a particular product category, territory, or licensee, but you will hold variation in the agreements to a minimum, to facilitate management of your licensing program, which will be a better-oiled machine to the extent that the license agreements you sign are uniform.

The license agreement will state what trademarks QP, as licensor, owns and is licensing, for what specific products, and for which specific territory or territories. QP will grant the licensee the right to use the licensed marks in connection with the manufacture, promotion, sale, and distribution in the territory of the licensed products, on specified terms and conditions.

The heart of the license is the "granting clause," where you grant the licensee the right, usually exclusive, but only in the specific licensed territory and only during the term of the agreement, to use the licensed marks in the manufacture, promotion, sale, and distribution of the licensed products. The term of the license will normally run three to five years, with the first contract year typically being a long year of eighteen months or so, to give the licensee lead time to ramp up production and prep the market. You may incentivize the licensee by giving it an option to renew the license for a few more years, provided it meets your required performance levels in the initial term.

The licensee will agree to pay you royalties at a rate equal to a specified percentage, often somewhere between 6 and 10 percent, of net sales of licensed products. You and your licensee may haggle over the definition, but "net sales" will essentially boil down to licensee's invoice price less returns. Royalties on licensed products will be considered earned the moment the licensee invoices the products, and you will insist the licensee invoice products no later than their shipment date. You don't want the licensee playing games with its invoicing that could either delay royalty payments or distort the sales performance picture. Royalties are due regardless of whether the licensee ever receives payment from its customers, because customer credit risk is the licensee's headache, not yours.

You will require the licensee to pay annual minimum royalties for each contract year, to guarantee the license earns you at least that much. Royalties will be payable quarterly, and sales must be reported quarterly. Though annual or semi-annual reporting is the norm in the publishing business, in most merchandise licenses you want to track performance quarter by quarter to forewarn you if the licensee's business starts falling off a cliff.

The licensee must also agree to satisfy or exceed specified minimum annual sales quotas. If the licensee fails to achieve the applicable quota in any year, you will have the right to terminate the license, whether or not they have been paying you the required minimum royalties. After all, in granting the license, you aren't just bargaining for the minimum royalties, you are bargaining for a successful branded product. A weak entry in one licensed category or territory can hurt your return there, and hurt your return in other categories and territories too.

Throughout the contract term, the licensee must diligently and continuously offer the licensed products for sale, ship orders promptly, and otherwise use best efforts to maximize sales. To preserve the *Hispaniola* brand's high reputation and goodwill, the licensee must sell and distribute licensed products only to pre-approved quality retailers in sync with your brand image.

You will require the licensee to spend a minimum percentage of its net sales each year, at least 2 to 3 percent, for advertising of licensed products, and on top of that, require it to chip in a small percentage along with the other licensees for cooperative advertising promoting the brand as a whole.

You want your royalty provisions to prevent things that could whittle down net royalties received. Royalties must be paid in full, without deductions or set-offs. With foreign licensees, withholding tax issues will crop up in some countries, just as they will in your foreign film distribution deals. Some foreign countries require a licensee to withhold taxes on outbound license payments. Your agreement will require that if the licensee is prohibited by foreign law from making payments free of withholding, the licensee must "gross up" its payment, remitting additional amounts necessary to make the actual amount received after withholding equal to the amount QP would have received had no withholding been required. Some foreign countries may impose taxes on QP, and in that case, you will make the licensee arrange payment of the taxes and send you official tax receipts to enable you to claim a foreign tax credit in the United States for any such taxes paid.

The licensee will promise to keep accurate books of account and records covering all sales, and you will have the right to inspect the books and audit inventory and sales records, imposing penalties if an audit reveals underreporting of royalties, an all too common temptation for unscrupulous licensees.

You cannot license your trademarks without monitoring the quality of the products licensed. Failure to include in the license agreement quality control provisions and to enforce them can create what is known as a "naked license," potentially resulting in a total forfeiture of your trademark rights.

In the agreement, you will make the licensee acknowledge that if the licensed products designed, manufactured, and sold by it were to be inferior in quality, design, material, or workmanship, as compared to your other branded products, your goodwill in the licensed marks and their favorable public recognition would be impaired. You will make the licensee represent and warrant that all licensed products will be of a high standard of quality suited to exploitation of the licensed marks to best advantage.

Before commencing production of any licensed product, the licensee should be required to furnish samples at its expense, including product packaging, and not to manufacture, promote, advertise, distribute, or sell items without QP's prior written approval. The licensee also should be required, whenever QP requests, to furnish free production samples, so that you can verify whether the actual production run lives up to the approved pre-production sample.

You also need to insist on the right to inspect any factory, warehouse, showroom, business office, retail store, or other facility used or occupied by the licensee or its subcontractors in making, promoting, distributing, or selling licensed products or packaging, to inspect and test the products, and to take any other action necessary or useful in your opinion to assure that the licensed products comply with your agreement.

You must include provisions in the agreement to make sure the licensee respects QP's trademark rights and recognizes that QP controls all trademark matters. The licensee must agree to use the licensed marks only in the forms your licensing division authorizes in writing, and to put on its packaging, advertising, and promotional materials any notices you require regarding the license and QP's trademarks and copyrights.

The licensee must acknowledge QP as the exclusive owner of the licensed marks, and promise not to do anything, during the license term or later, to challenge the validity of the marks and QP's exclusive ownership. The licensee must agree to execute any documents you may request to preserve QP's rights in the licensed marks. Since the continuing validity of each mark and registrations covering the goods licensed depends on the licensee's continuing use of the mark, the licensee must acknowledge that all uses it makes of the licensed marks, and any goodwill arising therefrom, run to QP's benefit alone as trademark owner, and that QP is entitled to register the licensed marks anywhere in the world. The licensee must agree not to file any trademark applications anywhere and not to take any other action detrimental, in your judgment, to QP's goodwill in the licensed marks.

To contend with counterfeiters and other trademark infringers, the licensee must agree to assist you, whenever you ask, in protecting the licensed trademarks. The licensee must immediately notify you in writing of any infringement it becomes aware of, but must not launch any lawsuit or other legal action without obtaining your prior written consent. You will decide in your discretion whether, when, and how to prosecute any infringement claims or lawsuits.

Depending on the category of licensed product, QP may provide most of the source artwork under nonexclusive license to the licensee, or may license the licensee to develop original artwork or to create derivative works from artwork QP provides, to be approved by QP prior to production. To a greater or lesser extent the license agreement will be a copyright license, as well as a trademark license.

To the extent QP licenses artwork, you will require the licensee to acknowledge QP's sole ownership of copyright in the artwork worldwide, and add quality control provisions detailing specifications as to how the artwork must be rendered on the licensed products and how the approvals process must run. You may also charge a separate royalty or fees, or increase the overall royalty rate, to reflect the value of the artwork QP supplies.

To the extent that artwork on or in the licensed products, packaging, advertising, or promotional materials is created or commissioned by the licensee, you will require that the licensee take all actions needed, under copyright and other applicable law of the licensed territory, to vest all rights in the artwork in QP's name. In the United States, you may require the licensee to reimburse QP's expenses in registering copyright in its name or registering copyright assignments in its favor, and require the licensee to ensure that any works created by its employees or freelancers constitute works made for hire under the Copyright Act, including providing you with signed work-for-hire agreements prior to production. Overseas, you will require analogous provisions tailored to each foreign territory's copyright law.

Product liability is a risk you need to consider when launching a merchandise licensing program, especially for toys and other children's products, and you want the brunt of that risk to fall on your licensees, since they are the manufacturers. Each licensee must promise to manufacture, advertise, sell, and distribute the licensed products in compliance with applicable laws and regulations, to pre-test products and provide truthful care and use labeling. Each licensee must keep you fully and immediately informed of any consumer complaint or government action relating to the licensed products, such as a Federal Trade Commission action, and act promptly under your direction to resolve the situation.

Of course, you will make each licensee agree to indemnify QP and its affiliates against any claims, losses, or expenses, including reasonable attorneys' fees, arising from any actual or alleged product defect or connected with the manufacture, advertising, promotion, sale, or distribution of the licensed products, the use of the licensed marks, or any breach by the licensee of the agreement. To backstop the indemnity, you will require the licensee to carry, during the contract term and for at least a couple of years after the term, product liability insurance and comprehensive general liability insurance with approved limits, naming QP as an additional insured.

If the licensee breaches the agreement, QP, among other rights and remedies, can terminate the agreement and the license by giving written notice of breach. If the breach is not curable, you'll make the termination immediate. If the breach is a failure to pay money due, the termination will take effect five business days after notice, giving the licensee a chance to pay up, if it can. If the breach is a non-money problem that can be fixed, for example, a failure to report sales to you on time, you will give the licensee ten business days to cure it.

As the end of the license term approaches, unless the licensee commits to renew or you renegotiate, QP will have the right to negotiate a new license with a new licensee, and to start design, manufacture, and marketing of a new licensed product line, including soliciting and taking orders for product to ship after the end of the old licensee's term. Finally, on termination of the agreement, all rights granted to the licensee will immediately and automatically revert to QP, subject only to a brief sell-off period of a few months to let the old licensee sell reasonable quantities of existing inventory on hand, provided sales are accounted for and royalties paid.

All in all, it's a lot of work.

But think how many dolls you're going to sell.

Hispaniola—The Music

You make a note to self to make sure Kurzweil's agreement, and whatever other music contracts you put together to produce the movie, give QP the right to use the music not only for the movie, but also for *Hispaniola* licensed products and entertainment, such as movie soundtrack albums, the animated television series you're considering licensing the Director of Companies' kids network to produce, video games, music boxes, theatrical musicals, and theme park attractions.

A hit title song would be the icing on the cake, you muse.

But you want somebody who can actually sing.

This will mean dealing with a real recording artist, her agent, and the record label she's signed to. And let's not forget the poor little songwriter. The songwriter is not going to sell and assign anyone his copyright in the musical composition. Instead, he'll license his music publisher to publish the music, let the publisher promote and market the song, let the publisher grant the record company a *mechanical license* to record the song, and let the publisher grant the singer a *performance license* to perform the song in concert.

QP is going to need a *synchronization license* from the music publisher to use the song in its movie, allowing you to "synchronize" the music in timed relation with the visual images in the film, and a separate synchronization license from the recording company to use the singer's recording of the song. The Copyright Act, you may recall from Chapter 1, doesn't have a work-made-for-hire provision in favor of the recording biz like the one in favor of the movie biz. So the recording company is going to make damned sure the singer assigns her copyright to them. You are also going to need a synchronization license from Kurzweil to use his music in the film, unless he sells you his musical score outright. If you get him to conduct the score, his services as conductor will be a work-for-hire owned by QP, and so will the performances of each member of the orchestra. And yes, you'll have to pay union scale.

Running the Numbers

You turn to the Accountant and say: Maybe you're right.

Huh? He peers up from the green-eyeshade glow of his Excel spreadsheet.

Maybe QP needs an outside equity investor, you concede.

> To fuel your licensing program, for whatever music you don't buy outright, you'll need to pay for more synchronization licenses to use the music in the cartoon show and video games, pay for mechanical licenses to use the music in soundtrack albums and music boxes, and pay for performance licenses to use the music in theatrical musicals and theme park attractions. It takes money to make money, you've come to realize hanging out with these people.
>
> At least we'll be able to save some dough using Kurzweil's film score, you shrug.
>
> Uh, not so fast, says the Accountant.
>
> Suddenly Marlow puts his head in the doorway, and says—
>
> Mister Kurzweil—he dead.

FURTHER READING

PRACTICAL

Want more contracts? For more on the role of contracts during the feature film production process and for numerous sample contracts, see Schuyler M. Moore, *The Biz,* 3rd ed. (Los Angeles: Silman-James Press, 2007), Mark Litwak, *Contracts in the Film and Television Industry,* 2nd ed. (Los Angeles: Silman-James Press, 1999), Mark Litwak, *Dealmaking in the Film and Television Industry,* 3rd ed. (Los Angeles: Silman-James Press, 2009), and Gunnar Erickson, Harris Tulchin, and Mark Halloran, *The Independent Film Producer's Survival Guide: A Business and Legal Sourcebook,* 3rd ed. (New York: Schirmer Trade Books, 2010). Dina Appleton and Daniel Yankelevits, *Hollywood Dealmaking: Negotiating Talent Agreements for Film, TV, and New Media,* 2nd ed. (New York: Allworth Press, 2010), focuses primarily on feature film contracts, but includes one chapter on reality TV negotiations and another on digital content deals. And for information on contracts geared specifically for screenwriters, see Brooke A. Wharton, *The Writer Got Screwed (but Didn't Have To): A Guide to the Legal and Business Practices of Writing for the Entertainment Industry* (New York: HarperCollins, 1996).

CONTRACT HISTORY AND THEORY

Several legal and media scholars have explored the historical importance of contracts to the media industries. Unlike the one-off talent deals we describe you negotiating for *Hispaniola,* the Hollywood studios of the 1920s, '30s, and '40s held most of their actors, writers, and directors under seven-year contracts, in which the studio reserved the option to dump them every six months. Recently, though, Tom Kemper's *Hidden Talent: The Emergence of Hollywood Agents* (Berkeley: University of California Press, 2009) and Emily Susan Carman's "Independent Stardom: Female Film Stars and the Studio System in the 1930s," *Women's Studies* 37, no. 6 (2008): 583–615, have suggested that short-term contracts were much more prevalent during Hollywood's Golden Age than previous historians had acknowledged. Mark Weinstein's "Profit-Sharing Contracts in Hollywood: Evolution and Analysis," *The Journal of Legal Studies* 27, no. 1 (1998): 67–112, offers a detailed exploration of Hollywood profit participation contracts, including Art Buchwald's infamous, though not unusual, 1983 "net profits" agreement with Paramount.

As you know by now, ideas are not copyrightable. Under some circumstances, however, ideas can be protected through contract law. Eric Hoyt's "Writer in the Hole: *Desny v. Wilder,* Copyright Law, and the Battle Over Ideas," *Cinema Journal* 50, no. 2 (2011), discusses the pivotal lawsuit against writer-director-producer Billy Wilder that enabled contract law to be applied to idea submission disputes in the state of California. The logic is this: when you pitch an idea to a producer, he enters into an implied contract with you. The implied contract is that if he uses the idea, then you get paid. That's the gist anyway. For additional legal discussions on the law of ideas and the application of contract law to ideas, see Melville B. Nimmer, "The Law of Ideas," *Southern California Law Review* 27, no. 2 (1954): 119–148, Benjamin Kaplan, "Implied Contract and the Law of Literary Property," *California Law Review* 42, no. 1 (Spring 1954): 28–39, and Lionel S. Sobel, "The Law of Ideas, Revisited," *UCLA Entertainment Law Review* 1 (1994): 10–96. But what *Desny v. Wilder* means for you today is that studios and networks will most likely require you to sign submission agreements holding them harmless before they come anywhere near you or your pitch.

Contracts, of course, also play a variety of important functions beyond the entertainment industry. If you decide to turn the art of law into your new profession, you will take a contracts course during your first year of law school, where you will have the joy of paying over one hundred dollars for a heavy book of important contract law decisions, possibly edited by your professor. But in the meantime, if you are looking for a more afford-

able and readable overview of contract law, we recommend Randy E. Barnett, *The Oxford Introductions to U.S. Law: Contracts* (New York: Oxford
University Press, 2010). Barnett opens with a "Short History of Contract
Law" and uses memorable examples to illustrate theories of contract law
throughout the book.

5

Rights of Privacy and Publicity

Fame is a fickle food
Upon a shifting plate

—Emily Dickinson, poem no. 1702

In his final year in office, California governor Arnold Schwarzenegger signed into law in the Golden State an "anti-paparazzi" bill enabling lawsuits against tabloids, television, and other media outlets that pay for and use material they know was improperly obtained in violation of a person's right of privacy. It was the latest milestone on a long and winding road of legal developments enlarging rights of privacy and publicity.

Simply put, the right of privacy is one's right to be left alone, and the right of publicity is one's right to control the use of his or her name, image, likeness, and voice for commercial gain. The right of privacy protects against some of the main drawbacks of fame, and the right of publicity tries to help ensure some of fame's compensations. If a celebrity is a magnet, think of the right of privacy and right of publicity as the north and south poles of the magnet, the one repelling unwanted intrusions, and the other attracting cold, hard cash.

If you hope to negotiate the next curve on your creative road trip with a celebrity like Ashleigh Somerset, or even just contend with ordinary people whose name, image, likeness, voice, or personal info finds its way into your works, you will need a road map to rights of privacy and publicity, just as a midwestern tourist doing Sunset Boulevard needs a map to the stars' homes. But be forewarned. Compared with copyright and trademark law, privacy and publicity rights are scattered across the map.

Here is why.

The U.S. Constitution sets the stage for copyright and trademark law. It is the source of power that allowed Congress to enact a Copyright Act, granting authors and artists copyrights in new literary and artistic works for a limited period of time, and to make federal jurisdiction over copyright exclusive. It is also the source of power that enabled Congress to horn in on the trademark game by enacting the federal Trademark Act, which exists side by side with state common law and statutory protection for trademarks. Though federal jurisdiction over trademark matters is nonexclusive, as the Trademark Act does not preempt state law, federal law now dominates the trademark arena in this country, and has spurred the adoption in the vast majority of states of a Model State Trademark Bill, resulting in a high degree of uniformity across the land even at the state trademark law level.

Yet although the Declaration of Independence talks of "Life, Liberty and the pursuit of Happiness," a catchphrase penned by Boston lawyer John Adams, and the Constitution provides certain fundamental private citizen's rights against encroachment by the government, such as the Fourth Amendment's "right of the people to be secure in their persons, houses, papers, and effects, against unreasonable searches and seizures," a right to protect one's privacy against encroachment by other private parties wasn't even on the Founding Fathers' radar screen. In the media-starved *Poor Richard's Almanack* age they grew up in, the notion that private folks might need a legal right to stop unauthorized use of their name, image, or likeness never even occurred to anyone.

TWO GUYS FROM BOSTON

Mass media would change that.

A century after adoption of the Constitution, in 1890, two more Boston lawyers, Samuel Warren and Louis Brandeis, came along and sketched out the right of privacy as we now know it—the idea that an individual should have a right to protect his or her name and likeness—in a *Harvard Law Review* article titled, aptly enough, "The Right to Privacy."

Viewing with alarm the fin de siècle rise of yellow journalism, epitomized by the no-holds-barred circulation war between Joseph Pulitzer's *New York World* and William Randolph Hearst's *New York Journal* (later fictionalized in Orson Welles's *Citizen Kane*), Warren and Brandeis feared the press's escalating technological reach into previously inaccessible regions of personal life. Old-time sanctions against libel and trespass may have sufficed in days gone by, but these could not adequately protect individuals from the "too enterprising press, the photographer, or the possessor of any other modern device for recording or reproducing scenes or sounds."

To uphold "the right to be let alone" and "the right to one's personality" against the onslaught of new media, they argued that brand-new legal remedies needed to evolve to draw a line in the sand between public and private life. Over the next century the remedies did evolve in one form or another in nearly all states. All states recognize some form of common law right of privacy and publicity, and most have enacted statutes on the subject as well.

Rights of privacy and publicity are still evolving state by state, though, forming a cross-country crazy quilt that can make celebrities, creative artists, media players, and their lawyers want to tear their hair out. Fifty states, fifty bodies of law. Do the math. You don't have time for a fifty-state tour. But we can get the basic lay of the land of rights of privacy and publicity if we go bicoastal.

GANGS OF NEW YORK

The Big Apple, where Brandeis and Warren's "too enterprising press" cut its teeth, remains today a daunting media metropolis, where danger lurks round every corner and up every alleyway for innocent law-abiding celebrities. So it should come as no surprise that New York state law provides celebrities and common folk alike with a reasonably sharp weapon to help keep the media gangs of New York at bay.

But it didn't come easy. Soon after the publication of Warren and Brandeis's *Harvard Law Review* article, several New York courts upheld the right of privacy until the issue came to a head, and a very pretty head at that, in the case of *Roberson v. Rochester Folding Box Co.* Miss Abigail Marie Roberson, through her guardian at law, complained that the defendants, without her knowledge or consent, had distributed thousands of lithographic prints bearing her photograph and likeness. Miss Roberson's image appeared on a poster beneath the words "Flour of the Family" along with defendant Franklin Mills Flour's brand name and logos of a flour chest, barrel, and sack, advertising their flour and displayed in stores, warehouses, and other public places, including—heaven forbid—saloons.

The trial court ruled that her right of privacy had been invaded, but the New York Court of Appeals reversed. Chief Judge Alton Brooks Parker, writing for the majority, opined prissily that the court's hands were tied due to lack of judicial precedent supporting the Warren and Brandeis thesis.

The *Roberson* decision provoked a public outcry. The next year, in 1903, the New York state legislature became the first lawmaking body in America to recognize a right of privacy, and for the rest of the twentieth century courts and state legislatures would keep leapfrogging each other to build on this new area of the law.

Meanwhile, Parker resigned the bench in 1904 to launch a disastrous bid for the presidency against Theodore Roosevelt. During his campaign, old-school Judge Parker refused to be photographed, provoking a tongue-lashing in the press from Miss Roberson when he remarked: "I reserve the right to put my hands in my pockets and assume comfortable attitudes without being everlastingly afraid that I shall be snapped by some fellow with a camera." But if Judge Parker didn't get New Media, T.R. did. The rest is history.

New York's right of privacy is enshrined in New York Civil Rights Law Sections 50 and 51. Under Section 50, a party that uses for advertising or trade purposes "the name, portrait or picture of any living person without having first obtained the written consent of such person, or if a minor of his or her parent or guardian, is guilty of a misdemeanor." Section 51 creates a private right to sue, stating that any person whose "name, portrait, picture or voice" is used within New York for advertising or trade purposes without prior written consent can sue the party so using his or her name, portrait, picture, or voice, to prevent and restrain such use, and to recover damages for any injuries sustained by reason of such use, plus, if the defendant knowingly used the person's name, portrait, picture, or voice, punitive damages.

Since this statutory right of privacy was considered a personal right, though, it would take a second legal home run under New York law to enable celebrities to cash in on their names and images in ways we today take for granted.

The federal Court of Appeals for the Second Circuit stepped up to the plate in 1953 in the case of *Haelan v. Topps Chewing Gum,* a playoff between two chewing gum makers over baseball trading cards. Haelan had signed up a string of ballplayers under exclusive licenses authorizing the use of their images on its cards. When Topps sold its own gum with photos of the same players without permission, Haelan cried foul. Topps argued that Haelan could not recover damages under New York's right of privacy, because the statutory right was a personal, non-transferable right. The court said that may be true, but turned around and created a new common law "right of publicity."

In addition to and independent of the New York statutory right of privacy, the court ruled that a ballplayer has a right in the publicity value of his photograph, including the right to grant an exclusive license to reproduce it on merchandise. Coupled with the personal right of privacy, here was a clear-cut economic right of publicity that a celebrity could take to the bank, freely transfer, license, and assign, and the celebrity, his or her licensee, or an assignee could sue in New York for money damages geared to the value of the endorsement.

That being said, the Empire State is still often regarded as a tough place to win a right of publicity case, and many New York celebrity plaintiffs prefer to rely on the federal Trademark Act surrogate "false endorsement," as we saw Ginger Rogers try to do in *Rogers v. Grimaldi* in Chapter 2.

Another limiting factor is that, although there have been attempts to steer a "dead celebrity" bill through the New York legislature, to date those attempts have been unsuccessful. So rights of privacy and publicity in New York are recognized only during a person's lifetime, and do not survive post-mortem. Yet, somewhere over the rainbow, there's a land where the dreams dead celebrities dare to dream really do come true.

CALIFORNIA DREAMIN'

Just as movie pioneer D. W. Griffith and media mogul William Randolph Hearst both vacated New York in the 1920s for California's sunnier climes, rights of privacy and publicity too found a warmer reception in the Golden State.

LA DOLCE VITA

California courts recognized a common law right of publicity in 1931, and the California legislature enshrined the right of publicity in statute in 1971. California Civil Code Section 3344 allows any living person to sue anybody else who, without prior consent, knowingly uses his or her name, voice, signature, likeness, or still or moving photograph in any manner on or in merchandise, or to advertise or sell products or services. The aggrieved party can recover statutory damages, or actual damages plus the offending party's profits, as well as punitive damages and an award of attorneys' fees.

In a nod to the First Amendment, Section 3344 exempts use of a name, voice, signature, photograph, or likeness in connection with any news, public affairs, sports broadcast, or political campaign. But as we saw in

Chapters 1 and 2 with the fair use defense to copyright infringement and trademark infringement, the statute is not the last word on what satisfies the First Amendment, or on what constitutes fair use of a name, voice, signature, photograph, or likeness in a creative work.

Most other states also recognize a common law right of publicity, and a majority have enacted right of publicity statutes, but most, like New York, still do not recognize a right of publicity enduring beyond the grave. In California, though, as usual, life imitates art.

THE UNDEAD

In *Lugosi v. Universal Pictures,* the heirs of actor Bela Lugosi, famed for the title role he created for the 1931 film *Dracula,* sued for an injunction and for recoupment of Universal Pictures' profits from licensing Lugosi's name and image on merchandise without Lugosi's or the heirs' permission, raising the question: Who's sucking whose blood now?

The California Supreme Court answered Lugosi's heirs with a wooden stake through the heart, ruling that, like rights of privacy, California's common law and statutory rights of publicity as they stood on the books at the time were personal to the artist and had to be exercised, if at all, by him or her during his or her lifetime.

The case catalyzed passage of the California Celebrity Rights Act, creating a "deceased personalities" right of publicity. Under Civil Code Section 3344.1, this post-mortem right of publicity is transferable by contract, will, or trust. It defines a "deceased personality" as someone whose name, voice, signature, photograph, or likeness has commercial value at the time of his or her death, whether or not in life he or she used these on merchandise or to advertise or sell things.

With an eye again on the First Amendment, however, the California legislature saddled the statute with an ill-drafted exemption big enough to drive a freight train through, for plays, books, magazines, newspapers, musical compositions, films, radio or television programs, material of political or newsworthy value, single and original works of fine art, and advertisements or commercial announcements for any of these things. It took the spirit of Fred Astaire tap dancing on into federal court to set things right.

In *Astaire v. Best Film and Video Corp.,* Mr. Astaire's widow sued a videotape producer for unauthorized use of film clips of Fred in a series of instructional dance videotapes. She claimed the company had violated her statutory post-mortem right to control the use of her husband's

Bela Lugosi, the master vampire actor

image, name, and likeness. The district court agreed, finding that the video maker had used Astaire's image in "merchandise" in violation of the statute, but the Ninth Circuit Court of Appeals reversed, ruling that the tapes fell under the statutory exemption for film, even though the videos were overtly commercial.

Not to be upstaged that easily, Mrs. Astaire formed a new dance team with the Screen Actors Guild and gained passage in 1999 of the Astaire Celebrity Image Protection Act, revamping Section 3344.1 to limit the types of uses of a deceased celebrity's name, voice, signature, photograph, or likeness that do not require consent of the heirs, stating that use in a play, book, magazine, newspaper, musical composition, audiovisual work, radio or television program, single and original work of art, work of political or newsworthy value, or ad or commercial announcement for any of these does not require the consent of the heirs, provided the work is fictional or nonfictional entertainment, or a dramatic, literary, or musical work.

The legislation also extended the term of post-mortem rights from fifty to seventy years.

As Bela might say, at the end of the day, immortality is a tough act to follow.

A WORLD WITHOUT PAPARAZZI

To show that it wasn't neglecting the privacy side of the privacy-publicity equation, California became the first state to enact an anti-paparazzi statute, in 1999, amid public outrage over Princess Diana's tragic death and celebrity anger at the increasingly reckless and obnoxious tactics of overaggressive photojournalists. Though existing California common law and statutes against trespass, intrusion, assault, battery, false imprisonment, stalking, and surreptitious recording of confidential communications had long been deployed in the vendetta against the paparazzi, California Civil Code Section 1708.8 created new causes of action for "physical" and "constructive" invasion of privacy.

Under California Civil Code Section 1708.8, any person may sue for "physical invasion of privacy" if someone else has knowingly entered his or her land without permission, the entry was made with the "intent to capture any type of visual image, sound recording, or other physical impression" of the person engaging in a "personal or familial activity," and the invasion was made in a manner "offensive to a reasonable person." Personal or familial activity includes, but is not limited to, the "intimate details" of one's personal life, "interactions" with one's family or significant others, and "other aspects" of one's private affairs or concerns.

Where the statute trumps old-fashioned trespass, which traditionally yielded miniscule money damages and was better suited to a law school hypothetical than a real world lawsuit, is in the stiffer penalties, which include general damages, special damages, treble damages, punitive damages, disgorgement of profits, and equitable relief in the form of injunctions and restraining orders.

But you can't yell "Get off my lawn!" at the paparazzi if they're not on your lawn. So Section 1708.8 added a tort called "constructive invasion of privacy," which triggers liability even if there is no entry onto the target's property. It occurs when someone attempts to capture a visual image, sound recording, or other physical impression of another person engaging in a personal or familial activity, the attempt is made in a manner that is offensive to a reasonable person, the person photographed, videotaped, or recorded had a "reasonable expectation of privacy," and a "visual or auditory enhancing device" is used, such as a telephoto lens or directional microphone.

Throwing mainstream investigative journalism a bone, the anti-paparazzi statute exempts law enforcement personnel and employees of governmental agencies or "other entities public or private" who, in the course and scope of their employment and supported by an "articulable suspicion," try to photograph, videotape, or record a person as part of an investigation of illegal or other fraudulent activity involving "a violation of law or pattern of business practices adversely affecting the public health or safety."

As first enacted, the anti-paparazzi statute left publishers and broadcasters immune from liability for using images or recordings captured in violation of the statute. It specifically said the sale, transmission, publication, broadcast, or use of any image or recording did not in itself constitute a violation, though a person who directed or caused someone to commit an invasion of privacy might be liable for compensatory and punitive damages. Thus, a publisher could not be held liable for publishing an image it obtained from a sinning paparazzi, as long as the publisher did not direct the violation. It left publishers free to buy invasive celebrity photos shot on spec by freelancers.

An amended bill signed into law by Arnold Schwarzenegger, which took effect in 2010, his final year in office, enables celebrities to sue media companies that sell, transmit, or publish offending images or recordings if they have "actual knowledge the images or recordings were obtained illegally." Counsel to the tabloids continue to probe the First Amendment chinks in this shining suit of privacy armor, and the courts are sure to be busy for years to come balancing privacy rights against the public's right to know in matters of public interest in celebrity-versus-paparazzi legal battles royale.

PUBLICITY STUNTS

With different laws of privacy and publicity in every state, lawsuits over these rights are quirky not only because of the idiosyncrasies of the celebrity and "ordinary" plaintiffs who bring them, but because of the idiosyncrasies of each state's laws. The results aren't always consistent, and aren't always right, which makes getting a handle on rights of publicity a difficult stunt. The overall trend in right of publicity cases, though, has been to expand the right to dragnet a widening ring of culprits, including celebrity look-alikes, sound-alikes, statuettes, and other artwork. Here are a few examples of particular interest to creative artists in film, video, video gaming, and other media:

A TALE OF TWO WIPEOUTS

In *Dora v. Frontline Video, Inc.,* surf legend Mickey Dora (aka Miklos Sandor Dora, aka Miki "Da Cat" Dora, aka "The Black Knight") sued the producer of a documentary video, *The Legends of Malibu,* chronicling the early days of California surfing, with film footage of famous surfers riding tasty waves, including Dora. He asserted that the use of the footage violated his California publicity rights.

A California court of appeal ruled Dora's claim bogus. The First Amendment was a total defense, because surfing was a matter of public interest, and Dora's contribution to the development of the sport was "the point of the program." The judge, writing perhaps under the influence of *Fast Times at Ridgemont High,* said in his opinion that the video maker was not required to obtain Dora's consent because surfing "has created a lifestyle that influences speech, behavior, dress, and entertainment, among other things."

But it's not always the surfers who wipe out in surf publicity right litigation.

In *Downing v. Abercrombie and Fitch,* things got gnarly when a group of well-known surfers whose photograph was used without permission in an Abercrombie catalog sued the hip clothier for surfing pics in a restricted area. The federal Ninth Circuit Court of Appeals ruled Abercrombie's First Amendment defense didn't hold water.

The court found the catalog to be commercial speech not entitled to the full First Amendment protection reserved for expressive works, and though the theme of Abercrombie's catalog was surfing and surf culture, a matter of public interest, the use of the plaintiffs' names and pictures was a different kettle of fish from *Dora.* His contribution to the development of the surf lifestyle and his influence on the sport was "the point of the program" in Frontline Video's documentary. He was depicted in it because his identity directly contributed to the story about surfing, which came under the protected public interest. In Abercrombie's catalog there was only a tenuous relationship between the surfers' photo and the catalog theme. Abercrombie used the photo "essentially as window-dressing to advance the catalog's surf-theme." The illustrative use of the photo did not contribute significantly to a matter of public interest, so Abercrombie could not avail itself of the First Amendment defense.

In general, newspapers, books, magazines and other publications, films, and television shows on matters of public interest are protected by the First

Amendment against claims of violation of privacy and publicity rights. They are also protected by the First Amendment against claims of defamation, unless the reportage is about an ordinary person and is actually false, or is about a public figure, is actually false, and is made with knowing or reckless disregard for its falsity.

You have a right to stay out of the public eye, unless and until you either make yourself a public figure, by running for Congress or becoming a surf celebrity, for instance, or make yourself a private person of public interest by getting caught up, intentionally or not, in a newsworthy event, by robbing a bank, for instance, or by being the unlucky teller that morning behind the bank counter.

HOW'RE WE GONNA SHOOT GOLF WITHOUT GUNS?

The Three Stooges delivered a posthumous poke in the eye on behalf of dead celebrity rights in *Comedy III Productions, Inc. v. Gary Saderup, Inc.*, when the licensing and merchandising company holding the rights of the late, great vaudeville and film comics Moe Howard, Curly Howard, and Larry Fine sued artist Gary Saderup, who specializes in charcoal drawings of celebrities, under California's dead celebrity publicity rights statute. Saderup had created a drawing of the Stooges and sold lithographs and t-shirts bearing reproductions of it. The case went all the way to the California Supreme Court, where Saderup argued that his work was protected by the First Amendment. The Court gave Saderup a pie in the face with a "balancing test" between the First Amendment and the right of publicity, based on whether the artist's work "adds significant creative elements" to the celebrity's likeness. Sizing up Saderup's Stooges pics, the Court found no such elements. Although they praised Saderup's "undeniable skill," the justices felt his skill was "manifestly subordinated to the overall goal of creating literal, conventional depictions of the Three Stooges so as to exploit their fame."

The Court's balancing test for publicity rights was modeled on the fair use defense to copyright infringement, focusing nearly entirely on whether the artist's work is "transformative." Saderup's was a more or less straight-up representational picture of the Stooges, so it was not "transformative."

The Court clarified that the right of publicity can't be used to control a celebrity's image by censoring disagreeable portrayals, so that caricature, parody, and satire enjoy a broad First Amendment immunity, and it said it was not holding that all reproductions of celebrity photographs are unprotected by the First Amendment, giving its blessing to Andy Warhol's famed silk-screen serigraph prints of Marilyn Monroe, Elizabeth Taylor, and Elvis Presley.

But the *Comedy III Productions* test raises the question:

How're judges supposed to play art critic without an art history degree?

Or as Curly put it in *Three Little Beers:*

How're we gonna shoot golf without guns?

Speaking of golf, Tiger Woods's licensing company hit a sand trap in Ohio federal court in *ETW Corp. v. Jireh Publishing,* when the Sixth Circuit Court of Appeals held that the First Amendment furnished a complete defense to his false endorsement claim under the Trademark Act against another enterprising artist.

Rick Rush, the self-styled "America's Sports Artist," is a well-established creator of limited edition serigraph paintings and prints depicting a wide variety of sports and sports figures of the genre no sports bar of quality should be without. When Tiger won the Masters Tournament in 1997, Rush painted a work titled "The Masters of Augusta," portraying Woods in three different golf poses before a ghostlike collage background depicting several past Augusta tournament champions in inspired full swing.

When Rush's art publisher sold prints and posters of the painting, Tiger's licensing arm sued, charging false endorsement. The Court of Appeals ruled the complaint a paper tiger. It found that the painting was more than a mere literal likeness of Woods. It contained a creative component that originated with Rush and was unique to his talent. His First Amendment right to artistic freedom outweighed Woods's property rights in the profits generated by his image. The Court of Appeals found that the painting contained transformative elements of significant expression beyond the imitation of a celebrity, which made it especially worthy of protection, and also less likely to interfere with the economic interest protected by Woods's right of publicity. The painting did not capitalize solely on a literal depiction of Woods, but rather contained a collage of images combined to artistically describe a historic event and to convey a message about the significance of his achievement in the 1997 tournament.

The outcome of the appeal in 2003 was a minor setback for the most lucrative franchise in the history of celebrity endorsement. The following year Woods became the first pro golfer to pass the $40 million mark in career earnings, and later that year he married Swedish model Elin Nordegren in a $1.5 million fairy-tale wedding. Tiger's fame was at the top of its game.

As Emily Dickinson said, fame is a fickle food.

FAR FROM THE MADDEN CROWD

Retired NFL running back Jim Brown is regarded as one of the greatest American professional athletes of all time, and he leveraged his fame in football into a long and successful second career as a film and television actor, while playing a real-life leading role as a social activist helping inner-city youths steer clear of street gangs and prison.

Electronic Arts develops and publishes video games, including the *Madden NFL* series, named for former Oakland Raiders coach and Pro Football Hall of Famer John Madden, which it has published for over two decades with great commercial success. Each Madden NFL game contains as many as 170 virtual teams and 1,500 virtual players. Electronic Arts has a licensing agreement with the NFL, but no agreement with Brown. In the games, virtual players on current NFL teams wear the names and numbers of real-life players, while players on historic teams are anonymous, represented by numbers and roster positions. The players compete in virtual stadiums, cheered by virtual fans and coached by virtual coaches, all designed by the games' graphic artists. A soundtrack, voice commentary, and sound effects accompany the action.

In 2009, in *Brown v. Electronic Arts, Inc.,* football legend took game publisher to federal district court in Los Angeles, charging false endorsement under the Trademark Act, and tacking on California state law privacy and publicity claims. Brown complained that Electronic Arts had misappropriated his identity and likeness by including him in the games as a player on two historic teams: the 1965 Cleveland Browns team and the All Browns team.

The character he claimed represents Brown in the game is anonymous, and wears jersey 37. Brown wore 32. Brown and his video doppelgänger have nearly identical stats. Brown said Electronic Arts altered the jersey numbers and made other superficial tweaks precisely to avoid being sued. He argued that this amounted to using his likeness in a false endorsement of the video game, whereas Electronic Arts protested that the First Amendment allows video game designers to use virtual characters that appear similar to celebrities.

The court said the Madden NFL video games are expressive works, akin to a painting that depicts celebrity athletes of past and present in a realistic sporting environment, as in the Tiger Woods "Augusta Legends" case. As such, video games are entitled to "as much protection as the most profound literature."

So, even assuming for the sake of argument that Electronic Arts used Brown's likeness, his false endorsement claim had to fail on First Amendment grounds. Under *Rogers v. Grimaldi,* as we saw in Chapter 2, a false endorsement claim under the Trademark Act brought against the creator of an expressive work can succeed only if the "public interest in avoiding consumer confusion outweighs the public interest in free expression."

The court observed that the Madden NFL series is creative in different ways than some of the other video games courts have held to be artistic speech, such as the *Grand Theft Auto* case, aka *E.S.S. Entertainment 2000, Inc. v. Rock Star Videos, Inc.,* which contain such creative elements as a story line and satires of real cities. But the lack of a plot in Madden NFL doesn't matter: "Video games do not have to be stories to qualify as expressive works."

Even though the Madden NFL games seek to realistically replicate NFL football, they use creative means to achieve that goal, with virtual stadiums, athletes, coaches, fans, sound effects, music, and commentary created or compiled by the games' designers. Manipulating virtual athletes and franchises at will, gamers interact with the designers' creative interpretation of real-world NFL game play. The virtual football season becomes itself a story line, as gamers navigate their athletes and franchises toward victory. That the designers used a realistic sports theme to express their creativity, as opposed to a sleazy, ultra-violent urban adventure like *Grand Theft Auto,* does not change the fact that the Madden NFL games manifest their designers' creative vision.

Applying the two-part *Rogers v. Grimaldi* test that helped Fellini end run Ginger Rogers, the court agreed with Electronic Arts' argument that the First Amendment provided a complete defense to Brown's false endorsement claim. First, the use of a legendary NFL player's likeness in a game about NFL football has a level of artistic relevance at least "above zero." Second, that being the case, the false endorsement claim could win only if the use explicitly misled consumers about the source or content of the work.

The Madden NFL character Brown claimed bears his likeness is one of thousands of virtual athletes in the games. Unlike most of the other characters, this virtual athlete is anonymous: he is identified only by a jersey number and his roster position as a running back. The character, and Brown's name, are not depicted on the games' packaging, advertising, or promotion. Although a Madden NFL gamer could assume from the circumstances that player number 37 represents Brown, it would take a leap of logic to conclude that the anonymous, misnumbered player in the games equates to Brown's endorsement of the games. Besides, the virtual player's mere presence in the game does not amount to an explicit attempt to convince consumers that Brown endorsed the games. Thus, Electronic Arts' use of Brown's likeness did not explicitly mislead consumers into thinking Brown is somehow behind the games or sponsors the product, and the use is protected by the First Amendment.

On that basis, the court called time out, dismissed Brown's false endorsement claim, and declined to take jurisdiction over the state law claims. Brown has appealed the case to the Ninth Circuit Court of Appeals.

A REPUBLICAN FORM OF GOVERNMENT

Under Article IV of the Constitution, the United States "shall guarantee to every State in this Union a Republican form of Government." This means no state governor may be a monarch, but Article IV says nothing against celebrities.

Which raises a conundrum: when a celebrity becomes a politician, or a politician a celebrity, what becomes of his or her right of publicity? While celebrities often litigate their rights of publicity, politicians normally steer clear of the commercial courts. So where can we find an actual case where a politician went to the mat over unauthorized use of his or her name, image, or likeness?

Where else but L.A.?

Shortly after Arnold Schwarzenegger's election as governor of California, an Ohio toymaker produced an Arnold bobblehead to add to its stable of topical political figures. The bobbling action figure wore a business suit, a bandolier, and an assault rifle.

The action-hero-turned-Governator was less than amused, especially about the rifle. His entertainment production company sent the toymaker a cease and desist letter, then sued in state court in Los Angeles in *Oak Productions, Inc. v. Ohio Discount Merchandise, Inc.*, claiming the bobblehead illegally exploited Arnold's image for commercial gain. The toymaker replied that it was a political parody and that the use of the governor's likeness without permission was protected speech under the First Amendment.

The stage was set for a precedent-shaping decision balancing a celebrity-politician's right of publicity and an entrepreneur's First Amendment right to lampoon him. Before any ruling in the case, however, the parties settled out of court. The settlement allowed sales of the Arnold bobblehead to bobble along, on condition that the toymaker remove the offending gun from the bobble's cold plastic hands and turn over a share of its profits to a children's charity sponsored by Schwarzenegger. Though the settlement left some big legal issues up in the air, it certainly seems the death knell for a bobblehead's Second Amendment right to bear arms. Then again, when they drafted the Bill of Rights, the Founding Fathers foresaw a lot, but they presumably didn't foresee bobbleheads.

DEALING IN RIGHTS OF PRIVACY AND PUBLICITY

With so much state-to-state variation in rights of privacy and publicity, how can you tackle them on a given creative project so as to steer clear of trouble?

First, since California law delivers industrial-strength rights of privacy and publicity, in most situations, if your creative project has a potential nation-wide audience, it is a good idea to think through how things would play out in California. Second, consider how things would play out in New York, the other jurisdiction where celebrity legal spats most often crop up. Third, if your celebrity or other "person of interest" is a resident of or spent a considerable portion of his or her career in a state other than California and New York, you should consider how things would play out under that state's law. For example, if you want to make a documentary about a country-western singer who spent much of his or her career in Nashville or Memphis, you would want to consider Tennessee law, and if he or she spent years playing gigs on the Austin music scene or in Lubbock, you would want to look into Texas law.

Here are a few rules of thumb to follow in your creative projects generally.

DRAMATIS PERSONAE

If some individual is going to appear in or be heard in your film, video, still photography, sound recording, or other creative work as an actor, model, singer, narrator, or other performer, get a signed written release from him or her waiving any right of privacy or publicity in connection with the work and permitting you to use his or her name, image, likeness, and voice. It doesn't matter whether they are a celebrity, a known talent, a paid performer, a volunteer, the girl or guy next door, your cousin, or your dearest bff. And it doesn't matter how you credit them or whether you credit them at all. Get a signed release.

A FACE IN THE CROWD

People out and about in public places normally have no reasonable expectation of privacy. So, normally, if you are filming, taking photos, or recording in a public place, and somebody drifts through your shot or appears as part of a crowd, and you don't single them out, it is generally considered okay not to get a written release from that person. But if you interview people on the street, you need to get each interviewee's permission to use him or her in your work. Either get it in writing or get it verbally in an "on camera" release, which you should keep for your files after editing your film.

The California right of publicity statute applies to still photographs, motion pictures, videotapes, or live television transmission of any person, if the person is "readily identifiable." A person is "readily identifiable" in a work when one who views the work with the naked eye can reasonably determine that the person depicted is the same person as the one who is complaining of its unauthorized use.

But if a work includes more than one person and the persons are not represented as individuals, but rather solely as members of a "definable group," it does not violate anyone's right of publicity. People are considered to be represented as a member of a definable group if they appear in the work "solely as a result of being present at the time" and have "not been singled out as individuals in any manner." The statute says a "definable group" includes, among others, the following examples: "a crowd at any sporting event, a crowd in any street or public building, the audience at any theatrical or stage production, a glee club, or a baseball team." Food for thought if you were thinking of joining a glee club.

THE ACCIDENTAL TOURIST

If you are producing a film, video, video game, or other work with a named fictional character, try your best not to name accidentally a living person who inhabits the real world in a brick-and-mortar setting resembling your fictional setting.

In productions with an adequate budget, the producer can afford a script clearance report from a specialty firm that will review the script and research character names against phone books and other databases in the vicinity in which your story takes place or is to be shot, and also research business names, locations, product names, artwork, music, and other items that might raise a privacy, publicity, copyright, trademark, or other legal conflict.

If you are on a shoestring budget, you need to make best efforts to do your own homework. Checking local phone directories online is a useful reality check, though with many people not listing, and many relying exclusively on their cell phones, opting not to have home phones at all, a phone directory is less relevant than it used to be. But a broader Internet search, turning up social network listings and whatnot, can go a long way toward avoiding a train wreck with an innocent nobody who just happens to have your character's name, live in the same city, play contrabassoon in an alternative metal band just like your character, and buy the same brand of tortilla chips.

If your character doesn't have to have a surname to tell your story, don't give the character a surname. If your character doesn't need a first name to tell your story, give them just a surname. Something like Marlow. And lose the contrabassoon.

THE CHEAPSKATE TEST

When a person's image, likeness, or voice has commercial value, because he or she is famous or just flat-out good-looking in the kind of exploitable way that helps sell sacks of flour, like Miss Abigail Marie Roberson, the right to exclude others from using the image, likeness, and voice becomes valuable. As with copyright and trademark, the flip side of the right to exclude is the right to license. Since everyone has a right to control the commercial use of his or her identity, if you come along and use it without permission, odds are someone is going to want you to pay for it. So, if you have a mind to use a person's name, image, likeness, or voice in a creative work, ask yourself these questions:

- Are you using the person's name, image, likeness, or voice to sell your artistic work or a product or service?
- Could you get the same thing by paying an actor or a model?
- Are you just too cheap to pay an actor or a model?

If the answers to these three questions are yes, then you can't use it without the person's permission. Abercrombie couldn't get away with it. Neither can you.

DON'T MIX RIGHTS

Remember not to mix up copyrights and publicity rights. They are separate rights, often owned by separate parties. Getting a license or permission from the copyright owner of a photograph, film, video, or audio clip does not give you the right to use the name, image, or voice of any person appearing in the copyrighted work. Conversely, getting a license or permission from a person whose name, image, or voice appears in a copyrighted work does not give you the right to use the copyrighted work itself.

BUYING ASHLEIGH SOMERSET

Like it or not, the commercial success of *Hispaniola* hinges on Ashleigh Somerset.

You need her permission to use her name, image, likeness, and voice to line up financing and distribution for the movie, and to publicize, promote, and advertise the finished product. In her actor's agreement, it is not enough that Quisqueya Productions extracts from her an airtight work-for-hire provision ensuring a clean chain of title for copyright. You must also get from her a clearly worded grant of the right to use her name, image, likeness, and voice as it appears on film, video, still photography, and audio recorded during the making of *Hispaniola*.

Besides, the Director of Companies is keen on having QP gin up a "Making of" program to promote *Hispaniola* while filling airtime on one of his cable channels, so you need to make that clear to Ashleigh up front and get it in writing. QP controls film publicity, and that includes exploiting her right of publicity within reasonable limits. It's part of what you're paying her for.

At the same time, you need to recognize that stars and their agents also have a vested interest, and need to have a substantial say in how you use their name, image, likeness, and voice to promote your film. Make sure her actor's agreement expressly allows QP to use still photos, film, and video clips from the shoot, whether used in the edited film or not, subject only to a limited right of approval in her favor. You should constrain her to a limited time frame of no more than a few days to accept or reject shots and clips you submit for approval, make clear that if she doesn't respond within that time frame, the material is deemed approved, and require that she accept a minimum percentage of materials submitted, so she can't paralyze the process by simply rejecting them all. Nice wording in the agreement about mutual cooperation and support in publicizing, promoting, and advertising the film for her and the film's mutual benefit will help set the right tone, and at the same time, it would be a good idea to say in her contract that on the off chance you fire her, or she walks off the set, you won't disparage her and she won't disparage QP, or the rest of the above-the-line talent, or the film.

Your right to use Ashleigh's name, image, likeness, and voice to publicize, promote, and advertise the movie as part of the deal she makes with you as lead actress does not give you the right to plaster her lovely face on product packaging for the Hispaniola doll series or the rest of your licensed junk. If you wish to deploy Ms. Somerset's formidable publicity rights in service of your movie merchandise, you will need a separate agreement with her.

In an *endorsement agreement* a celebrity licenses his or her name, image, likeness, and/or voice for use in promotion of endorsed products or services in specified media, in exchange for compensation that often consists of an annual base minimum, bonuses, or escalation of the base upon achievement of certain sales benchmarks for the brand endorsed, or royalties based on a percentage of products or services sold. Your endorsement agreement with Ashleigh will need to detail what products she is endorsing, will contain a number of other provisions analogous to those in a trademark licensing agreement, and will have to specify what, if anything, Ashleigh has to do for you in promoting your products besides letting QP use her name, image, likeness, and voice.

You would be better off negotiating this with her up front, at the time you negotiate her actor's agreement with its merchandise participation, and make sure QP gets an express right to sublicense it to its various authorized *Hispaniola* trademark licensees whom you plan to enlist to churn out and market the dolls, the video games, and so on. Author Bonnie Charlotte may need a piece of Ashleigh too, to promote her book series, so you had better sort that out up front as well, because it also affects QP's bottom line.

Ordinary People

Below-the-line talent has rights of privacy and publicity too. In every production the stars and directors, who negotiate big salaries far in excess of any guild or union pay scales, and possibly including profit-sharing, are referred to as above-the-line talent. Below-the-line talent do the bulk of the work on the film and include everyone else, from gaffers to sound engineers to makeup artists and background actors. All of these people also have rights of publicity—they just aren't worth very much. But just because you don't have to pay a person to give up their rights doesn't mean you don't need to make the person give them up. In your contracts with all below-the-line talent, you need clear written permission, without additional compensation, to use their names, images, likenesses, and voices, as well as a waiver of any privacy or publicity right claim they might otherwise have. Most of these worker bees will be tickled pink to see their bright shining faces pop up in "The Making of Hispaniola" and can be counted on to tell all their friends to tune in.

Life Story Rights

Behind "The Making of Hispaniola" lies a very personal backstory: Bonnie Charlotte, teenage daughter of a blacklisted screenwriter, makes good as a novelist, then throws herself into a four-decade teaching career with a dedication that would make Mr. Holland and his opus blush, then makes an against-all-odds twenty-first-century comeback when the box office success of *Hispaniola* the movie delivers CPR to the drowning girl-pirate-novel genre.

That is why, in your option and purchase agreement with Bonnie, you had the foresight to pick up her "life story rights" for the purpose of producing "The Making of Hispaniola." There is no fixed legal definition of the term *life story rights*, but agreements to option them, typically granted to a production company in return for a modest option payment, to be credited to a more substantial purchase price if the option is exercised, normally cover rights of privacy and publicity as well as defamation, granting the producer the right to portray the person and his or her life, exploits, personal experiences, and biographical incidents in a film or television production. The person granting the life story rights usually agrees to cooperate in providing additional information and materials and in helping obtain releases from relatives, friends, and others who are part of his or her life story. With Bonnie, while you were at it, you got her to option QP the right to make a film or a made-for-TV biopic about her, an option that put another smile on the Director of Companies' face. Two guesses who Mom is going to insist be attached as screenwriter, when the time comes to exercise that option.

Come to think of it, you're a pretty fascinating part of the *Hispaniola* backstory too.

Guard your life story rights as if your life depended on them.

And your rights of privacy and publicity in whatever deals you strike.

Because Emily Dickinson warned you.

FURTHER READING

PRACTICAL GUIDES

For additional guidance in drafting your own release forms and life story rights agreements, the best print resource is Michael C. Donaldson's *Clearance and Copyright: Everything You Need to Know for Film and Television,* 3rd ed. (Los Angeles: Silman-James Press, 2008), 231–257. Donaldson nicely weaves hints and comments throughout the sample agreements. Unlike several other books on the market that simply provide the boilerplate of contracts, Donaldson highlights the critical passages, points out other areas you can tailor to your needs, and encourages you to reflect on the agreement you are drafting.

LEGAL HISTORY AND THEORY

Privacy and publicity lawsuits raise many fascinating questions about who controls the image of celebrities—the individual, the estate, corporations, or the public? Many of the lawsuits discussed briefly here have received extensive scrutiny by other writers. For *Haelan Laboratories v. Topps Chewing Gum,* 202 F.2d 866 (2d Cir. 1953), see Melville B. Nimmer's still incisive "Right of Publicity," *Law and Contemporary Problems* 19, no. 2 (1954): 203–223.

For a terrific analysis of *Lugosi v. Universal Pictures,* 603 P.2d 425 (Cal. 1979), see Jane M. Gaines, *Contested Culture: The Image, the Voice, and the Law* (Chapel Hill: University of North Carolina Press, 1991). Peter L. Felcher and Edward L. Rubin, "The Descendibility of the Right of Publicity: Is There Commercial Life After Death?" *The Yale Law Journal* 89, no. 6 (1980): 1125–1132, more broadly considers the questions surrounding estates and publicity rights.

Alicia M. Hunt, "Everyone Wants to Be a Star: Extensive Publicity Rights for Noncelebrities Unduly Restrict Commercial Speech," *Northwestern University Law Review* 95 (2001): 1605–1659, examines the implications of expanded publicity rights for commercial speech and addresses *Dora v. Frontline Video, Inc.,* 18 Cal. Rptr. 2d 790 (Cal. Ct. App. 1993), and *ETW Corp. v. Jireh Publishing, Inc.,* 99 F. Supp. 2d 829 (N.D. Ohio 2000).

For more on publicity rights and free speech, see Eugene Volokh, "Freedom of Speech and the Right of Publicity," *Houston Law Review* 40 (2003):

903–930, which also analyzes *Comedy III Prods., Inc. v. Gary Saderup, Inc.*, 21 P.3d 797 (Cal. 2001).

Downing v. Abercrombie and Fitch, 265 F.3d 994 (9th Cir. 2001) is profiled by Erin C. Hansen in "The Right of Publicity Expands into Hallowed Ground: Downing v. Abercrombie and Fitch and the Preemption Power of the Copyright Act," *UMKC Law Review* 71 (2002): 171–192.

Although the parties settled the Arnold Schwarzenegger bobblehead skirmish out of court, William T. Gallagher provides an overview of the issues at stake in "Strategic Intellectual Property Litigation, the Right of Publicity, and the Attenuation of Free Speech: Lessons from the Schwarzenegger Bobblehead War (and Peace)," *Santa Clara Law Review* 45 (2005): 581–615.

Jim Brown lost his lawsuit against Electronic Arts, but use of the likenesses of actors and athletes in video games continues to be a contested issue in courtrooms, union negotiations, talent deals, and law reviews. The publicity rights of unpaid college athletes have generated particular scrutiny—see Beth A. Cianfrone and Thomas A. Baker III, "The Use of Student-Athlete Likenesses in Sport Video Games: An Application of the Right of Publicity," *Journal of Legal Aspects of Sport* 20 (2010): 35–68. For coverage of SAG and AFTRA's negotiations with video game publishers for voice residuals, see Richard Verrier and Ben Fritz, "Video Game Voice Actors Worry They're Getting Shortchanged," *Los Angeles Times*, December 7, 2009, http://articles.latimes.com/2009/dec/07/business/la-fi-ct-actors7-2009dec07, accessed October 30, 2010.

Finally, you can always return to that classic law review article, without which this chapter and the aforementioned publications might not exist: Samuel Warren and Louis Brandeis, "Right to Privacy," *Harvard Law Review* 4, no. 5 (1890): 193–216.

CHAPTER **6**

Internet and New Media

> Inside the flat a fruity voice was reading out a list of figures which had something to do with the production of pig-iron. The voice came from an oblong metal plaque like a dulled mirror which formed part of the surface of the right-hand wall. Winston turned a switch and the voice sank somewhat, though the words were still distinguishable. The instrument (the telescreen, it was called) could be dimmed, but there was no way of shutting it off completely.
>
> —*Nineteen Eighty-Four,* by George Orwell

In 1984, Microsoft's MS-DOS 3.0 upgraded MS-DOS 2.0, the 3.5-inch floppy diskette debuted, Hitachi sold the first 1 MB chip, Dell Computer was launched, author William Gibson coined the term "cyberspace" and used it in his cyberpunk novel *Neuromancer,* USC School of Engineering student Fred Cohen coined the term "computer virus" and showed how to write one, *Beverly Hills Cop* and *Ghostbusters* were tops at the box office, Dire Straits recorded *Brothers in Arms,* the first CD album to sell a million copies, Megadeth recorded its demo tape, *1984 Demo,* Apple's Macintosh kicked off with a Super Bowl ad entitled "1984," directed by up-and-coming filmmaker Ridley Scott, Bill Gates made the cover of *Time* magazine, and Facebook founder Mark Zuckerberg was born. Also born in 1984 were the first five top-level Internet domains, in a memorandum discreetly titled "Request for Comments: 920."

Writing in 1949, George Orwell didn't get New Media completely right.

But he got one thing absolutely right: there's no way of shutting it off completely.

"Request for Comments: 920" was issued under the auspices of the Defense Advanced Research Projects Agency (the U.S. Department of Defense's R&D office) and the Internet Advisory Board (now the Internet Architecture Board). It created the .mil and .edu domains, reflecting the military-academic collaboration in the 1960s and '70s that had built the Internet's backbone, the ARPANET (Advanced Research Projects Agency Network). It created the .gov domain, reflecting Big Brother's gentle guiding hand in the process. It threw nonprofits a bone with the .org domain. And it signaled loud and clear that the Net was open for business with the .com domain.

Today's laptops, notebooks, and smartphones aren't Big Brother's telescreen. Instead of one monolithic agenda and a single top-down message, there are millions of agendas and billions of scattershot messages streaming through the ether. In the creative industries, the Internet and its wonderful world of e-commerce, coupled with the mass proliferation of digital media, devices, and apps it has spawned, have caused seismic shifts in the way the players with a stake in the game think about copyright, trademark, publicity rights, and contracts.

COPYRIGHT MEETS THE INTERNET

Ever since the Copyright Act of 1790, Congress has had to overhaul the statute once a generation or so to play catch-up with new media. When the World Wide Web evolved in the 1990s into a content-rich school, playground, and marketplace, and the PC or Mac became as obligatory a fixture in middle-class American households as Big Brother's telescreen in Winston Smith's wee seedy crib, it was inevitable that Congress, prodded by entertainment and software companies on the one hand and Internet service providers on the other, would have to step up and amend the Copyright Act yet again. It was inevitable too that Big Business and Big Think would come to blows over copyright and the Internet.

INTERNET ANGELS AND DEMONS

The battle between Hollywood and the digerati over copyright in digital media resembles the fictional clash over religion versus science between the Catholic Church and the Illuminati in Ron Howard's *Angels and Demons*, based on the Dan Brown page-turner. Ordinary Web-surfing souls can feel at times as caught in the digital crossfire as Tom Hanks dodging bullets in ill-lit Vatican chapels in the dead of night. Every self-respecting media giant from Viacom to YouTube and every think tank from Harvard's Berkman Center for Internet and Society to the Electronic Rights Foundation has a dog in this fight.

THE SWORD AND THE SHIELD

Congress took a stab in 1998 at mediating the tension between entertainment companies adamant to protect their lucrative copyrights and Internet service providers trying to earn an honest buck in the dot-com boom by enacting what it dubbed, with typical congressional hyperbole, the Digital Millennium Copyright Act (DMCA).

It was a great if not a grand compromise. The studios, in a lobbying offensive spearheaded by the Motion Picture Association of America, wanted to protect their copyrights from wholesale infringement on the Web, and so did the software companies. They fought for an anti-circumvention rule to prevent consumers from bypassing copy-protection schemes. Internet service providers, hosting companies, and interactive sites, on the other hand, were angling for immunity from liability for the IP violations of their users. As the quid pro quo for their support of the anti-circumvention rule, they sought safe-harbor provisions sheltering them. The DMCA, a part of the Copyright Act, implemented the lobbyists' bargain by handing copyright owners a very big sword, and Internet service providers a very big shield.

Circumvent This

The DMCA sword is an anti-circumvention provision forbidding anyone to "circumvent a technological measure that effectively controls access" to a work protected under the Copyright Act. The DMCA criminalizes production and dissemination of technology, devices, or services intended to circumvent digital rights management (DRM) measures that control access to copyrighted works. It also criminalizes the act of circumventing DRM measures, whether or not there is actual infringement of anyone's copyright.

The DMCA makes it a crime to circumvent anti-piracy measures built into most commercial software, except for innocent purposes such as computer repair, computer security system testing and research, and limited exemptions for nonprofit libraries, archives, and educational institutions. It outlaws the manufacture, sale, or distribution of code-cracking devices used to illegally copy software. When it was enacted, the anti-circumvention rule was credited with paving the way for film studios' commercialization of DVD technology, then in its infancy, because it gave the studios a nice warm security blanket to calm their jitters about releasing first-run movies on a disc that could be copied an unlimited number of times with ease. At least their digital rights management software could not legally be sidestepped. Of course, reality is another matter. DVD-ripping tools and other circumvention devices and software, legal only in the limited educational exemptions mentioned above, are casually available on the Internet and widely used.

Giving the First Amendment the customary nod in order to avoid constitutional challenge, Congress installed a crack of daylight in the anti-circumvention rule. The DMCA states that nothing in it affects rights, remedies, limitations, or defenses to copyright infringement, including fair use. This means that, at least in principle, the fair use defense to copyright infringement remains alive and well on the Internet.

Under the DMCA, the Librarian of Congress—who, as the name suggests, runs the Library of Congress, but is also the Copyright Office's overlord—is supposed to review the anti-circumvention measures every three years and carve out specific exceptions that make sense in terms of fair use. This special administrative procedure has so far produced only a small batch of exceptions.

For instance, the librarian gave film schools a gold star in 2006, excepting from the anti-circumvention regime audiovisual works included in the educational library of a college or university's film or media studies department, when circumvention is done for the purpose of making compilations of portions of the works for educational use in the classroom by media studies or film professors. And for techies and gamers, the librarian excepted computer programs and video games distributed in formats that have become technically or commercially obsolete and that require the original media or hardware as a condition of access, when circumvention is accomplished for the purpose of preservation or archival reproduction of published digital works by a library or archive.

Most recently, in the summer of 2010, the librarian granted an exemption at the Electronic Frontier Foundation's request for "jailbreaking" an iPhone. Apple had argued that copyright law precludes users from installing unapproved programs on its iPhones, but the librarian determined that when you jailbreak a smartphone in order to make the operating system on the phone interoperable with an independently created application that has not been approved by the maker of the smartphone or the maker of the operating system, modifications made purely for the purpose of such interoperability are fair uses.

Meanwhile, in federal court, the DMCA has fostered several epic clashes between Internet angels and demons. The Motion Picture Association of America slaughtered RealNetworks in San Francisco district court in 2009 in *RealNetworks v. DVD-CCA*, when the court enjoined RealNetworks from selling its RealDVD software, which enabled users to copy DVDs and store them on a computer hard drive. The MPAA argued that RealNetworks violated the DMCA by circumventing anti-piracy measures the studios had embedded in their film DVDs precisely to prevent ripping. RealNetworks has appealed to the Ninth Circuit Court of Appeals to lift the injunction, arguing that the trial court applied an incorrect legal standard in that it was wrong to presume RealDVD would cause the film industry irreparable harm, and that the court failed to consider the public interest. The Electronic Frontier Foundation argues that the major movie studios used the suit against RealNetworks to thwart innovation. In addition to the RealDVD copying software, RealNetworks had been planning to roll out a prototype DVD player that would copy DVDs and store movies on a hard drive, and the studios certainly wanted to nip that in the bud. The studios contend they are only protecting their films from those seeking to profit from the creation of piracy tools.

Shake Down, Break Down, Take Down

The DMCA shield is a "safe harbor" insulating "intermediaries" such as Internet service providers and other online service providers against claims based on copyright infringements committed by the providers' users. Immunity is strictly conditioned, however, on the intermediary following a "takedown notice" procedure set up by the statute.

If the intermediary receives a takedown notice from a copyright owner complaining that content posted by an end user and stored on its server or displayed on its site infringes its copyright, the intermediary must promptly remove the complained-of material from the server it hosts or the Web site it operates. The intermediary must do so without evaluating the merits of the claim, because the DMCA took intermediaries out of the business of refereeing infringement beefs. If the intermediary does not abide by the notice, it loses its immunity and exposes itself to copyright liability. The intermediary can restore the content only if the end user comes back with a counternotification certifying that the content is noninfringing, and the copyright claimant thereafter fails to sue.

The DMCA has come under fire from freedom of expression advocates for making it too easy for copyright claimants to bully Web site operators into taking down allegedly infringing content that may in fact not infringe. When Web site operators receive a takedown notice, it is in their normal self-interest not to challenge it, even when the infringement claim is dubious, because there is no legal downside to blindly obeying a take-down notice.

Criticized by the digerati on the one hand for its chilling effect, the take-down notice regime on the other hand arguably helped foster search engines, e-commerce sites, social networking, and user-generated content sites. Google, Inc., was founded a month before enactment of the DMCA, anticipating the safe harbor, and the company acknowledges the DMCA's role in its success. YouTube, MySpace, Facebook, and Twitter didn't exist in 1998. Without the safe harbor they arguably would never have gotten off the ground. A dozen years after enactment of the DMCA and the ensuing explosion of social media, the spectacle of congressmen in their sixties feverishly tweeting their constituent fan base during the 2010 midterm elections simply boggled the mind.

Read the terms and conditions of any user-generated content or interactive Web site, and odds are you will find policies, terms, and conditions tailor-made to put its operator squarely inside the safe harbor, where it makes business sense to be. For instance, Linden Lab's Second Life is a place to "be yourself, free yourself," in the Internet's largest user-created 3D virtual world community, but the Second Life terms of service (http://secondlife.com/corporate/tos.php) make quite clear that:

> 4.4 If properly notified, Linden Lab responds to complaints that User Content infringes another's intellectual property.
>
> Intellectual property infringement on the Service is a violation of this Terms of Service, and you agree not to engage in such infringement. It is our policy to respond to notices of alleged copyright infringement that comply with the Digital Millennium Copyright Act and to terminate the accounts of repeat infringers in appropriate circumstances. We operate an intellectual property complaint process for complaints that User Content infringes another's intellectual property, the details of which are available in our Intellectual Property Policy. Linden Lab reserves the right to disable, delete or terminate, without notice, any user's Content or access to the Service if that user is determined by Linden Lab to infringe or repeatedly infringe.

Visit Second Life's DMCA page (http://secondlife.com/corporate/dmca.php), and you will find that:

> Linden Lab will respond to allegations of copyright violations in accordance with the Digital Millennium Copyright Act (DMCA). The DMCA provides a process for a copyright owner to give notification to an online service provider concerning

alleged copyright infringement. When a valid DMCA notification is received, the service provider responds under this process by taking down the offending content. On taking down content under the DMCA, we will take reasonable steps to contact the owner of the removed content so that a counter-notification may be filed. On receiving a valid counter-notification, we generally restore the content in question, unless we receive notice from the notification provider that a legal action has been filed seeking a court order to restrain the alleged infringer from engaging in the infringing activity.

Just in case you get a bit too wrapped up in your avatar to distinguish which way is up anymore, Linden Lab, Inc., goes on to point the way:

Please note that these notifications and counter-notifications are real-world legal notices provided outside of the Second Life environment.

And in case you and your avatar still didn't get the message, Second Life's DMCA FAQs helpfully explain:

How does Linden Lab determine who "wins" and "loses"?
Linden Lab does not adjudicate the substance of the copyright claim: we do not declare winners and losers. Your copyright in an item is determined in the real world, by real-world processes including the DMCA. The DMCA process allows users of an online service to resolve copyright disputes using the adjudication systems available in the real world.

. . . and speaking of adjudication systems available in the real world, for a real dose of reality you and your avatar should try the U.S. District Court for the Southern District of New York.

That is where Viacom initiated a full-frontal assault on YouTube's DMCA safe harbor in 2007. After shotgunning the video-sharing site with over a hundred thousand takedown notices regarding Viacom-owned programs spotted on YouTube, the TV and film conglomerate sued YouTube and its parent company Google in *Viacom International Inc. et al. v. YouTube, Inc. et al.*, seeking a billion dollars in damages.

Viacom argued that YouTube should be liable for contributory copyright infringement because of its knowledge of, and apparent willful blindness to, pervasive copyright infringement by the video site's users. Viacom alleged that some of these users frequently upload copyrighted shows, hurting Viacom's revenues while boosting ad revenue gain for YouTube, and asserted that the site allowed and even encouraged infringement, pointing to internal YouTube e-mails to suggest that managers and employees knew full well about the prevalence of unauthorized content uploads on their site.

YouTube countered that since it followed the DMCA takedown notice procedure when Viacom notified it, the safe harbor rendered the company bulletproof. Aside from abiding by the takedown notice procedure, the safe harbor also requires online service providers to implement a policy to terminate users who become "repeat infringers," and to inform users of the policy. YouTube had wisely crafted and implemented a "three strikes" law for users, under which it terminates a user after three incidents of apparent infringement.

In the summer of 2010, the district court granted summary judgment in YouTube's favor, ruling that an online service provider's generalized knowledge of copyright infringement on its site, even knowledge of prevalent infringing activity, is not enough to destroy its DMCA safe harbor. The court underscored Congress's legislative rationale for enacting the DMCA, to limit the liability of service providers and thereby ensure that the efficiency of the Internet will continue to improve and that the variety and quality of services on the Internet will continue to expand. Rejecting Viacom's arguments, the court held that the safe harbor is available unless the service provider has actual knowledge of specific and identifiable infringement, and then fails to act expeditiously to remove or disable access to the infringing user-provided content.

Viacom tried to analogize YouTube's serving of uploaded infringing content to peer-to-peer file-sharing networks. The U.S. Supreme Court addressed such networks in 2005 in *MGM Studios Inc. v. Grokster,* a landmark decision in which the Court held that one who distributes a device with the object of promoting its use to infringe copyright is liable for the resulting acts of infringement by third parties. But in *Viacom v. YouTube,* the Court decided that *Grokster* and other peer-to-peer cases have little application to online service providers such as YouTube, because peer-to-peer file-sharing networks are not covered by the DMCA safe-harbor provisions. Differentiating Grokster from YouTube, the Court noted that whereas peer-to-peer networks exist for the near-exclusive purpose of violating copyrights, service providers such as YouTube have numerous other, non-infringing purposes and uses.

The moral of the story—unless the ruling gets overturned on appeal—is that copyright owners, not online service providers, bear the burden of policing for infringements. If a service provider receives from a copyright owner a takedown notice identifying an alleged specific infringement, the provider must promptly remove the allegedly infringing material or else lose the safe harbor. But the DMCA does not impose on the service provider any monitoring or removal requirement if the service provider simply has general knowledge that infringement is widespread, or even rampant.

Viacom's appeal to the Second Circuit Court of Appeals is currently pending. Hopping on the bandwagon, and consolidated with the Viacom case, shortly after Viacom sued YouTube, England's most prestigious soccer league dogpiled in a copyright infringement class action, *The Football Association Premier League Limited et al. v. YouTube, Inc. et al.*, joined by the Ligue de Football Professionnel, the governing body for the major French soccer leagues, the Fédération Française de Tennis, organizers of the French Open, and two U.S. music publishers to boot. Like Viacom, they accuse YouTube of allowing users to upload and distribute media in violation of the plaintiffs' copyrights.

As we said, everyone has a dog in this fight. Bob Seger may have put it best at the dawn of the dot-com age in his hit single "Shakedown" from the *Beverly Hills Cop II* (1987) soundtrack (and, yeah, last time we looked, you could hear it on YouTube):

> *Shake down, break down, take down*
> *Everybody wants into the crowded line.*

TRADEMARKS TRAFFIC THE INTERNET

The fact that Web sites can feature information and other content about brands, sponsored or not, flattering or not, can promote and sell branded products and services via e-commerce, and can have domain names which may be the same as or similar to a brand name or company name has made trademark owners, large and small, excited about the opportunities the Internet creates, but anxious about the risks and dangers the Internet presents. The same goes for celebrities.

Legal developments addressing such anxieties affect creative artists distributing content online in two principal ways. First, statutes and legal mechanisms designed to mediate conflict between a trademark owner or celebrity, on the one hand, and the registrant of a domain name that is identical or arguably confusingly similar to a trademark or celebrity name, nickname, or associated slogan, on the other, mean that any creative artist planning to launch or collaborating on a Web site showcasing content needs to take care in the selection and use of an appropriate domain name, much as you conducted trademark availability searches in Chapter 2 for the portfolio of trademarks that became the Hispaniola brand, to avoid a potential conflict that could result in your having to change your domain name after launch. Second, evolving case law in the area of contributory trademark infringement, which has thus far tilted in the direction of insulating online service providers in a way roughly comparable to the DMCA safe harbor discussed above, means that any creative artist posting content that incorporates trademarks or celebrity names, images, or likenesses to a user-generated content site can expect that the online service provider, if faced with a takedown notice from the trademark owner or celebrity, is going to yank your content, even if your trademark or celebrity references clearly constitute fair use, so that the trademark owner or celebrity will tend to have de facto veto power over your work, unless you are in a position to put up a fight.

SHADY CHARACTERS IN CYBERSPACE

Fast on the heels of the copyright lobby's victory lap after scoring the Digital Millennium Copyright Act, trademark owners clamored for a Digi-Act of Congress to call their own. They had a particular ax to grind with that dodgy species of bad actor known as the cybersquatter, who registers a domain name containing a trademark with no intent of launching a legitimate Web site, angling to sell the domain name to the trademark's owner or, in the owner's worst nightmare, the highest bidder.

Congress responded in 1999 with the Anticybersquatting Consumer Protection Act (ACPA), an add-on to the Trademark Act, enabling a trademark owner to sue anyone who, with a bad-faith intent to profit, registers, traffics in, or uses a domain name that is identical or confusingly similar to a distinctive mark, is dilutive of a famous mark, or is a specially protected trademark, word, or name of the Red Cross or the International or U.S. Olympic Committees. "Trafficking" here means any sort of transaction for money that you can imagine.

To determine whether a domain name registrant has a bad-faith intent to profit, courts may consider many factors, including these nine outlined in the statute:

- the registrant's valid trademark or other IP rights in the domain name
- whether the domain name contains the registrant's legal or common name
- the registrant's prior use of the domain name in bona fide offering of goods or services

- the registrant's bona fide noncommercial or fair use of the trademark in a site accessible by the domain name
- the registrant's intent to divert customers from the trademark owner's online location that could harm the goodwill represented by the mark, for commercial gain or with the intent to tarnish or disparage the mark
- the registrant offering to transfer, sell, or otherwise assign the domain name to the mark owner or a third party for financial gain, without having used the mark in a legitimate site
- the registrant's providing misleading false contact information when applying for registration of the domain name
- the registrant's registration or acquisition of multiple domain names that are identical or confusingly similar to marks of others
- the extent to which the trademark is distinctive or famous.

Tossing the First Amendment the usual bone, the ACPA says that bad-faith intent shall not be found in any case where a court determines that the domain name registrant believed, and had reasonable grounds to believe, that the use of the domain name was fair use or otherwise lawful. This is meant to allow things such as gripe sites, if done in good faith. If you sincerely hate Brand W, go ahead and register the domain name www.brandwsucks.com, and complain as much as you like. But don't use it as a pretext to hold Brand W up for the big bucks.

DOMAIN NAMES OF THE RICH AND FAMOUS

Many trademark owners and celebrities prefer not to track down and chase a cybersquatter through federal court for money damages of dubious collectibility, when what they really want is to retrieve a domain name. Instead of suing under the ACPA, they can pursue a streamlined process under the Uniform Domain Name Dispute Resolution Policy (UDRP).

The UDRP was established in 2000 by ICANN, the Internet Corporation for Assigned Names and Numbers, a nonprofit corporation that manages the assignment of domain names and IP addresses. It allows aggrieved trademark owners, celebrities, and other individuals to challenge bad-faith domain name registrations in an expedited arbitration proceeding to compel transfer of the domain name that is far less costly than court litigation.

Any domain name registrar worth its salt is accredited by ICANN. All accredited registrars authorized to register names in the generic top-level domains, or country code top-level domains that have signed up to the UDRP, must agree to abide by the UDRP. In turn, anyone who registers a domain name in one of these domains must consent that disputes over the domain name may be resolved under the UDRP.

ICANN has issued procedural rules governing UDRP cases, and has accredited a list of dispute resolution service providers empowered to decide cases, the best known of these being the WIPO Arbitration and Mediation Center based in Geneva, Switzerland. The fees charged by dispute resolution service providers to handle a case range from around a thousand to several thousand dollars, depending on the number of arbitrators appointed.

A UDRP case starts with the complainant filing a complaint with a dispute resolution service provider chosen by it, and footing the bill for the provider's fees. The provider then notifies the domain name registrant about the case, and the registrant has twenty days to respond. Failure to respond on time is treated as a default. Of course, when the registrant is the typical cybersquatter who wishes to stay under the radar, default is common. A panel of one or three arbitrators is appointed to decide the dispute; it considers the evidence, usually submitted electronically, and makes a decision. If the decision is that the domain name in question should be canceled or transferred, the panel orders the domain name registrar to do so. The panel cannot order either side to pay money damages.

To win, the complainant must establish that the domain name is identical or confusingly similar to a trademark in which the complainant has rights, that the registrant does not have any right or legitimate interest in the domain name, and that the registrant registered the domain name and is using it in "bad faith."

If either party is unhappy with a UDRP decision, it can challenge the decision in court. A complainant losing a UDRP proceeding can then bring a lawsuit against the domain name registrant in federal court invoking the ACPA. A domain name registrant losing a UDRP proceeding must either throw in the towel or file suit against the complainant within ten days to prevent the ICANN-accredited registrar from transferring or canceling the domain name.

In addition to its use to retrieve domain names for well-known brands, the UDRP has been used in numerous high-profile celebrity domain name cases. The celebrity usually wins.

For instance, a WIPO arbitration panel ruled in favor of Jay Leno in 2009 in his UDRP action to recover *thejaylenoshow.com* from a cybersquatter. *Leno v. Zambrano* pitted the popular NBC talk show host against a Texas real estate agent who had registered the domain name in 2004 and used it to redirect visitors to his real estate Web site. Because the UDRP rules do not specifically talk about rights of publicity, a celebrity complainant will either show ownership of his or her name as a registered trademark or argue common law trademark rights, which is what Leno did.

When the cybersquatter originally grabbed this domain name, Leno was the host of *The Tonight Show*. When NBC plugged Leno into prime time on *The Jay Leno Show* in 2009, *thejaylenoshow.com* suddenly became a must-have domain name for the network. Never mind that when NBC swapped Leno back into late night in 2010, the show morphed into *The Tonight Show with Jay Leno*. Leno won *thejaylenoshow.com* fair and square in his WIPO proceeding. All NBC had to do then, as it got set to launch *The Tonight Show with Jay Leno*, was to go retrieve *thetonightshow.com* and *thetonightshowwithjayleno.com* from enterprising domainers who had registered them and were basking in the reflected glory of Leno's footlights, and to decide once and for all what time it wants Leno to clock in for work.

BREAKFAST AT TIFFANY'S

One used to have to go down to Fifth Avenue early in the morning and moon around like Audrey Hepburn outside the display windows of Tiffany and Company to be able to admire genuine TIFFANY® jewelry in quiet. But nowadays you can simply surf the Web over breakfast in the privacy of your own home, munching Kellogg's® Pop-Tarts® and sipping Starbucks VIA® Ready Brew, while admiring the handiwork of America's most famous jewelers. The company has a perfectly gorgeous Web site at www.tiffany.com. But, yikes, this is expensive stuff. As long as you're online, you may as well do a bit of bargain hunting. See if you can get a deal on eBay. But wait a second. How do you know whether the TIFFANY® jewelry a given seller on eBay is putting up for auction is genuine or fake?

Tiffany and Company realized that a lot of supposed Tiffany items offered on eBay were counterfeit, and took eBay to court in 2004. Tiffany argued that eBay was quite aware that a large percentage of the products advertised on the site as Tiffany items were not the real deal, because Tiffany had sent eBay scads of notices of claimed infringement under eBay's Verified Rights Owner (VeRO) program. eBay had also received complaints from customers about counterfeit Tiffany goods they had innocently purchased online.

In response, eBay removed offending listings, suspended some sellers, and implemented some technical anti-fraud measures. Still, though, there remained a lot of Tiffany counterfeits on eBay. Tiffany charged, among other things, that eBay should be liable for contributory trademark infringement for facilitating and profiting from the counterfeit sales. Nevertheless, the U.S. District Court for the Southern District of New York ruled in eBay's favor, and the Court of Appeals for the Second Circuit upheld the district court's ruling in the spring of 2010 in *Tiffany (NJ) Inc. v. eBay, Inc.*

Back in the good old brick-and-mortar days of 1982, the U.S. Supreme Court in *Inwood Labs v. Ives Labs* had created a test for contributory trademark infringement that it applied to product manufacturers and distributors. It said that if a manufacturer or distributor intentionally induced another party to infringe a trademark, or if it continued to supply its product to a party it knew or had reason to know was engaging in trademark infringement, then the manufacturer or distributor was liable for contributing to the infringement. The Court of Appeals in *Tiffany v. eBay*, as the first appellate court to consider contributory trademark infringement in the online marketplace, decided to extend the *Inwood* test to online service providers. It ruled that a service provider should be held contributorially liable for trademark infringement if it either intentionally induces another to infringe a trademark, or if it continues to supply its service to a party it knows or has reason to know is engaging in trademark infringement.

As applied to eBay, the key question was whether the site had continued to supply its online auction services to sellers it knew or had reason to know were selling counterfeit Tiffany goods. When Tiffany alerted eBay to specific infringements, eBay acted promptly and removed the listings. Under its VeRO program, eBay removed allegedly infringing listings within twenty-four hours of receiving a complaining notice. Tiffany argued that eBay should nevertheless be liable because it knew that sales of counterfeit Tiffany merchandise on eBay were widespread.

The Second Circuit, however, upheld the district court ruling that a generalized knowledge of trademark infringement does not amount to contributory infringement. A service provider must have more than a general knowledge or reason to know its service is being used to sell counterfeit goods. To be held liable, eBay would have had to have knowledge of specific sellers posting fraudulent listings, and thereafter fail to act. Because eBay's practice was to promptly remove challenged listings upon receiving notice, the Court of Appeals affirmed that Tiffany had failed to demonstrate that eBay was supplying its service to sellers it knew or had reason to know were selling counterfeit Tiffany goods.

The moral of the story—unless the ruling gets overturned on further appeal to the U.S. Supreme Court—is that trademark owners, not online service providers, bear the burden of policing for infringements. Under *Tiffany v. eBay,* an online service provider will be liable for contributing to trademark infringement only when it continues to service a specific user that it knows, or has reason to know, is infringing trademark. This result, based on case law precedent, resembles the result reached in *Viacom v. YouTube* discussed above, applying the statutory DMCA to copyright infringement, and in fact the district court in *Viacom v. YouTube* expressly acknowledged that the Second Circuit ruling in *Tiffany v. eBay* a few months earlier influenced its decision.

In much the same way that YouTube responded promptly when Viacom sent it copyright infringement takedown notices, eBay under then CEO Meg Whitman acted promptly and removed listings when Tiffany notified it of specific trademark infringements, and that is what saved both online giants . . . for the time being at least. In the summer of 2010, Tiffany filed a petition for a writ of certiorari, asking the U.S. Supreme Court to accept an appeal of *Tiffany v. eBay,* making the point that a lot has changed since the Supreme Court last looked at contributory trademark infringement, in 1982, when dot-coms didn't exist and Jerry Brown was governor of California for his first couple of terms in office.

Although *Tiffany v. eBay* concerned counterfeiting, its logic can be applied to other types of trademark infringement as well. The Second Circuit ruled that a generalized knowledge of trademark infringement does not amount to contributory infringement, and that a service provider must have more than a general knowledge or reason to know its service is being used to infringe trademarks. If an online service provider receives notice from a disgruntled trademark owner that content posted by a user infringes its trademark, the only prudent thing for the service provider to do is to promptly remove the challenged content, since not to act would put the service provider at risk. Thus, if a creative artist uses in a work a trademark (for instance, on any product that happens to appear in a film, or in a cartoon that parodies the trademark), and then uploads the work to a user-generated content site, he or she cannot expect the online service provider to defend the work if the trademark owner, rightly or wrongly, complains. Even if the trademark use is fair use, you can expect the work to be removed from the site, unless you are prepared to go to the mat with the trademark owner.

TERMS AND CONDITIONS PERMEATE THE INTERNET

Watch out.

Operators of social networking and user-generated-content sites change their terms of service from time to time, in furtherance of their business models and in pursuit of the content streams and revenue streams that feed them. They don't normally make a big fanfare about it when they do, and they sometimes try to slide changes quietly under the table, a tactic that occasionally backfires in controversies swirling around ownership of user-generated content, user privacy, and operator exploitation of private data for commercial gain.

For instance, Facebook had to beat a retreat in early 2009 from a change in its terms of use, when users protested it was claiming ownership of photos and other materials posted to the site. Facebook denied having such an intention, but it yanked the protested change of terms. Then in late 2009, Facebook caught flak when it changed its privacy policy in tandem with its rollout of new privacy settings. The change made certain information, including lists of friends, publicly available. Users who had set their list of friends as private were forced without notice to go public, sparking an outcry from digital rights advocates like the Electronic Frontier Foundation, and making Iranian dissidents scatter for cover, deleting Facebook accounts so their contacts could not be hounded by Ahmadinejad's goons. Yet again, in the fall of 2010, it emerged that many popular Facebook apps, such as FarmVille, had been transmitting users' Facebook ID numbers to dozens of advertising and Internet tracking companies, including IDs of users who set all their information to be private. Facebook acted right away to disable the offending apps and announced it would introduce new technology to address such privacy breaches, but it left another big question mark hanging over privacy on the site.

Facebook is not (yet) Big Brother. Up to a point, Facebook doesn't have much alternative except to listen to its users, since the site itself provides them with the social networking tools that facilitate their protests on any subject, including against Facebook itself. As pressure from shareholders mounts, however, Facebook may come to ignore such protests in favor of bringing in cash from advertisers and others in a position to pay to mine the vast amounts of data it accumulates.

As a creative artist tempted from time to time to post your work online, you should read the terms of use or comparable boilerplate of any Web site you may consider using as a vehicle to share your art, make sure they're not pulling a fast one on you at the outset, and be alert to changes in terms of service that try to pull a fast one down the road.

Here's what Facebook had to say about intellectual property rights in your content and sharing your information, when we last looked.

2. Sharing Your Content and Information

You own all of the content and information you post on Facebook, and you can control how it is shared through your privacy and application settings. In addition:

1. For content that is covered by intellectual property rights, like photos and videos ("IP content"), you specifically give us the following permission, subject to your privacy and application settings: you grant us a non-exclusive, transferable, sub-licensable, royalty-free, worldwide license to use any IP content that you post on or in connection with Facebook ("IP License"). This IP License ends when you delete your IP content or your account unless your content has been shared with others, and they have not deleted it.

2. When you delete IP content, it is deleted in a manner similar to emptying the recycle bin on a computer. However, you understand that removed content may persist in backup copies for a reasonable period of time (but will not be available to others).

3. When you use an application, your content and information is shared with the application. We require applications to respect your privacy, and your agreement with that application will control how the application can use, store, and transfer that content and information. (To learn more about Platform, read our Privacy Policy and About Platform page.)

4. When you publish content or information using the "everyone" setting, it means that you are allowing everyone, including people off of Facebook, to access and use that information, and to associate it with you (i.e., your name and profile picture).

5. We always appreciate your feedback or other suggestions about Facebook, but you understand that we may use them without any obligation to compensate you for them (just as you have no obligation to offer them).

So, on one hand, you own your content, but on the other hand, you grant Facebook a free license to use any copyrightable content you post. The license ends when you delete it, but not if you have shared it with anyone else and they haven't deleted it. If you publish content using the "everyone" setting, everyone will have access to that information, and your content will be out there for the taking.

The terms of service agreement for YouTube takes a comparable tack regarding IP rights in your content. In Section 4.D:

> You agree not to use the Website . . . for any commercial use, without the prior written authorization of YouTube.

But Section 4.E goes on to say that

> Prohibited commercial uses do not include:
> uploading an original video to YouTube, or maintaining an original channel on YouTube, to promote your business or artistic enterprise; . . .

In other words, YouTube basically encourages you to share your art. In Section 6.B, you take responsibility for your content:

> You shall be solely responsible for your own Content and the consequences of submitting and publishing your Content on the Service. You affirm, represent, and warrant that you own or have the necessary licenses, rights, consents, and permissions to publish Content you submit; and you license to YouTube all patent, trademark, trade secret, copyright or other proprietary rights in and to such Content for publication on the Service pursuant to these Terms of Service.

In Section 6.C, you retain ownership, but you license YouTube:

> For clarity, you retain all of your ownership rights in your Content. However, by submitting Content to YouTube, you hereby grant YouTube a worldwide, non-exclusive, royalty-free, sublicenseable and transferable license to use, reproduce, distribute, prepare derivative works of, display, and perform the Content in connection with the Service and YouTube's (and its successors' and affiliates') business, including without limitation for promoting and redistributing part or all of the Service (and derivative works thereof) in any media formats and through any media channels. You also hereby grant each user of the Service a non-exclusive license to access your Content through the Service, and to use, reproduce, distribute, display and perform such Content as permitted through the functionality of the Service and under these Terms of Service. The above licenses granted by you in video Content you submit to the Service terminate within a commercially reasonable time after you remove or delete your videos from the Service. You understand and agree, however, that YouTube may retain, but not display, distribute, or perform, server copies of your videos that have been removed or deleted. The above licenses granted by you in user comments you submit are perpetual and irrevocable.

In Section 6.D, you say your content doesn't violate IP rights belonging to any third party:

> You further agree that Content you submit to the Service will not contain third party copyrighted material, or material that is subject to other third party proprietary rights, unless you have permission from the rightful owner of the material or you are otherwise legally entitled to post the material and to grant YouTube all of the license rights granted herein.

If you guessed by now that YouTube has Digital Millennium Copyright Act terms more or less like those of Second Life, you guessed right. So does the highly successful and more exclusive Funny or Die comedy video Web site (www.funnyordie.com), which combines user-generated content with original, exclusive content, and describes itself as "a place where celebrities, established and up-and-coming comedians and regular users can all put up stuff they think is funny. At the same time, the site hopes to eliminate all the junk that people have to pick through to find videos. That means around here you get to vote on what videos are funny and what videos deserve to die."

What you don't get to vote on is Funny or Die's terms of use.

Section 5.B of the terms of use (www.funnyordie.com/about/terms) makes you represent and warrant that you own or have the necessary licenses and permissions to use and authorize Funny or Die to use all patent, trademark, trade secret, copyright, or other proprietary rights in any of your submissions to enable inclusion of them in the Web site, and have the written consent, release, or permission of each and every identifiable individual person in any submission to use his or her name or likeness. It says you retain all of your ownership rights in your submissions, but by submitting, you grant Funny or Die a worldwide, nonexclusive, royalty-free, sublicenseable and transferable license to use, reproduce, distribute, prepare derivative works of, display, and perform the submissions in connection with the Funny or Die Web site and Funny or Die's business, including promoting and redistributing part or all of the Funny or Die Web site (and derivative works thereof) in any media formats and through any media channels. It also says you grant each user of the Funny or Die Web site a nonexclusive license to access your submissions through the Web site, and to use, reproduce, distribute, prepare derivative works of, display, and perform such submissions.

Section 5.C makes you agree not to submit material that is copyrighted, protected by trade secret, or otherwise subject to third-party proprietary rights, including privacy and publicity rights, unless you are the owner of such rights or have permission from their rightful owner to post the material and to grant Funny or Die all of the license rights granted per the terms; to publish falsehoods or misrepresentations that could damage Funny or Die or any third party; to submit material that is unlawful, obscene, defamatory, libelous, threatening, pornographic, harassing, hateful, racially or ethnically offensive, or encourages conduct that would be considered a criminal offense, give rise to civil liability, violate any law, or is otherwise inappropriate; to post advertisements or solicitations of business; or to impersonate another person. Funny or Die warns you that it will remove content and submissions if notified that it infringes on another's intellectual property rights. Funny or Die reserves the right to remove content and submissions without prior notice. Funny or Die will also terminate a user's access to its site, if they are determined to be a repeat infringer, namely, a user who has been notified of infringing activity more than twice or has had a submission removed from the Web site more than twice. Funny or Die reserves the right to decide whether content or a submission is appropriate and complies with its terms of service for violations other than copyright infringement and violations of intellectual property law, such as, but not limited to, pornography, obscene or defamatory material, or excessive length.

Seriously, though, folks . . .

To post or not to post, that is the question, and it is a question you alone can answer.

As the Facebook, YouTube, and Funny or Die terms illustrate, even though an operator may stop short of grabbing ownership of your work, the license you grant the operator is quite open-ended. And keep in mind, once a creative cat's out of the bag in cyberspace, it can run far from home, and easily stray. You may retain copyright in theory and stand a snowball's chance in hell of enforcing it in practice.

Don't get us wrong. We have nothing against sharing. But if you're thinking of parking your creative work in a de facto public domain with private Web site strings attached, you at least ought to think twice. It's your bicycle. If you want to leave it unlocked all day and night on the commons, that's up to you. But you should weigh in the balance, on a case-by-case basis, the upside of the positive exposure you can realistically hope to gain from posting the work against the downside of disqualifying the work from school credit and protection, competitions and other special exhibition opportunities, and the ultimate downside of downright theft.

Finally, there is a reasonably safe place to leave your bike on the commons, sponsored by the kind of folks who would never steal your bike, but do expect you to share it with others. It calls into play another set of trade-offs, which you also have to weigh in the balance, and which may or may not be of practical value to you as you pursue your creative art.

Creative Commons (creativecommons.org), a San Francisco–based non-profit corporation founded by legal scholars Lawrence Lessig and James Boyle along with other like-minded collaborators, fosters sharing of artistic and intellectual works consistent with the rules of copyright. The idea is simple. Prior to the mid-1970s, authors had to formally register their works with the U.S. Copyright Office and comply with other formalities (such as inclusion of the © symbol) to receive protection. The Copyright Act of 1976, however, rendered copyright protection automatic. Even if you didn't mind fans and ordinary citizens sharing and tinkering with your work, they were still technically infringing on your copyright and violating the law. Through Creative Commons, authors and creators can stake out a middle ground—enabling users to do certain things but not others.

Creative Commons has devised a menu of a half dozen licenses that allow authors and artists who publish their works to retain copyright, while relaxing the old-school "All Rights Reserved" stance in favor of a more generous, nuanced reservation of rights. For instance, at the liberal end of the spectrum, an "Attribution" license lets others distribute, remix, tweak, and build upon your work, even commercially, as long as they credit you for the original creation, while at the restrictive end of the spectrum, the "Attribution Non-Commercial No Derivatives" license allows redistribution, letting others download your work and share it with others, as long as they mention you and link back to you, but they can't change your work in any way or use it commercially.

You can also turn to Creative Commons as a site to find music, photographs, and videos to sample in your own work. One thing to remember, though, is that much of the media on Creative Commons contains a "Share Alike" license. This means if you use media in your project that you obtained through a Creative Commons "Share Alike" license, then your project will also need to be available to creators under a similar license. You may want this. But keep in mind you will no longer hold exclusive control over your media project and, for this reason, will not be able to enter into a contract with many commercial distributors. Like everything else on the Web, make sure you understand the consequences before you click upload or download.

HISPANIOLA—THE WEB SITE

Sometimes you get lucky, sometimes you don't.

You've been summoned to the *Nellie* for a follow-up with the Director of Companies, the Accountant, the Lawyer, the Banker, and the Agent to troubleshoot the budget for *Hispaniola* the movie, but you're still scrounging around for music and you haven't plugged the gaping gap in your financing. A lot hinges now on Marlow and Bonnie, and a lunch they took this afternoon in Sherman Oaks. It took Marlow no time at all to track down Roland Kurzweil's grandson, the late composer's sole heir, so thank God, the score to *A Pirate's Life* is not an orphan work. But the heir has a jam-packed schedule, and it took forever setting up a meeting to convince him to fork it over. Your creative dreams hang in the balance as you loiter outside the Galleria on Ventura Boulevard, and Marlow and Bonnie swing by to pick you up.

Well? you demand impatiently as you scrunch into the back seat of the Aston Martin.

Marlow says, RK3 is no spring chicken—

RK3?

Roland Kurzweil III—he likes to be called RK3—

Whatever, you sigh.

—but he's done very well for himself in the retail piano biz.

Has he?

You'll recognize him when you meet him.

How so?

You must've seen him in the Sunday *Times*.

Really?

Does ROLLIE, THE KING OF THE BABY GRANDS® strike a chord?

The guy with the crown, in the stroller, shaking an eighth-note rattle?

Yes, and the cable commercials: YOU'RE GONNA LIKE THE WAY YOU SOUND.®

That's RK3?

Bottom line, says Bonnie, he's filthy rich.

Bottom line, you ask, how much cash does he want for RK1's film score?

He doesn't want cash, says Marlow.

He doesn't?

He wants equity.

You groan.

And he happens to have a few spare million to invest.

He does?

He likes the project. He simply told us to ask you how much you need.

He did?

O.P.M., baby, O.P.M., chuckles Marlow.

You didn't want to give up any equity in Quisqueya Productions except as a last resort, but the time has come to resort to the last resort. As Marlow barrels down the Sepulveda Pass in a race against rush hour, you guesstimate how many millions you can soak RK3 for in exchange for a 25 percent piece of your transmedia dream. RK1's musical score and RK3's money will bury the shortfall in the film budget with plenty to spare. You contemplate the far-out ways a serious cash infusion in QP could help you leverage the Internet and new media to roll the Hispaniola saga out across multiple platforms.

For instance, what would it take to launch an interactive *hispaniolaonline.com*?

A place where visitors can select pirate avatars of their very own and customize them with garish pirate threads, jewelry, tattoos, weapons, and other gear bought with virtual pieces of eight, can outfit virtual pirate ships and cruise a virtual Caribbean hooking up with like-minded pirates, can fight battles, walk the plank, learn to swim, learn to party, feast on virtual buccaneer barbecue, swill virtual Puerto Rican rum, and smoke virtual Cuban cigars. To blueprint and build *Hispaniola Online*, you'll need some of RK3's money, and you'll need more contracts. You will use the same essential building blocks that built the contracts you put together in Chapter 4, tweaked to fit the architecture of Web 2.0.

You've had your eye on an up-and-coming interactive Web design firm out of Burbank that is getting a lot of buzz. Maybe you'll approach them. But one thing's for sure. The Web site design and development contract must be very clear about the deliverables. Just as a real estate investor would do in a brick-and-mortar construction project, you will pay them in installments, approve their work one stage at a time, and make sure the payments you make don't get ahead of the work they complete. Also, the firm is not going to be working exclusively for you, so you at least want to make them commit to build your site on a first-priority basis. If you like their stuff on the interactive site, you may want to spend a few more RK3 bucks and hire them to produce iPhone and Facebook apps for you, so you may as well bargain fixed pricing for these up front.

Your contract for *Hispaniola* the handheld video game will essentially be a trademark and copyright license, with QP as licensor and a video game publisher as licensee. *Hispaniola Online*, in contrast, is going to be a work commissioned by QP and owned by QP lock, stock, and barrel. So your Web site development and design agreement will need provisions to ensure the copyright in each strand of creative content woven into this dreamscape of a site flows first into the design firm's hands, so they can turn around and deliver an assignment of everything to QP, much as your film production contracts for *Hispaniola* the movie make the rights flow first into QP's hands, so QP can turn around and deliver the domestic rights in perpetuity to the studio under the negative pickup agreement and deliver overseas licenses to the foreign distributors under the distribution agreements.

The Web design firm will have to enlist legions of animators, graphic artists, musicians, voices, and programmers to create *Hispaniola Online*. Some may be employees, some freelance independent contractors, but you'll make the firm obtain work-for-hire agreements and waivers of moral rights from every last one of them. All of the content any of them create or contribute must be a work made for hire owned by the firm, so that the firm can then sell and assign the copyright to QP. Each worker bee will also have to give the Web design firm representations and warranties, backstopped by indemnities, analogous to those you obtained from Bonnie for her book, Bobby for his script, and Ashleigh and Vic for their performances in *Hispaniola* the movie, and analogous to the ones the animator creating *Hispaniola* the cartoon will give the Director of Companies' kiddy network for her animation work.

You will grant the Web design firm a limited license to use QP's Hispaniola copyrights and trademarks exclusively for the purpose of creating the Web site, its virtual world, avatars, and accessories, and you will make the firm make its worker bees promise to use your IP only for that purpose. The firm must also deliver QP at no additional cost a perpetual nonexclusive right to each worker bee's name, voice, likeness, and photos, for publicity and promotion of the site, in case you want to release promotional "behind the scenes" footage and stuff online, or produce a "Making of Hispaniola Online" film, TV show, or Webcast.

Since the Web design firm uses programmers, and commercial software applications used in interactive design and development projects of this sort are vigorously protected by copyright, you must make the firm represent and warrant that it has all needed licenses in third-party proprietary software sufficient to turn around and grant QP a license in perpetuity enabling you to launch, host, and maintain the Web site, and you must make the firm back it up with a good stiff indemnity. You can't launch *Hispaniola Online* and then have some software maker pop out of the woodwork and put the bite on you for license fees.

Hispaniola Online will have a virtual Caribbean, a virtual duty-free shop on each island, loads of avatars, ships, weapons, food, beverages, and buried treasure.

Have you forgotten anything?

Oh yeah.

One last thing.

Hispaniola Online will have terms of service.

Lots of them.

Now that RK3's money will be priming the Hispaniola pump, it occurs to you that you ought to shop around for a new lawyer. Marlow has been a good egg throughout this process, but you can't keep freeloading on the old gent's professional expertise now that you can afford to hire your own hired gun.

Marlow swings a left onto Via Marquesas. The *Nellie* lies in its slip without a flutter of sails. The wind is calm. The Marina stretches before you like the beginning of an interminable waterway, but this time around you see daylight at the end of the tunnel, thanks to other people's money.

Well? the Director of Companies demands impatiently. He stands looking to sea as you ascend the gangplank, sporting his meticulously weathered Greek fisherman's cap.

Try this on for size, you say: Music by Roland Kurzweil.

I smell posthumous Oscar, crows the Director of Companies, lighting up a Montecristo.

Add one more credit while we're at it, you say: Executive Producer Roland Kurzweil III.

Yes! yes! yes! squeals the Accountant and high fives you.

The Lawyer whips open her briefcase and dishes out four reams of paper, one for the Banker, one for the Agent, one for the Director of Companies, and one for little old you. She issues four Montblanc pens. The four of you keep on signing till you get tennis elbow.

This calls for a drink, crows the Lawyer.

Uh-uh, says the Director of Companies. No time.

What's the hurry? she asks.

He turns to you and says: Go pack your bags, kid.

Right now?

Right now. The corporate jet's waiting.

What for?

You're going to Puerto Rico.

FURTHER READING

SOFTWARE AND INTELLECTUAL PROPERTY

Before copyright lawyers and scholars turned their attention to broad questions of "new media," they had already generated a great deal of litigation and writing on intellectual property law and computer software. Douglas E. Phillips, *The Software License Unveiled: How Legislation by License Controls Software Access* (New York: Oxford University Press, 2009), reviews many of the key historical and legal developments. Phillips incisively critiques the current model of software license agreements, both the proprietary licenses and the free software licenses. Similar to the case with terms of service, the deck is stacked in those "end user license agreements"—adhesion contracts for software users—we frequently encounter navigating across the net.

To read a practical guide written by an advocate of free software, see Andrew M. St. Laurent, *Understanding Open Source and Free Software Licensing* (Sebastopol, Calif.: O'Reilly Media, 2004). To his credit, St. Laurent's book is as clearly written as a guidebook to computer software can be.

Christopher M. Kelty, *Two Bits: The Cultural Significance of Free Software* (Durham: Duke University Press, 2008), historicizes the free software movement and argues for its social value. In one of his later chapters, Kelty provides a fascinating ethnographic study of the early years of Creative Commons.

COPYRIGHT IN THE DIGITAL AGE

Several scholars and critics today are confronting the pressing questions of copyright's role in the digital age. How should the law apply to software, the Internet, and new media? How can we as a society balance property rights with cultural access and expression?

In *The Wealth of Networks: How Social Production Transforms Markets and Freedom* (New Haven: Yale University Press, 2006), Yochai Benkler sees new restrictions, like the Digital Millennium Copyright Act, as limiting the tremendous democratizing power of the Internet. Lawrence Lessig and James Boyle, cited in Chapter 1, have also forcefully addressed these questions. See the work of Lawrence Lessig, *The Future of Ideas: The Fate of the Commons in a Connected World* (New York: Vintage Books, 2002), *Free Culture: The Nature and Future of Creativity* (New York: Penguin, 2005), *Code, Version 2.0* (New York: Basic Books, 2006), and *Remix: Making Art and Commerce Thrive in the Hybrid Economy* (New York: Penguin Press, 2008). See also James Boyle's *Shamans, Software, and Spleens: Law and the Construction of the Information Society* (Cambridge, Mass.: Harvard University Press, 1996) and *The Public Domain: Enclosing the Commons of the Mind* (New Haven: Yale University Press, 2008).

For a clear, incisive analysis of the Digital Millennium Copyright Act and digital rights management restrictions, see Jessica Litman, *Digital Copyright* (New York: Prometheus Books, 2001). The Digital Millennium Copyright

Act, among other things, technologically prohibits certain uses of copyrighted material that would otherwise qualify as fair uses. Tarleton Gillespie's *Wired Shut: Copyright and the Shape of Digital Culture* (Cambridge: MIT Press, 2007) warns against the desire to find "technological fixes" to complex cultural problems and also highlights some of the negative consequences that the DMCA and digital rights management have caused.

Finally, Edward Lee Lamoureux, Steven L. Baron, and Claire Stewart, *Intellectual Property Law and Interactive Media: Free for a Fee* (New York: Peter Lang, 2009), provides a useful introduction to intellectual property law and the challenges facing content owners and users in the digital environment.

COURTSIDE SEATS

You can access many of the *MGM Studios, Inc. et al. v. Grokster, Ltd. et al.* 545 U.S. 913 (2005) documents online at www.copyright.gov/docs/mgm/index.html. In addition to the Supreme Court's opinion in favor of MGM, you can find more than fifty amicus curiae (friend of the court) briefs. The briefs range from arguments favoring MGM by the American Federation of Musicians and the commissioner of Major League Baseball to arguments supporting Grokster by Creative Commons and the American Civil Liberties Union (ACLU). Legal scholars Pamela Samuelson, Jack I. Lerner, and Deirdre K. Mulligan wrote one of the most thoughtful briefs, representing the views of "Sixty Intellectual Property and Technology Law Professors and the United States Public Policy Committee of the Association for Computing Machinery" in favor of Grokster. These law professors argue the "case is fundamentally about technology policy, not about file sharing or copyright infringement," and call attention to a rift between Northern California technology companies and Southern California entertainment industries that is as contentious as the Giants-Dodgers baseball rivalry. See www.copyright.gov/docs/mgm/tech-law-profs-usacm.pdf, p. 2 (accessed November 1, 2010). The case reached a conclusion in the nation's highest court, but most of the current debates about file sharing echo the same arguments inscribed in the many amicus curiae briefs.

Many of the documents from the *Viacom v. YouTube* litigation are also available online at http://dockets.justia.com/docket/new-york/nysdce/1:2007 cv02103/302164 (accessed November 1, 2010). There are some fascinating nuggets and revelations in these documents if you can make it through the mountains of civil procedure matters and legalese.

USER TERMS AND AGREEMENTS

Here is where we found the Web site user agreements:

Facebook, "Statement of Rights and Responsibilities," Last Revision: October 4, 2010, www.facebook.com/terms.php (accessed November 1, 2010).

Funny or Die, "Terms of Use," Dated: October 2010, www.funnyordie.com/about/terms (accessed November 1, 2010).

Second Life, "Terms of Service," Last Updated and Effective Date: October 6, 2010, http://secondlife.com/corporate/tos.php (accessed November 1, 2010).

YouTube, "Terms of Service," Dated: June 9, 2010, www.youtube.com/static?gl=US&template=terms (accessed November 1, 2010).

We are confident you will have the pleasure of reading and evaluating many more of these agreements, which will probably have grown in length by the time this book reaches you.

Epilogue

There is a pause of profound stillness aboard the *Nellie*, then a match flares, and the Director of Companies' plump face appears, with an aspect of concentrated attention, and as he takes vigorous draws at his cigar, it seems to retreat and advance out of the night in the regular flicker of his Dunhill lighter. The light goes out. He laughs.

What? says Marlow.

Opening night jitters, he admits, turns to you, and asks: What time's the red carpet?

Seven, you reply, gazing out over the Marina.

The Director of Companies smiles at you and says: You nailed it, kid.

You like the film?

I like the fact you came in under budget.

Couldn't have done it without my lawyer, you say, with a deferential nod to Marlow.

Lawyer? snorts the Director of Companies. Who ever said Marlow's a lawyer?

He's not?

The Director of Companies shakes his head.

But, rumor has it he worked for the studios for decades as a—

As an accent coach, says the Director of Companies.

Accent coach?

He's simply the best.

He is?

Kid, you gotta get out more.

'Spose so. Now you understand where Marlow got the dough for the Aston Martin.

Nobody would ever guess he was born and raised in Wichita, adds your host.

You stare at Marlow. So . . . you're . . . not . . . English?

Nope, Marlow replies with a gentle smile. And we're not in Kansas anymore, Dorothy.

Marlow ceases, and sits apart, indistinct and silent, in the pose of a meditating Buddha.

Nobody moves for a time.

Well, guys, says the Director of Companies. It's showtime.

You raise your head.

The offing is barred by a black bank of clouds, and the tranquil waterway leading to the uttermost ends of the earth flows somber under an overcast sky strafed by floodlights off to the east—seeming to lead you way, way back, to an afternoon once upon a time in an ill-lit curio shop, a chance encounter with a used book, a ship named *Hispaniola*, and an accent coach who knows a thing or two about the art of law.

APPENDIX   1

How to Register a Copyright

Registering your copyright in a work you create is not mandatory, but it can have its advantages, as we saw in Chapter 1. Here's how to register a copyright with the U.S. Copyright Office.

THE APPLICATION

An application for copyright registration requires three things:

- a completed application form
- a nonrefundable filing fee
- deposit of a copy or copies of the work.

Nowadays most applications are processed within a few months, but processing time varies depending on your choice of application method and the Copyright Office's work backlog. A copyright registration is effective on the date the Copyright Office receives all required elements of the application in acceptable form. This normally means the certificate of registration has a retroactive effective date, earlier than the date it is issued. For instance, if you file your application on September 30 with everything in order, and the Office issues the certificate on December 1, the effective date of the registration is September 30.

HOW TO FILE

The best, quickest, and cheapest way to register most claims for literary works, visual arts works, performing arts works, sound recordings, and motion pictures and other audiovisual works—in short, every kind of work that interests you— is by filing an application online through the Copyright Office's "electronic Copyright Office" (eCO), at its Web site, www.copyright.gov. The advantages of online filing include:

- an inexpensive $35 filing fee
- the fastest processing time
- online status tracking

- secure payment by credit or debit card
- the ability to file deposit materials electronically.

A second, slower filing method is to download from the Copyright Office Web site a barcoded fill-in Form CO, which you complete on your PC, print out, and mail to the Copyright Office, together with payment by check and the required deposit materials. Paper applications on Form CO are not processed as quickly as eCO filings, though, and the $45 filing fee makes it slightly more expensive, not to mention the cost of paper, printer ink, and postage, and the associated collateral damage to the environment.

The third and slowest alternative, also requiring a $45 fee, is to file a copy of one of the old-school copyright application forms on paper. These can be obtained from the Copyright Office only via snail mail: Form TX (literary works); Form VA (visual arts works); Form PA (performing arts works, including motion pictures); Form SR (sound recordings); and Form SE (single serials). It is best to avoid these old-fashioned forms whenever possible, since online registration is cheaper and so much faster.

Another advantage of applying online via eCO is that you will automatically receive a dated email receipt from the Copyright Office confirming that your application was received. If you file a paper application, you won't receive acknowledgment of whether or when your filing is received, unless you go to the trouble of sending it by registered or certified mail, return receipt requested.

WHO CAN FILE

Only the following parties are entitled to file an application:

- The *author* is the person who created the work or, if the work is a work made for hire, the employer or other party for whom it was made. If you create a work as a work for hire, as explained earlier, you don't own the copyright, so you can't file an application.
- The *copyright claimant* is either the author or a party who has obtained ownership of all of the author's rights under the copyright.
- An *owner of exclusive rights* is somebody who obtains ownership of any one or more of the exclusive rights contained in the overall copyright, and such an owner can apply for registration of a claim in the work to the extent of the owner's interest, even though the rights may be limited in time, place, or media.
- An *attorney or agent* can file an application on your behalf, if you authorize him or her to do so.

WHAT TO FILE

Let's assume you apply online through eCO or on paper using fill-in Form CO. You may or may not be able to complete the application by yourself, depending on the complexity of the work, its authorship, and its ownership. If in doubt, it is best to consult a lawyer experienced in registering copyrights. The main items of information you need to include in the application are these:

- First, regarding the work to be registered, you must include the type of work (e.g., motion picture/audiovisual work), the title of the work (e.g., *Hispaniola*), the year of completion, and, if the work has been published, the date and country of publication. Titles of registered works are filed alphabetically in the indexes and catalogs of the Copyright Office, but the title itself is not copyrighted or protected by copyright, since titles are not copyrightable. A search of Copyright Office records will often reveal the same title for two or more entirely different works by different authors.

- Second, about the author or authors, you need to identify each (unless the work is anonymous or pseudonymous), including full name, if an individual author, and organizational name, if a corporation or other organization, and you need to indicate each author's country of citizenship and domicile, because citizenship and where an author lives affect rights under international treaties. If the author is an individual, stating his or her year of birth is optional, though the Copyright Office likes this information to help identify authors for search purposes, and disclosing the year of death is required, if the author is dead. You also need to say whether each author's contribution to the work was a work made for hire, or is anonymous or pseudonymous. Notice that corporations and other organizations can be authors only on a work that is a work made for hire. If it is a work made for hire, the individual who created the work is not named in the application or in the resulting registration. If there are multiple authors, you need to indicate each author's contribution to the work (e.g., text/poetry, editing, script/play/screenplay, and so forth).

- Third, you need to provide the name and address of the party claiming ownership of the copyright, who will be either the author or authors of the work, or someone to whom the copyright has been transferred. If the claimant is not the author of the work, you must indicate whether ownership was acquired by written agreement, by will or inheritance, or by other means.

- Fourth, if the work contains or is based on previously registered or previously published material, or material in the public domain, or material not owned by the claimant, you must enter a limitation of the copyright claim being applied for. This kicks in whenever you apply to register a derivative work unless all the underlying works are unpublished and unregistered works owned by you. Any previously registered, published, or public domain material and material other people own will be excluded from the scope of your copyright, and you must identify the new material on which your claim in the derivative work is based. For example, if your work is a movie based on a previously registered novel and a previously registered screenplay, you would indicate that the novel and the screenplay each are excluded material, identify them as "text," and describe your new material as "all other cinematographic material." If your work is a new arrangement of a public domain song, you would indicate that the song is excluded material, identify it as "text" and "music," and describe your new material as "new arrangement."

- Fifth, you can, if you wish, designate a contact person, such as your attorney, agent, or assistant, for members of the public to contact to request rights or permission to use your copyrighted work, with address, email address, and telephone contacts. These become part of the Copyright Office's searchable online public records.

- Sixth, you can, if you wish, designate a correspondence contact, such as your attorney, agent, or assistant, for the Copyright Office to contact if they have any questions about your application.

- Last, but not least, you need to designate the person to whom you would like your registration certificate mailed.

DEPOSIT REQUIREMENTS

Along with your copyright application, you need to deposit a copy of the work or, for some kinds of applied art and sculptural art works, surrogate materials. The specific deposit requirements and number of copies required vary depending on whether, where, and when the work has been published, on the type of work, and the medium in which the work is rendered, but in general you must submit the following.

- If the work is unpublished: one complete copy or phonorecord.
- If the work was first published in the United States: one or two complete copies or phonorecords of the *best edition* (the required number of copies depending on the type of work).
- If the work was first published outside the United States: one complete copy or phonorecord of the work as first published.

Although copyright registration is optional, there is a *mandatory deposit* requirement for works published in the United States. The owner of a copyright or, to be more precise, the owner of that portion of the copyright granting the exclusive right of publication, has a legal obligation to deposit within three months after publication two complete copies of the work. Failure to deposit, if the Copyright Office tracks you down and demands it, can result in fines and other penalties. The good news is that depositing the best-edition copies along with a copyright application simultaneously satisfies the mandatory deposit requirement. So an owner who has to fork over a mandatory deposit anyway is almost always better off applying to register, and killing two birds with one stone, so as to gain the benefits of copyright registration.

The "best edition" of a work is the one the Library of Congress considers best for its purposes. If two or more editions of a work have been published, the one of the "highest quality" under Library rules is generally the best edition. But for some types of works, the Library imposes quite finicky criteria, because its purposes, at the end of the day, are archival, serving as it does as the nation's central repository of books, recordings, photographs, maps, audiovisual works, and other research materials. For example, if one edition of a book is printed on acid-free paper, and another edition is printed on plain paper, the acid-free version is the best edition, but other criteria also come into play, such as quality of binding, illustrations, and size.

For motion pictures, film is considered the superior medium. The Copyright Office stipulates a hierarchy of preferred film and video formats. For film, a 70mm positive print, if the original production negative is greater than 35mm, is better than a 35mm positive print, which is better than a 16mm positive print. For video, Betacam SP is better than Digibeta, is better than DVD, is better than VHS cassette.

For phonorecords, compact digital disc is better than vinyl disc, is better than tape, and open-reel tape is better than a cartridge, which is better than a cassette, while quadraphonic is better than stereophonic, true stereophonic is better than monaural, but monaural is better than electronically rechanneled stereo.

Depositors can request authorization to deposit something other than the best edition of a work by seeking "special relief." Requests for special relief have to say why the applicant can't send the best edition, and what the applicant proposes to submit instead. A special relief request spells extra work, so it's worth making only if the added trouble outweighs the expense or difficulty of providing the best edition.

Different types of works have different deposit requirements. If the work is a motion picture, for instance, the deposit requirement is one complete copy of the unpublished or published motion picture, together with a separate written description of its contents, such as a synopsis, a continuity, or a press book. If the work is a literary, dramatic, or musical work published only in a phonorecord, the requirement is one complete phonorecord. In the case of sculptural or other works reproduced in three-dimensional copies, instead of the real thing in 3D, the Copyright Office wants and requires surrogate *identifying material* in the form of 2D photographs or drawings, paper or electronic, which fit a lot better in their file drawers and computers than statues and such. There are other special deposit requirements for many works of the visual arts such as toys, fabrics, and oversized materials, and for computer programs, video games, and other machine-readable audiovisual works. The details are spelled out in a set of Copyright Office information circulars readily downloadable from its Web site.

You can file an application online using eCO even when you must submit a hard-copy deposit, as required under the mandatory deposit requirements for published works. The eCO system prompts you to specify whether you intend to submit an electronic or a hard-copy deposit. If you are making a hard-copy deposit, eCO issues you online a printable barcoded shipping slip, keyed to your application, to attach to your mail-in deposit.

If you use fill-in Form CO instead, you mail the form, fee, and deposit in a single package. You can find specific addresses for the different types of mail-in filings, with different zip code extensions for different types of works, at the Copyright Office Web site.

EXAMINATION

After you apply to register a copyright, you may receive a letter, email, or phone call from a Copyright Office staff person asking for further information. Copyright applications are reviewed to check that all required information has been included on the form, that the deposit complies with requirements, and that the work appears to be copyrightable. If all is in order, you should receive in the mail a certificate of registration confirming that your work has been registered. However, if the Copyright Office examiner considers the application unacceptable, for instance, because he or she thinks your deposit does not comply with the requirements, or considers your work uncopyrightable, you should receive a letter explaining why your application is being rejected, and giving you 120 days to respond.

Bear in mind, the Copyright Office and its examiners aren't always right. An examiner sometimes makes a mistake about what is and isn't copyrightable. Nobody's perfect. If you feel a mistake has been made, but cannot persuade the examiner to see things your way, you can appeal the decision to the Copyright Office. If the office's decision on appeal is not in your favor, you can sue the Register of Copyrights, who heads the Copyright Office, in federal district court, and ask a judge to decide whether or not your work is copyrightable. Federal judges have the power to compel the Register of Copyrights to register a copyright, and also have the power to compel the Register to cancel a registration. Of course you'd rather not go there, but on rare occasions, when the stakes are high, copyright owners occasionally do.

How to Register a Trademark

Registering a trademark you either use or intend to use is not mandatory, but can have its advantages, as we saw in Chapter 2. Here's how to apply to register a trademark with the U.S. Patent and Trademark Office.

THE APPLICATION

An application for trademark registration requires two things:

- a completed application form
- a nonrefundable filing fee.

Nowadays most applications are examined within a few months, but processing time varies depending on your choice of application method and the Trademark Office's work backlog.

HOW TO FILE

Online application through the Trademark Office's Web site at www.uspto.gov, using its Trademark Electronic Application System (TEAS), is a far better and less expensive way to apply to register a trademark than paper filing. Trademark applications are much more expensive to prepare and file than copyright applications, and usually require much more work for the applicant, legal counsel, and the Trademark Office examiner assigned to examine the mark, but paper filing makes things worse. Paper applications are not processed as quickly as TEAS filings, and the Trademark Office actively discourages paper filings by charging a higher filing fee of $375 per class of goods or services. In practice, this makes paper filing of trademark applications, except in highly unusual circumstances, a thing of the past. The advantages of online filing include:

- a reduced filing fee of $275 or $325 per class
- faster processing time
- online status tracking
- secure payment by credit or debit card
- the ability to file supporting materials electronically
- an automatically issued email receipt for your filing.

WHO CAN FILE

The applicant entitled to file a trademark application must be the person or company using the mark or having a bona fide intent to use, or an entity closely affiliated with that person or company. An attorney can file an application on your behalf, if you authorize him or her to do so.

You might or might not be able to complete an application online using TEAS by yourself, depending on its complexity in terms of the form of mark, the goods or services of interest, facts surrounding your use of the mark, and other issues that may affect its registrability. TEAS and the Trademark Office's other online offerings are reasonably user friendly, but the difficult part of online filing is the underlying legal analysis. Deciding what ingredients to include in a trademark application calls for a seasoned knowledge of trademark law and practice, and tends to be less cut and dried than preparing a copyright application. There are numerous ways to foul up. If you have a trademark in mind, but are in doubt as to what to include in your trademark application, it is best to consult an experienced trademark lawyer.

Law firm professional fees to file trademark applications vary, but roughly speaking, the total official and professional fees to apply for and register a trademark in one class will mount up to at least one thousand dollars. Trademark lawyers normally quote their fees for preparing and filing applications on a flat, fixed-fee basis. A number of online operators on the Internet promote trademark filing services at cut rates, but like the man says, you get what you pay for, and what online operators provide often does not include legal advice. If you do hire a trademark lawyer to handle your application, he or she should strategize with you on the form of the mark to apply for, the filing basis or bases, the identification of goods and services and other particulars, and should factor in your actual or intended use of the mark, your marketing and related business plans for the mark, and your timetable for launch.

WHAT TO FILE

The main items you need to include in an application are these:

- *Applicant.* The applicant can be an individual, a company, or another legal entity. You must spell the applicant's name right, because only extremely minor corrections are allowed after filing. You must state the citizenship of the applicant, which in the case of a legal entity is the jurisdiction under whose laws it is formed. It is permitted to have joint applicants, but keep in mind that joint applicants jointly control the application.
- *The Mark.* The form of the mark set out in the application depends on whether it is a word mark, a word mark in stylized letters, a design mark, or a composite mark.

If the mark is a word mark, the applicant has the option of applying in *standard character format,* simply typing the word mark into the TEAS application template, which means the applicant claims the right to use the word mark in any lettering format whatsoever. This allows the flexibility in an intent-to-use application to settle on the lettering style of the mark at a later date, and the freedom in use-based and intent-to-use applications to change the lettering style of the mark in future without filing a new trademark application. Alternatively, a word mark can be filed in stylized letters, but then the application protects the mark in that specific stylization, which may be appropriate if the lettering style is part of the distinctive character of the mark and an element of it that you especially wish to protect.

For design marks, composite marks, and word marks filed in stylized letters, the applicant must submit via the TEAS template a jpeg image of the mark, which may be done in black-and-white or color. You also have to submit a short description of the mark in words. A filing without color claim, of a black-and-white image, is appropriate when you would like to reserve the freedom to render your mark in any color or colors. On the other hand, if the color or colors of your mark are part of its distinctive character, and you plan always to render it in those colors, an application with color claim is appropriate.

When filing a composite mark, in addition to including a jpeg image of the entire composite, you separately state the word mark portion, called the *literal element*, in letters, numbers, or other typographical symbols. This helps the Trademark Office index your application for searching purposes. Just as Marlow found other people's marks when he conducted a pre-filing availability search for you, other people are going to find your mark when they conduct future trademark searches and type in your literal element or portions of it, or search for marks indexed with design codes referencing the design elements contained in your design or composite mark. You actually want people who in future may think of adopting a trademark similar to yours to search and find yours, so that they can be put on actual notice, and hopefully rethink their plans to avoid conflict with you.

- *International Class.* To help pigeonhole the goods and services covered in trademark applications and registrations, and make trademark searches more meaningful, the myriad types of goods and services floating about in the world of commerce, from abacuses to zoot suits, are listed and sorted in excruciating detail into forty-five different classes, called International Classes, according to an international treaty classification scheme called the Nice Classification. Guidelines defining each class and the things included or excluded in them are found on the Trademark Office Web site in the Trademark Manual of Examining Procedure (TMEP), a set of guidelines the Trademark Office's examining attorneys follow when reviewing incoming trademark applications. Also available online is the U.S. Acceptable Identification of Goods and Services Manual, containing an enormous database searchable by keyword showing acceptable classification and wording for most goods or services under the sun. In every new trademark application, the applicant must group the goods and services it wishes to file for into one or more classes. What is at stake, among other things, is the Trademark Office's fee, to the tune of $325 per class. Trademark lawyers also tend to base their fees, in part, on the number of classes applied for.
- *Goods and Services.* Within the one or more classes you elect to apply for, you must specifically list the goods and services you want to cover. To compile this list, the Acceptable Identification of Goods and Services Manual keyword search feature is a helpful tool. An application listing goods or services in a way fairly consistent with the manual won't run into questions from the examining attorney, whereas a list that departs substantially from it may. If your list of goods and services is simple, and you are willing to toe the line of the manual verbatim, you can opt to use a streamlined application template called

TEAS Plus. This form straitjackets you into filing only for goods and services worded exactly as listed in the manual, in return for which you pay a reduced filing fee of $275 per class, since such applications are less expensive for the office to process. A nice savings if your goods and services are plain vanilla, but if they need customized wording, TEAS Plus is not for you.

- *Filing Basis.* There are two bases on which a U.S. applicant can file to register a U.S. trademark application. You can file under Section 1(a) of the Trademark Act based on actual use in interstate commerce, but this requires that you actually sell the specified products or services before filing. Alternatively, you can file under Section 1(b) of the Trademark Act based on a bona fide intent to use the mark in interstate commerce for the goods or services applied for. But an intent-to-use application can ripen into a registration only after filing of a statement of use, demonstrating that you have started using and are using the mark in interstate commerce. A majority of trademark applications these days are filed on an intent-to-use basis. Intent-to-use applications have the priority advantage we already mentioned, and enable the applicant at the early planning stages to find out prior to brand launch whether or not its trademark will encounter problems at the Trademark Office or with third parties.
- *First Use Dates.* If your application is based on use, then as a part of the application, you must include a statement of the date of first use of the mark anywhere in the world and the date of first use in U.S. interstate commerce. These dates should normally be supported by sales paperwork such as invoices, contracts, or shipping documents. If the exact dates are unknown, it is all right to submit approximate dates, but it is important to have backup records to be able to prove the use dates in case a Trademark Office examiner or third party challenges you down the road.
- *Specimen of Use.* If your application is based on use, then as a part of the application, or sent separately, you need to deposit a specimen of use in the form of a scan or digital photograph in jpeg or PDF format, showing current use of the mark for one item of goods or services in each class applied for. A specimen of use for goods should typically be a tag, label, packaging, or container for them, or a display associated with them. Advertising or promotional material is generally not acceptable as a specimen for goods, but a Web site page that displays a product and provides a means of ordering it counts as a display associated with the goods as long as the mark appears on the Web page in a manner in which the mark is associated with the goods, and the Web page provides a means for ordering the goods online. A specimen of use for services should show the mark as actually used in the sale or advertising of the services. Acceptable specimens may include brochures, leaflets, newspaper or magazine advertisements, trade show displays and the like, or, in the case of a mark for film production services, for instance, an advertisement for the film or an appearance of the mark in the film credits.
- *Declaration and Signature.* Last, but not least, you or your attorney must electronically sign the application, and a declaration saying the statements made in it are true. You should provide the Trademark Office an email address where correspondence and notices affecting the application can be sent to you or your lawyer. As soon as the completed application and payment are submitted online, TEAS assigns it an application serial number, and sends an electronic return receipt containing the application details submitted.

ACKNOWLEDGMENTS

We borrowed a lot of ideas and other cool free stuff to write this book.

Marlow we borrowed from Joseph Conrad. *Heart of Darkness* was first published in 1899 and Conrad died in England in 1924, so his works are in the public domain. Francis Ford Coppola and John Milius drew freely from *Heart of Darkness* to pen their now classic screenplay for Coppola's *Apocalypse Now.* Coppola hit a production snag or two along the way, but the end result panned out well, so we took a page out of their book and got free mileage from Conrad by hijacking Marlow. While we were at it, we borrowed the yacht *Nellie,* the Accountant, the Lawyer, the Director of Companies, ripped chunks of prose verbatim from *Heart of Darkness,* and ferried them wholesale up the Thames to Marina del Rey, brick by brick, the way the London Bridge was transplanted to Lake Havasu, because that's the kind of thing you can do with public domain stuff. We chartered Jim Hawkins and the good ship *Hispaniola* rent-free from Robert Louis Stevenson, and made a dog's breakfast of *Treasure Island* with impunity, because it too is in the public domain.

Conrad, Umberto Eco, Ian Fleming, Ethan and Joel Coen, Emily Dickinson, and George Orwell put in words, some copyrighted, some not, a few things we felt shed special light on the topic of each chapter, so we made fair use of those words to put our point across. For the same reason, we threw into the mix a song lyric here and there written by folks like Bob Seger and System of a Down. But what we can get away with in an educational book and what you can get away with in your creative work are two different things. We wouldn't dare use the same lyrics in a song, unless it were something transformative, like 2 Live Crew's rap parody of Roy Orbison's classic "Oh, Pretty Woman."

We have a lot of other people to thank for their support, ideas, and other cool free stuff.

Without our intrepid editors Alison MacKeen, Sarah Miller, and Phillip King at Yale University Press, there would be no book. We thank them each for letting us play in Yale's sandbox, and for their encouragement, support, comments, and editorial wizardry throughout the production.

Without our illustrator Jacqueline Jocson, MFA candidate in Animation and Digital Arts at the USC School of Cinematic Arts, there would be no pictures bringing Lucia Bonaire and the pirates of *Hispaniola* to life. Thanks, Jax, for your wonderful art.

Eric Hoyt was completing his Ph.D. at the USC School of Cinematic Arts during the writing of this book, and his quick mind, brilliant research, and broad knowledge of the entertainment industries inform every page of the book. Kiran Dharsan and Rebecca Samson of Seiter Legal Studio provided insightful and extensive guidance and suggestions on various drafts of the book. Anne Metcalf supplied invaluable editorial support. Tom Seiter supplied his wit and judgment about popular culture. Joe and Henry Metcalf offered steady encouragement and moral support.

We are grateful for our many stimulating conversations with, and comments on this book and related material from, our fellow professionals John Caldwell, Jennifer Holt, Jack Lerner, Tom Kemper, Paul Reidl, Rose Auslander, Greg Victoroff, and Damian Broadley.

We wish to thank Dean Elizabeth M. Daley of the USC School of Cinematic Arts, Associate Dean Michael Renov, and other organizers of the Visible Evidence XVI Conference for the opportunity to present portions of the "fair use" material in Chapter 1 in a panel presentation on intellectual property law for documentary filmmakers, joined by Eric Hoyt and fellow USC Critical Studies Ph.D. candidate Brett Service. Ellen presented an early draft of Chapter 3 at the 2008 Digicult Symposium in Paris and thanks Professor Jostein Gripsrud of the University of Bergen and the Norwegian Research Council for the generous invitation. Bill also wishes to thank the International Trademark Association and his moderator and colleague Jennifer McEwan for the opportunity to present portions of the material in Chapter 5 on rights of privacy and publicity in a panel on "Celebrities and Trademarks" at the 2010 INTA Annual Meeting in Boston.

We dedicate this book to the memory of our sister, Rosemary Seiter Morrison. Her kindness, bravery, and wit inspired us every day of our lives. Rosemary was a brilliant lawyer whose deep commitment to social justice touched everyone she knew.

Above all, thank you, gentle reader, for putting up with us, with the law, with Marlow, Bonnie, and the rest of our cast of characters. Whether you create a book, a script, a film or TV show, cartoon or graphic novel, video game or interactive Web site, a doll or a toy, the pleasure of the process lies in the anticipation of an audience you hope may enjoy the end product half as much as you enjoy bringing it to them. In this case, the pleasure has been all ours, because, at the end of the day, it's all about the pleasure of your company.

INDEX